THE DISABILITY RIGHTS MOVEMENT

From Deinstitutionalization to Self-Determination

Duane F. Stroman

University Press of America,® Inc.
Lanham · New York · Oxford

CONTENTS

Preface   v

Acknowledgements   vii

Chapter 1   Defining and Counting Disability in a Changing
World   1

Chapter 2   A Brief History of the Disability Rights
Movement   43

Chapter 3   The Disabled as a Minority Group   83

Chapter 4   Wave I of Deinstitutionalization—Persons
with Mental Illness   119

Chapter 5   Wave II of Deinstitutionalization—Persons
with Mental Retardation   147

Chapter 6   Early and Multiple Waves of Change for
Persons with Physical Disabilities   179

Chapter 7   The Growing Wave of Self-Determination   207

References   243

Index   259

PREFACE

For over twenty years I have been teaching a sociology course on disabilities that focused on the social meanings of disability and the social interactions of persons with and without disabilities. My book, *The Awakening Minorities: The Physically Handicapped (1982),* was an attempt to bring the minority group perspective to those with a range of disabilities. But that book is now dated as much has occurred that has changed the scene of those with disabilities. One significant change has been the development of new models of the interaction between people with and without disabilities captured under the rubric of medical and social models of disability. A second change has been in the language used to describe disabilities. A third change has been in the proliferation of disability rights organizations and their rich activities, aided by the electronic revolution, which have had a significant impact on creating the legislation which has greatly altered services for those with disabilities.

Despite these profound social changes, no textbook existed which adequately introduced the beginning student to the very diverse and growing population of persons with disabilities who form the largest minority group in this country. This book is my attempt to satisfy that need by looking at disability from multiple perspectives within sociology. The first perspective is to look at the evolving definition of disability as it moves from medical definitions of impairments in the body and brain to definitions that incorporate the social attitudinal and behavioral practices of society that limit functional activities of humans. It secondly looks at the social advocacy movement that has transformed the lives of many with disabilities. This perspectives focuses on the organizational component, the methods and the rationales by means of which the hopes and dreams of those with disabilities could be better achieved. Thirdly it reexamines the minority perspective by comparing the ways in which the minority with disabilities is like and unlike the historical racial and ethnic minorities. The book then documents the three major waves of deinstitutionalization involving those with mental illness, mental retardation and physical disabilities. This historical analysis examines how a number of social forces came together to depopulate custodial institutions for the disabled and increase their empowerment and opportunities. The last chapter looks at evolving changes that continue to increase the empowerment of those with disabilities and their supporters by giving them an ever-increasing say in the management and payment of the services they need to achieve or maintain the fullest life possible. This movement of self-determination is still unfolding as this book goes to press.

ACKNOWLEDGEMENTS

The author wishes to thank the World Health Organization for permission to reprint Table 1.2, An Overview of the ICF, found on page 26 of this work as first published by the World Health Organization, *International Classification of Functioning, Disability and Health.* 2001. p. 11.

The author also wishes to thank the administration and trustees of Juniata College for the sabbatical leave of absence during the fall of 2001 when much of this manuscript was written.

The author also wishes to thank Lacey Rhodes at Juniata College for her untiring assistance in reformatting many pages of my original manuscript into the style desired by the University Press of America.

CHAPTER I
DEFINING AND COUNTING
DISABILITY IN A CHANGING WORLD

THE ISSUES IN THIS CHAPTER

This book is about the disabled as a minority group whose members, along with many supporters, have been engaged in a social movement for decades. This movement has involved many different activities from diverse groups of people who have been socially labeled as disabled. The disability rights movement is a diverse social movement for several reasons. First, it is composed of a very diverse group of human beings. Second, different constituencies of this social movement have sometimes wanted different things. And thirdly, these diverse collectivities of the disabled have been responded to in different ways by society depending on how their disabling conditions were viewed. We will start off by noting that defining and counting disability is a challenge because there are multiple social perspectives on defining disability and counting it. In contrast to racial minorities or even ethnic minorities, the diversity of those with disabilities is much greater for several reasons:

>Their disabilities may be highly visible to invisible.

>Their disabilities may vary from minor to severe in comparison to being either present or absent.

>They are the largest minority group in the country—around 55 million and growing.

>They form an open membership group that anybody can join at any time as a result of injury, disease or simply attribution.

>Most people will experience a disability in their lifetime if we include those with chronic diseases and those who will experience older age.

>They have many allies who care about them—parents, children, friends, spouses, siblings, and professionals. In a sense, they too are

part of the disability rights movements because the lives of those with disabilities impact on them deeply.

>They may be born with the disability or acquire it during their lifetime and this mode of acquiring at various times of the life cycle has immense consequences.

>They form a very diverse group of citizens because of the encompassing nature of a general definition of disability: a blind person at age 7 or 87, a quadriplegic wheelchair user, a person with profound retardation, a person with schizophrenia or a hundred other psychiatric disabilities, a frail elderly person in a nursing home, an amputee, a deaf person, a veteran exposed to agent orange, an autistic person with mild retardation who also has diabetes, cancer, scoliosis, and arthritis.

>They have been studied by a variety of academic and professional disciplines which use different conceptual tools to define them with diverse purposes for analyzing them.

This chapter will focus on a number of issues related to the study of disability. First, we will briefly note that multiple disciplinary perspectives are involved in the study of disabilities. Medical science focuses on the symptoms, causes and treatment of disabilities, while psychology looks at the personal meanings and other impacts that disabilities have on their recipients, while sociology focuses on societal reactions to those with disabilities ranging from stereotyping, discrimination and legislation. Political scientists focus on the forces that shape legislative responses to disability and the impacts of such legislation while disability theorists give special although certainly not exclusive focus on the personal and social responses to disability. Recognizing these different but often highly overlapping perspectives will enable the reader to grasp some of the multiple levels at which the student of disabilities can focus their attention. Second, we will contrast two major models—the medical model and the social model in how they view the origins of disability and "treatment". Third, we will explicate the social model more fully since the medical model has been the dominant model for so long that the more recent social model requires a fuller explanation of how it is constructed. Fourth we will look at the different definitions of disabilities that agencies of the U.S. government use and how this produces different numbers of disabled. Fifth we will analyze some of the major correlates of disabilities to understand more fully how disabilities both cause and are influenced by other characteristics of the population. Finally, we will look at an emerging definitional synthesis of disability from the World Health

Organization that combines elements from both the social and medical models

MULTIPLE PERSPECTIVES IN THE STUDY OF DISABILITY

Multiple approaches have been taken in the study of disability. Each approach has its utility but each has its limitation because it does not include what each of the other approaches contains.   Some perspectives may combine two or more of these approaches. Disability is a "contested concept" that has been and is defined in many different ways.   There is no national and even less international agreement on how to define it generally or in broad concepts, how best to measure it, or how much "disability" there is.   In fact, the amount of disability varies hugely by how it is conceptually defined and then measured by one of the three ways by which information about it is collected—censuses, surveys of the population or administrative registration that reports on persons with specified disorders.   At the outset we need to note that research has enormously increased human understanding of disabilities even though much needs to be investigated and understood yet.   Three aspects of this complexity of disability language will be briefly explored: its change over time, its cultural and societal variation and the different approaches and definitions of disability that come from various personal, organizational, and disciplinary perspectives.

GENERAL TO SPECIFIC PERSPECTIVES.   Either the focus of study or the definitions of disabilities used may range from the **most general approach** of describing all disabilities, to describing some **category or subset** or all disabilities (such as sensory impairments, or mental impairments or physical impairments), to describing a very **particular type of disability** such as Tourette's syndrome, or paraplegia, hearing impairment, profound retardation, and depression. For example, the Disability Resources Organization with a web site at "http://www.disabilityresources.org" lists 170 specific disabilities on one of its pages and notes that there are over 200 neuromuscular disorders.   A fairly common global or general definition of disability is "a physical or mental problem that prevents someone from functioning at a normal rate or level" while a subset of all disabilities would be "cognitive disabilities" and in turn a subset of cognitive disabilities would be "autistic disorder" defined as the "presence of markedly abnormal or impaired development in social interaction and communication and a markedly restricted repertoire of activity and interests." (American Psychiatric Association, *Diagnostic and Statistical Manual of Mental Disorders.* 1994, 66). Developing a definition that will encompass all disabilities is very difficult if not nearly impossible. Altman's 20 page article on this very topic came to the conclusion: "Part of the difficulty of defining disability has to do with the fact that disability is a complicated, multidimensional concept. Because of the extensive variety in the nature of the problem, a global definition of disability that fits all circumstances, though very desirable, is in reality nearly impossible." (Altman, 2001, 97)

    MEDICAL VERSUS SOCIAL MODELS OF DISABILITY. The **individual or medical or clinical approach** to the definition of a disability focuses on a set of identifying symptoms. It locates these symptoms in a person. The medical approach may give both a short general definition of a particular disability and then a longer more detailed list of symptoms. For example, the fourth edition of the *Diagnostic and Statistical Manual of Mental Disorders* (1994, 629, 649-50) first states "**Antisocial Personality Disorder** is a pattern of disregard for, and violation of, the rights of others." But then the Manual gives a more detailed clinical description of this disability as follows:

    A. There is a pervasive pattern of disregard for and violation of the rights of others occurring since age 15, as indicated by three (or more) of the following:

    (1) failure to conform to social norms with respect to lawful behaviors as indicated by repeatedly performing acts that are grounds for arrest

    (2) deceitfulness, as indicated by repeated lying, use of aliases, or conning others for personal profit or pleasure

    (3) impulsivity or failure to plan ahead

    (4) irritability and aggressiveness, as indicated by repeated physical fights and assaults

    (5) reckless disregard for safety of self or others

    (6) consistent irresponsibility, as indicated by repeated failure to sustain consistent work behavior or honor financial obligations

    (7) lack of remorse, as indicated by being indifferent to or rationalizing having hurt, mistreated, or stolen from another.

    B. There is evidence of Conduct Disorder . . . before age 15 years.

    C. The occurrence of antisocial behavior is not exclusively during course of Schizophrenia or a Manic Episode.

    D. The individual is at least age 18 year

    This detailed operational definition lists a number of symptoms, some of which are optional from within a list of symptoms that can used to clinically determine if an individual has Antisocial

Conduct Disorder. At the same time there may be individual variations on the frequency and intensity of such things as impulsivity, deceitfulness, lack of remorse, reckless disregard for the safety of self or others and law-breaking behaviors. Thus this definition provides a threshold at which the disorder is to be regarded as present but there may be degrees of severity of it that this threshold definition does not attend to. In contrast to this model is the social model which focuses on the social origins of disability—such as people defining a given condition as disabling when it is not, creating artificial barriers to participation from curbs and steps to lack of accessible bathrooms or buses for wheelchair users, and to social stigma and discriminatory behaviors that flow from and reinforce that stigma. Embedded in these two models are assumptions about causes of disability. A **causal approach** looks at the origins of the disability. The causes may be variously defined as genetic, environmental toxic, injuries, diseases or having social environmental origins. This approach is often used in combination with the symptom approach. The information derived from that causal approach is often used for interventions that may range from prevention, treatment, and rehabilitation, to cure for the disability.

EXPERIENTIAL APPROACHES TO DISABILITY. The **experiential approach** to disability is the framing of what it is like to be disabled in some way either as described by the disabled person or by observers as they describe the changes a person goes through as they learn about the disability and then deal with all its medical and social unfoldings. This experience may vary greatly by the nature and severity of disability, its course over time, the responses and supports of friends, family, and professional caregivers, the policies of agencies and various levels of government, the prognosis for the disability, its visibility and many other factors. This narrative approach may be biographical or autobiographical and offer rich and interesting details on how a person reacted to either a disability they had from birth or one that occurred within their lifetime. Some medical sociologists and anthropologists have focused extensively on the range of experiences of persons with disabilities as they cope with a changing body or mind, the social responses of friends, family, and coworkers to changes in functionality and the meaning this has for their self identity.

SEVERITY OF DISABILITY. The **severity approach**, which often overlaps with the legislative approach described below, notes that very mild forms of impairment may result in no or minimal disability or functional limitation. Thus a person with hypertension which is being treated by medicine may not be able to run 100 yard dashes, yet is not impaired in doing the tasks important to him and that enable him to maintain a job. The regulations of Section 504 of the Americans with Disabilities Act thus are not concerned with minor impairments but with "a physical or mental impairment that **substantially limits** (emphasis added) one or more **major life activities**" (emphasis added). These major life activities are then defined by such things as "caring for oneself, performing manual tasks, walking, seeing, hearing, speaking, breathing, learning, working, and participating in community activities." (LaPlante, 1992, 1). A sufficient severity of disability is usually required to entitle a person to medical, insurance or government benefits.

LEGISLATIVE DEFINITIONS OF DISABILITY. Legislation definitions are ones that defines disability in terms of the processes that must be undertaken and/or the symptoms that must be present for a person to be eligible for benefits. For example, the Social Security Act as amended stipulates that multiple criteria must be met through a bureaucratically regulated process that involves physicians making 'medical determinations' of disability for a person to be eligible for Supplemental Security Income on the basis of a disability. As of January 2001, eligible individuals could get $530 in monthly benefits while eligible couples could get 1.5 times that amount or $796 monthly. These rates are adjusted annually using the prior year's rate of inflation. To be eligible for benefits, a person must meet three different kinds of criteria. (1) The first criterion is to have income below each year's "Federal Benefit Rate" defined above for individuals and couples. (2) The second criterion is to have "countable real or personal property" below $2,000 for an individual or $3,000 for a couple. These first two criteria then stipulate dollar income or asset limits that do not involve age or disability. (3) The third criterion involves one of three conditions that a person a must meet to be eligible for benefits: (1) be age 65 or older, or (2) be blind—"A 'blind' person is someone whose vision, with use of correcting lenses, is 20/200 or less in the better eye or who has tunnel vision of 20 degrees or less" or (3) be disabled—"A 'disabled' person age 18 or older is someone who meets the Social Security disability insurance program definition of disability. That is, he or she:

1. Must be unable to engage in substantial gainful activity (SGA) due to a medically determinable physical or mental impairment; and
2. The impairment can be expected to last for at least 12 months in a row or result in death.

There is no minimum age limit. A person under age 18 is eligible if he or she meets conditions (1) and (2) above. ("Definition of Disability

For a Disabled Worker's Benefits", 2001)

While there is additional information available on these requirements, it is important to note that physicians must make the determination when a person is unable to engage in "substantial gainful activity". For persons over 18 and not in school, the most important criterion relates to their **employability**. Thus, Social Security legislative definitions of disability are dependent on medical or clinical definitions of disability but go beyond them by adding qualifiers about age or the duration of the disability as well whether it impacts on working at a relatively high level of productivity in a job.

Two other legislative definitions have been important to those with disabilities. The first is the definition contained in the 1973 Rehabilitation Act: "Any mental or physical handicap that limits at least one major life activity such as walking, seeing, hearing, speaking, breathing, working and performing manual tasks." This definition was useful in specifying what was meant by "major life activities". The 1974 amendments to the 1973 Rehabilitation Act and 1990 Americans with Disabilities Act contains three types of disabling processes that legally may be the basis for some type of accusation of discrimination —the first is a medical definition while the next two are social definitions. The wording of the 1990 ADA act says a disabled person is:

(1) Any person with a physical or mental impairment that substantially limits one or more major life activities.
(2) Any person with a record of such an impairment.
(3) Any person who is regarded as having such an impairment.
(Social Security Disability Planner, 2001)

It is important to note that unlike the first part of this definition which indicates a medical approach which locates the impairment in the person, the next two definitions specify environmental processes that may result in some discriminatory treatment even though the individual currently has no impairment but is treated as if they do. Thus, a person who at one time had depression or cancer which left a paper trail in health and/or employment records might be treated as impaired even though the conditions were in remission or cured. Or people who once knew a person in some "special education" class might regard that person as one with mental retardation even though in fact they were not. Thus the ADA of 1990 was important in recognizing that discrimination may occur based on the presumption of the presence of disability even when there is no disability present.

Section 504 of the Rehabilitation Act of 1973 as amended also uses this definition of disability in prohibiting discrimination against "qualified individuals with disabilities" in those worksites or educational agencies that receive federal financial aid. This law defines "qualified individuals with disabilities" as "persons who meet legitimate skill, experience, education or other requirement of an employment position that he or she holds or seeks and who can perform the 'essential functions' of the position with or without reasonable accommodation." Thus Section 504 protects the civil rights of individuals with cerebral palsy, visual impairment, chronic illnesses such as AIDS, cancer, diabetes, mental retardation, former drug users, spinal cord injuries, specific learning disabilities, and speech disorders among many other conditions. ("Section 504 of the Rehabilitation Act of 1973, 1997.1).

VARIATIONS IN TYPES OF DISABILITIES. If we use the medical model of disability which objectives symptoms or sets of symptoms for impairment, then researchers can create categories of disability which share certain similarities. However, one limitation to this approach is that many persons may have one or two or three or more disabilities at the same time. If we count disabling conditions singly we will have more disability than if we count persons with disabling conditions since we can count persons only once.

The approach of the World Health Organization (Weiss, 2001) has been to define major types of impairments as structural or functional abnormalities in three areas:

1. psychological
2. physiological
3. anatomical.

Psychological disabilities are also labeled as "cognitive disabilities" which may in include two subcategories of mental illness and mental retardation. If those conditions happen to persons before the age of 19 they may be included among "developmental disabilities". However, some developmental abilities include physiological and anatomical conditions occurring during the first 18 years of life. Physiological and anatomical definitions will apply to conditions that often limit functioning in one or more areas. They may be diseases such as heart disease, arthritis, diabetes, AIDS, hearing or visual impairments, or spinal cord injuries or amputees. This definitional approach may lead to various other classifications and counts of those with disabilities.

For example, in 1996 the U.S. Bureau of the Census calculated that 19.7% of the population had a disability. Of this 19.7%, 9.5% had a "severe" disability and 10.2% had "not severe" disabilities. In 1996, about 2.4% or 3,640,000 million Americans had "ADL Limitations." ADL Limitations involve "activities in daily living" such as getting around the house, getting in and out of a bed and chair, taking a bath or shower, dressing, eating, and toileting by themselves. In that same year, a larger group, 3.6% of the population or 5,434,000 Americans, had limitations in the somewhat less severe category of --IADL— Instrumental Activities of Daily Living such as going outside the home to go shopping, being able to keep track of money and pay bills, preparing meals, doing light housework and using the telephone. (Weiss and Lonquist, 2000).

Persons with physical disabilities often get more attention in the literature than do persons with mental disabilities—variously called cognitive, intellectual or psychological, mental or psychiatric disabilities. This may be due to the heavy historical weight of the medical model and its focus on observable symptoms, the greater preponderance of physical disabilities, and perhaps the lesser stigma associated with physical than mental disabilities.

CONTRASTING PERSPECTIVES ON THE ROLE OF LANGUAGE IN CAUSING DISABILITY.   The constructionist or social constructionist view of language and knowledge that has emerged in the last part of the 20th century in a number of disciplines in the social sciences and humanities is that language does not finally reveal the *essentials* of a real world outside ourselves but is socially used to construct, invent and reinvent our interpretation or conceptual framing of that world.   There are variations in the constructionist view that could be seen as varying along a continuum from a "strong" constructionist approach that argues that the use of invented concepts is very important or paramount in understanding the external world to a weak constructionist view where conceptualizations of external phenomena are subject to some social influences but in the end the real world's essential nature and characteristics can be well understood by our social framing of them even though these are subject to change and modification over time. Two of the fields of study where supporters of social constructionism and essentialism have debated are in the areas of women's and gay studies. Essentialists in these fields would hold that the "categories" of gender, sexuality (like masculine or feminine) or sexual orientation (heterosexual, homosexual, bisexual, asexual) are categories embedded in the biology and psychology of individual rather than being culturally shaped by language and a range of social influences. In contrast, constructionists would argue that such concepts are historically invented and reflect the views of particular social groupings that may vary over time. A middle view is that there are real biological and psychological forces at work in shaping such things as sexual orientation, but that our framing of them and our social reaction to them are subject to changing cultural value sets. The field of disability studies has been undergoing the same debate on the causes and locations and meanings of impairment, disability and handicap.

The seventh chapter title in Mark's book *Disability* (1999, 137) is this question: "Does language disable people?" Her evidenced argument is that "language is used to separate disabled people from 'normal' society" and that it is "used to characterize the experiences of disabled people as being different and separate from the rest of society." It does this by playing a role in distancing disability from the everyday world and by helping to turn it into a 'master status" that defines the person with a disability as different and not fully human. As part of the evidence she uses to support her answer that language is one of the "causes" of disablement, she points out that (1) disability language often labels people as different, (2) that this difference is evaluated negatively, and (3) researchers and service providers are often rewarded for creating new terms or categories for disabilities which at the time of their invention are evaluated as less negative but over time often become new pejorative terms. She also makes the point that language is not only talk or just description but also action.

> For example, the vocabulary used to identify impairments is frequently used as terms of abuse: a persons who is not aware of their surroundings and fails to notice something important may be derided as 'blind", a person who fails to listen as 'deaf;' while a person who fails to understand something may be taunted with the term 'retard'. Such attacks feed back into our images of disabled people. The assumption is that blind and deaf people cannot interact effectively with their surroundings and that people with learning difficulties have no capacity to understand at all. In other words, using impairments as terms of abuse generalizes and exaggerates the effect they are seen as having. (Mark, 1999, 138)

PERSPECTIVES ABOUT THE HISTORICAL CHANGES IN THE LANGUAGE ABOUT DISABILITY. One of the challenges that researchers in the area of disability studies face is the changing language in the field. This may be due to several social forces. One of these is the development of new concepts to define or redefine older nomenclature that is often less particular, less specific. Secondly, researchers and organizations may gain stature or enhance their reputations by elaborating on new forms or meanings of some form of human variation. The other social force is currently entitled "political correctness" where new terminology is judged better and less stigmatizing than some older terminology.

As a researcher I have been often perplexed about the changes in nomenclature in the field of disabilities studies. The general pattern is that over time our categories have become much more detailed, differentiated and complex. Old concepts that decades earlier had been the newest and scientific terms of the day become loaded with negative connotations that may be seen as damaging to the lives of those with disabilities and rejected in formal discourse or popular discourse as politically insensitive. This is compounded by the value associated with scholarly/scientific or human services "advances" that emphasize new and "better" terms to replace older terminology. Several examples should help illustrate this. For many decades the word "handicap" was used popularly and appeared in the titles of two key pieces of legislation—the 1975 Education for Handicapped Children Act (renamed in 1990 as "IDEA"—the Individuals with Disabilities Education Act) and the 1984 Voting Accessibility for the Elderly and Handicapped Act. But sometime in the mid 1980s this word was seen as inappropriate or demeaning and was dropped in formal discourse. The World Health Organization in its new definition of disability has dropped the word "handicap" from its lexicon even though in some countries around the world it is still in use. Marks (1999, 139) writes, "Whilst 'disability" is the term used in the UK to describe social barriers, the term 'handicap' has wider currency at the international level. In the UK, the term 'handicap' has been rejected by many commentators in favor of impairment because of the patronizing connotations of being 'cap-in-hand' that is begging."

A second example is the changing nomenclature for persons with mental retardation. In *Inventing the Feeble Mind*, Trent (1994) reports that the terminology used by professionals in that field has changed greatly over the course of 150 years. As the terms used by the professionals became popularly used they often became terms of degradation. Hervey Wilbur, who opened the first school for those with mental retardation in 1848 in Barre, Massachusetts, was one of the first to distinguish gradations among those with mental retardation—then designated as the "feebleminded" or "idiots". Moving from the highest to lowest functioning he saw four levels—*simulative idiocy* involved limited delays in being able to carry out ordinary duties and enjoyments; *higher-grade idiocy* included those who could eventually go to school; *lower-grade idiocy* included those who might be capable of self-support under good management or in asylums; and *incurables* for whom development was very limited. Later in that century this last category was sometimes referred to "asylum grade" or "low functioning idiots". In the late 1800s other popular terms were dunce, simpleton, fool and imbecile. In 1910 the Committee on Classification of the Feeble-Minded of the American Association for the Feeble-Minded defined a child as retarded if the child was two or more years mentally below his or her chronological age or if as an adult the person failed to score at a mental age above 12 (using the early intelligence tests of that era). In 1910 the British Royal Commission on the Care and Confinement of the Feeble-Minded defined "mentally defectives" "scientifically" by specifying three levels of feeble-mindedness (the most generic term of this era) as follow: *feebleminded* (capable of earning a living under favorable circumstances but incapable of competing on equal terms with their normal fellows or managing their affairs with ordinary prudence; *imbeciles* (were incapable of earning their own living but could guard against common physical dangers), and *idiots* (so deeply defective from birth or an early age that they were unable to guard against common physical dangers. (Tyor and Bell, 1994). The American Association on Mental Retardation at one time had a very similar classification of levels of retardation. The AAMR has offered nine revisions of its definition of mental retardation since 1921, five of them since 1959, in order to be more precise and to replace terminology that the leadership of the association perceived had become degraded and/or outdated. The 1992 definition essentially requires that three criteria must be met to be labeled mentally retarded:

> *Mental retardation* refers to substantial limitations in present functioning. It is characterized by significantly subaverage intellectual functioning, existing concurrently with related limitations in two or more of the following applicable adaptive skill areas: communication, self-care, home living, social skills, community use, self-direction, health and safety, functional academics, leisure and work.   Mental retardation manifests before age 18. (AAMR, *Mental Retardation,* 1992,1).

Perhaps its change in 1973 was the most significant when it shifted its definition of subaverage intellectual functioning from one to two standard deviations below the IQ norm of 100. Before that, all four categories of subaverage intellectual functioning—mild, moderate, severe and profound—had been a component of the definition of mental retardation(Trent, 1994). But by excluding those with mild subaverage intellectual functioning (about IQ 70 to 85), the numbers of those categorized as mentally retarded was cut by over half. Ingredients in this change involved a growing criticism of the inhumane conditions in institutions for the mentally retarded, the high costs of institutionalization for those who were marginally deemed to need that type of care, and the other influences of the larger disability rights movement. The "moron" or "high grade mental defective" of 1910 became a "mildly retarded" person in 1980, the "imbecile" a "moderately retarded" person, and the "idiot" or "low grade mental defective" a "severely" or "profoundly" retarded person. (Stroman, 1989). However, starting in 1992, the AAMR ended its "deficit" approach to mental retardation by dropping the four categories of mild, moderate, severe and profound and replacing them with a more contextual approach about the relative use of four increasing levels of support—intermittent, limited, extensive, pervasive. (Smith, 2000).

The premier organization of professionals in the field of mental retardation has been renamed multiple times to try to escape the popular degradation of terminology for mental retardation over time. The American Association for the Study of the Feeble-Minded, founded in 1876, became the American Association of Mental Deficiency in 1933, and was renamed the American Association of Mental Retardation in 1987. In 2001 it was having its membership vote on a new name from a selected list of six possible new names or they could suggest their own. Some of the new possibilities included: American Association on Cognitive Developmental Disabilities, and American Association on Intellectual Disabilities. (Vote, 2001)

The situation in the United States has followed a similar path as in the United Kingdom where there is a tendency to see the language of the current generation as an "advance on ill-informed and immoral earlier generations." (Marks, 1994, 29) In the United Kingdom those called "mentally subnormal" in an earlier generation are now referred to as "learning disabled" even though the earlier term was no more pejorative in its time than learning disabled is now. Marks adds (1994, 29), "New inoffensive terms often function as euphemisms, and it doesn't take long for previous offensive connotations to 'catch up' with new 'politically correct' terms. She also points out, "It is important only to point out that, despite our criticisms of previous statutory and informal categories of disability, these were not consciously used by speakers at the time in order to be pejorative."

MEDICAL AND SOCIAL PARADIGMS OF DISABILITY

Two contrasting paradigms of the field of disability studies—the medical/clinical and the social paradigms exist. While we will present only these two major contrasting paradigms, some scholars have described a continuum of definitions that go from a rigid biomedical model to a rigid social model with various shades of each in several sub-models that combine varying degrees of both models in between the two extremes. The medical/clinical view in postmodernist thought is often called by different names—like realism, essentialism, and scientific positivism. It is most closely equated to the belief in the natural science approach that we can objectively understand and measure the external world. Many social scientists also argue the same way—that their verbal formulations of the world accurately portray it in objective ways. In contrast, the position of constructionism or social constructionism or post-structuralism is that our knowledge about the external world is finally a social construction that is dependent on social relations and the cultural context in which those ideas and constructs are created. They do not believe human constructions of reality can be value-free or totally objective. While each tends to interpret the world of disability research, advocacy, and treatment modalities from their own perspective, we will go on to evaluate both the benefits and limitations of each of these perspectives and argue that both are needed to develop a comprehensive view of the nature of a range of disabilities and their origins. In the field of disability studies Marks (1999, 17-18) argues that the medical or essentialist

> model of disability draws upon a realist philosophical approach which argues that some things (such as impairments) exist independently of the way in which they are socially constructed. There is, at least in principle, an objective, accurate truth, located in an external material reality, which is potentially discoverable. By contrast, post-structuralist theory argues that we can only ever grasp 'versions' of the world. There is no direct perception. The logic of the post-structuralist argument is that not only disability but also impairment is socially constructed. Post-structuralist

theory thus challenges the notion of stable, prior or essential characteristics or identities of people in favor of a much more fluid socially constructed subject.   Identities can be seen as sites of enunciation which constitute positions.   This raises problems for the disability/ability binary, which places individuals firmly on different sides of an essential divide.

Various other models or paradigms of disability have been developed.   These models most rather clearly fall into either the medical or social models even though particular disciplines or authors given them their own particular explications.   By looking at these distinctive approaches to defining disability we see that contrasting assumptions exist in different models as to what is to be focused on in the definition and the fuller description and analysis of a particular disability or "disability" as a global or general concept.   Two approaches that provide the sharpest contrast are the medical and social paradigms of disability (Weiss and Lonquist, 2000; Weitz, 2001; Higgins, 1992; Hahn, 1985, Zola, 1985.).   Table 1.1 shows these contrasts.   The **medical model** is both the oldest and the predominant model.   The assumptions it makes and its focus on the individual and the problems they face have been popularly held and often used by the mass media but are slipping as the disability rights movement has made strong thrusts in conceiving of the disabled as a minority group whose self-consciousness as an aggrieved minority has been growing over time (Stroman, 1982; Fleischer and Zames, 2001).   The medical model assumes that the social, political and educational world constructed mainly by the nondisabled requires adjustments by the disabled to fit into it rather than remaking those social, political and educational conceptualizations and practices that disable those with human variations in their bodies and/or psyches.

The medical model uses a definition of disability derived from health professionals and organizations that focus on some loss or abnormality in function that only a minority of people experience. Their focus is on the causes, symptoms, and interventions that will help that individual or others who have a similar disability.   In the past nearly all agencies serving the disabled have adopted the medical model of disability which involved assessing and devising intervention plans on how individuals can compensate for individual deficiencies. In contrast, the social model focuses on how existing social arrangements handicap individuals.   Social modelers argue that the very process of "professionals" assessing and certifying someone as disabled in order to get them legally entitled to services has the

Table 1.1 Medical and Social Models of Disability

COMPAR-ISON POINT	MEDICAL MODEL	SOCIAL MODEL
Location of impairment or disability	The **impairment** occurs in the individual due to genetic or birth defect, disease or injury. This impairment leads to a loss or abnormality in psychological, physiological, anatomic structure or functioning. The focus is on individuals not on the policies and practices of government and other organizations.	While impairments do exist in individuals, physical structures in the environment (lack of ramps e.g.), social prejudices and discrimination against those with impairments exist in many ways at many societal levels which **DISable** individuals who otherwise could function more fully if they did not exist.
Causes of impairment	Causes of impairments may be conceptualized at the cell, tissue, physiological structure or organ system level. It may also be described in terms of behavior at a functional level.	The critical focus should be on the types of disability that arise from policies and practices that disable or exacerbate individual disabling conditions arising from social values, social definitions and social practices.
Diagnosis	Diagnosis lies with trained professionals who understand the origins of disability that come from injuries, diseases, or various anatomical, chemical imbalance, physiological or genetic origins	Diagnosis in the social model focuses on the minority-like experiences of the disabled who experience a variety of forms of discrimination and who protest those practices in a variety of advocacy, self-advocacy and self-help social movements.
Federal legislation with this focus	Social Security Disability Insurance; Medicare, Supplemental Security Income; Titles I-IV of the Rehabilitation Act of 1973; Workmen's Compensation Laws	Architectural Barriers Act of 1968; Sections 501, 503, 504 of Title V of the Rehabilitation Act of 1973; The Education of All Handicapped Children Act of 1975; Voting Accessibility Act for the Elderly and Handicapped Act of 1984; Americans with Disabilities Act of 1990.

Central focus in treatment	Treatments often focus on providing some level of custodial care in earlier times and now on eradicating or minimizing the disability insofar as possible through education, surgery, medication, physical and/or mental rehabilitation by a variety of professional therapies.	Treatment involves changing the whole social system of practices to eliminate or reduce social conceptions of disability, reduce practices which exacerbate existing impairments, change the built environment and products so that they will be enabling of people with human variation in functioning rather than DISabling. Self-determination has emphasized control of services and funding by those with disabilities.
Role of professionals	Professionals are those who diagnosis and treat those with disabilities. Professionals are seen as those who know most about disabilities and their treatment and determines what happens.	Professionals may assist those with disabilities but in this model those with disabilities are citizen consumers who are to be in charge of determining the services they need and in controlling and evaluating those services.
Social Movements	Early efforts to get vocational rehabilitation programs that would enhance the functioning levels of those with impairments	Seen in a variety of Disability Rights Movement activities in the 1960s, the Independent Living Movement starting in the 1970s, and the Self-Determination Movement in the 1990s.
Prevention	Focuses on identifying and stopping events or conditions that lead to the original individual impairment.	Focuses on changing those attitudes and policies and physical structures that cause or worsen disability by undermining independence skills and attitudes and accessibilities of those defined as impaired.
Measurement	This public health model measures the extent and severity of disability in the population using measures of impairment or measures of activity/functioning level	This model is not concerned with materialistic measurement but rather focuses on changing socially oppressive structures and barriers to equality in all realms of life.

consequence of socially stigmatizing them which in turn creates dependency on the disabled status and reliance on professionals to evaluate their progress toward full functionality. As a consequence those with disabilities often define themselves as flawed, see themselves as needing the help devised by others, and end up supporting the system which has vested economic interests to maintain their disability (Albrecht, 1992; Higgins, 1992; Weitz, 2001).

Most people are familiar with the medical model which involves locating an impairment in the individual. Typically this impairment is seen as caused by a genetic inheritance, exposure to toxic elements inside or outside the womb, injury, disease, or sometimes to human neglect or abuse. And the rest of the model involves trying to detect the nature of the causes and the implications these have for rehabilitating the individual to a former state before the disability occurred or a more desirable condition if the disability has always been present.   The social model is somewhat more difficult to understand because it recognizes that the social world of ideas and constructs are not mere depictions of the real world but are conceptual constructions and reconstructions of it. In this sense, some disabilities are not simply a discovered part of the real world but are ideas that are invented about how to "frame" and interpret them and then reframe and reinterpret the world we are always revising. One of the best explications of this process of creating and sustaining the ideas of disabilities is *Making Disability: Exploring the Social Transformation of Human Variation* (1992) by sociologist Paul Higgins.   He argues with convincing evidence and illustration that disability is made and sustained over time by the following eight mutually reinforcing complex processes:

(1) FRAMING DISABILITY involves conceptualizing various forms of human deviation variously as abnormal, sick, flawed, deviant, defective, incomplete, evil and deficient in some way. We categorize such persons, count them and analyze their characteristics so they are found to be older, poorer, less likely to work, be married, have completed as much schooling as others and therefore deficient in some ways. By individualizing disability we seem to take it out of the hands of the those with disabilities and put in the hand of able persons who frame what it is like to be disabled.

(2) MANUFACTURING DISABILITY recognizes that many forms of disability are the products of injuries, war, work, poverty, self-disabling practices, and poverty. To deal with this, a entire disability business has developed as seen in what Albrecht (1992) calls The

Disability Business. About 20% of the population is found to need the services of vocational rehabilitation programs, supported employment services, vocational and substance abuse counselors, drug and medical equipment companies, providers of residential services for those with mental retardation, special education teachers, researchers who investigate the outcomes of developmental disability services, government agencies providing services to those with a variety of developmental disabilities, sheltered workshops, half-way houses for releases from institutions, physical and occupational therapists, and so on.

(3) DEPICTING DISABILITY is the process of naming disability and the disabled by the nondisabled. The names and depictions throughout history have shown them as odd, poor, beggars—cap-in-hand, that show what disability is, that it is not good, and that puts them down. This framing of them in stories, pictures, fund raising programs to help the poor souls who are cripples, retards or suffering from life's blows leaves a picture of them as undesirable and often needing medical or other professional help. Periodically as some "names" become stereotyped and politically incorrect they are deleted—e.g. the term handicapped has largely been dropped, or replaced with new terms. Thus terms for mental retardation that were scientifically correct in one era—idiots, moron, and imbeciles were replaced with newer ones—mild, moderate, severe and profound retardation that were replaced again in 1992 by four intensities of exterior supports (intermittent, limited, extensive, and pervasive) that are needed rather than individual deficits. The media often use those with disabilities to show them also as poor, dependent, defective, evil, as monsters or villains or sometimes as charitable cases who need our help. Their disability becomes their defining characteristic.

(4) CONSTRUCTING DISABILITY IDENTITIES occurs in the interactions between the nondisabled and the disabled where the "Nondisabled people often spoil disabled people's identities, making them tainted, even less than fully human."(Higgins, 1992,120). This interaction is often approached with stereotyped frames and reinforced by the extensive segregation of the disabled from the rest of the world.

(5) With the exception of most persons with developmental disabilities, the majority of people who become disabled grow up with the stereotypes of disability before they experience disability firsthand. Thus the EXPERIENCE OF DISABILITY first comes through the world created by the nondisabled about the seriousness of the problems of the disabled. "Taking their view as how the world objectively is,

nondisabled people may dismiss disabled people's experiences as delusional . . . too subjective, or irrelevant." (Higgins, 1992, 149).

(6) SERVICING the flawed disabled involves complex sets of entitlement laws, a huge variety of servicing organizations, a hierarchy of service professionals, a stratification of services among unequals all of which tends to further "handicap" the disabled by making them even more dependent on those who assume they know better than those they help as to what, when and how they need services. Some argue that the service system makes the disabled more passive and in some ways more disabled than when they entered the system that treats them as patients, cases, or clients. Higgins writes (1992, 186), "Servicing transforms disabled people into passive individuals who are unlike the rest of us. It preserves our social practices and arrangements that hamper disabled people."

(7) With a play on spelling, POLICY(ING) DISABILITY involves creating public policies that police people by keeping them in their place although that is seldom the announced intention of such legislation or agency action. Much policy for the disabled has been seen as a "charity" or handout for the handicapped. The more fortunate expect the assistance they give to the less fortunate to earn their gratitude and not to be requested as a "right". But such policies have segregated, emphasized self-support, made the disabled exceptional people, produced dependence and passivity, and exacerbated disability.

(8) MANAGING DISABILITY involves the complex set of attitudes, laws, policies, practices and institutions that persevere over time. Higgins writes (1992, 227), "We make disability. Typically, we have made disability a defect to be endured by individuals. We have made less worthy those we made disabled. We have portrayed them as dangerous, evil, pitiful, or maladjusted. Interactions between disabled and nondisabled people have often been awkward, the identities of disabled people spoiled, and the experience of disability too often dissatisfying. We directed disabled people to put themselves in the hands of professionals, who so often worked on a 'broken' person instead of serving a fellow citizen. Our policies have intentionally, at times unwittingly, and at other times in spite of good intentions typically oppressed disabled people."

As Higgins argues in his book and as we will elaborate later in this chapter and other chapters, the very same processes that have created a minority group of those with impairments or distinct ethnic or racial identities will have to be used to change the image, the policies and practices that shape the lives of all citizens whether they be minorities or not.

EVALUATING THE SOCIAL AND MEDICAL MODELS

Those persons who espouse one of these models often criticize the other model. Instead of looking at the criticisms of each model from the stance of the opposing viewpoint, let us look at the strengths of each model.

The **medical model** poses some strengths which are important:

1. It not only looks at the impairment and the processes which have produced it but at ways of reducing or eliminating the functional limitations that flow from it: whether they be mobility limitations, cognitive limitations, sensory limitations or other limitations. Many devices have been invented to minimize visual, hearing, and mobility limitations from eye glasses and hearing aids to motorized wheelchairs and lifts in vans. Medications and training technique have been developed to assist individuals with learning disabilities and cognitive disabilities. Educational programs have been devised to minimize segregation and promote community inclusion and socially healing contacts between those with and without disabilities.

2. The very categorization of the variety and sources of disability that form the basis of the medical model allow society to measure the dimensions of the problem. There are extensive reports on the epidemiology of different types and severities of a range of disabling conditions. These public health reports allow us to plan for types of services needed and the training programs needed to keep the supply of relevant professionals or various support services available to assist individuals in dealing with a wide assortment of disabling conditions.

3. The public health approach to impairments also allows for the development of prevention programs in a variety of functional areas where research has shown the types of "causes" for some form of disability. Prevention programs ranging from helmet laws to reduce brain injuries, amniocentesis to discover pre-birth anomalies, immunizations programs to reduce the effects of contagious diseases like German measles, lead-paint decontamination programs to reduce mental retardation, air-bag regulations to reduce spinal cord injuries are just a few of the significant steps that have been taken to reduce the costs of impairments (See Pope & Tarlov, 1991)

4.   The rigorous scientific approach that has been part of the medical model enables us to understand the very biological, chemical and genetic roots of many impairments and thus to develop efforts at remediation and prevention.   The social model does not purport to investigate the non-social roots of impairments to determine either the possibilities of prevention or techniques of possible remediation.

5.   The clinical model also makes us aware of the many secondary conditions that may arise from or be associated with various forms of disability.   These secondary conditions may include decubitus ulcers, physical deconditioning, contractures, cardiopulmonary conditions, and depression.   This knowledge can be used for initiating a variety of prevention or intervention measures. (Pope & Tarlov, 1991).

The strengths of the **social model** are certainly identifiable also:

1.   By focusing on the social environment this model helps people recognize that not all or even necessarily the most important "causes" of disability are rooted in genetics, disease, injury or human biology or physiology.   Rather, this model makes us aware that a complex system of mutually supporting beliefs and practices can impact those with disabilities by: stigmatizing them as less than full humans, isolating them by policies of confinement or the built environment, making them overly dependent on professionals rather than helping them develop responsible behaviors, robbing them of independent decision making that others enjoy, undermining their self-confidence in their many capabilities, over-generalizing the significance of some impairment, and defining them as tax-eaters rather than tax-contributors.

2.   This model makes us aware that preventing the presence or severity of disability does not rely solely in inoculating the physical body from harm but involves inoculating the social person from social harm by giving such persons the authority to make decisions with assistance when needed, the responsibility to live with their decisions, the freedom to be regarded as an equal in all social processes, and the rights and privileges afforded all citizens.

3.   This model recognizes that reliance on the medical model as defined in federal, state and agency laws and practices may be an additional source of disability by isolating the disabled, making them dependent on professionals for defining their condition and the services they need and for how long they need them, and by not altering the built environment for the restrictions it imposes.   This model would argue for **"demedicalization"**—diminishing the power of professionals who operate under the systems of beliefs and practices that are a part of the medical model.   Power and authority for decision-making should be

transferred to the disabled and in the case of the cognitively disabled to them and those who support them. Having that power to determine their own lives would augment their skills, include them in their natural communities and promote gains in equality.

4. This model lends itself to the experiential aspect of examining the role of disability in the lives of persons with impairments. Biographical narratives about the unfolding awareness of an impairment provide insight into the personal aspects of how people respond to stares, invasive questions, the loss of functioning, the adjustments they must make at school, home, work and in the community, and the strategies they develop to deal with changes in the intensity of the disability. The medical model tends to treat the body rather than the whole person in their environment.

5. This model is particularly helpful in exploring the historic development of policies that impact on those with disabilities and how various disability rights groups have developed strategies to combat service agency assumptions on loss of ability from sit-ins, public education campaigns, self-help programs and the like.

AN EMERGING SYNTHESIZING PARADIGM

An emerging paradigm synthesizes the strengths of the medical and social model by recognizing that disabilities are products of both medical and social processes that impact on body and chemical psyche as well as the mind and personality as they function in social contexts of sets of expectations that vary by age, gender, and social settings of many variations.

The Committee on a National Agenda for the Prevention of Disabilities began its work in the late 1980s and produced its report in 1991 under the title, *Disability in America: Toward a National Agenda for Prevention* (Pope and Tarlov, 1991). This committee recognized that changing terminology and the emergence of competing models of disability made it difficult to develop a model that was acceptable to various disability rights groups, various disciplines involved in research in this area, and terminological differences that exist among nations. Using the ideas of Saad Nagi, this twenty-three member committee and its staff developed the following overview of terms as found in Figure 1.1. This model still had a heavy lean toward the medical model and did not give adequate attention to the social aspects of defining disabilities and the architectural, technological, policy and social barriers in the form of interpersonal and institutional forms of discrimination that impact on the disabling process.

For years the World Health Organization has worked on developing a conceptual scheme that would allow for a more standardized definition and perhaps even standardized measurement and thereby meaningful and comparable data on disability worldwide. The World Health Organization published its *ICIDH: International Classification of Impairments, Disabilities and Handicaps* in 1980. Its latest revision, adopted in 2001, modified its language by replacing three words from the title with those of "functioning, disability, and health". The new title, *International Classification of Functioning, Disability and Health,* popularly referred to as *ICF, is* a new model of classification that incorporates ideas from both medical and social models on disabilities.

The new classification model is relatively complex as is shown in Table 1.2. It is also dependent on the list of definitions given below. This model focuses on three simultaneous dimensions of disablement— **impairments, activity limitations,** and **participation restrictions.** (Fujiura and Rukowski-Kmita, 2001). It is important to study the components of Table 1.2 to understand what they are and their possible interconnections. While impairments may lead to activity limitations, they may not. And while activity limitations may lead to participation restrictions, they may not. Participation restrictions come not only from body/mind related activity limitations but may also come from without as well—by barriers erected or imposed by stigma which undermines the desire to participate to lack of transportation or employment discrimination or a large range of inhibiting factors that the disability studies approach has described. (Brown, 2001)

Important definitions for understanding the model presented in Table 1.2 are as follow:

"**Body Functions** are the physiological functions of body systems (including psychological functioning)."

"**Body Structures** are anatomical parts of the body such as organs, limbs and their components."

"**Impairments** are problems in body function or structure as a significant deviation or loss."

"**Activity** is the execution of a task or action by the individual."

"**Participation** is involvement in a life situation."

"**Activity limitations** are difficulties an individual may have in executing activities."

"**Participation restrictions** are problems an individual may have in involvement in life situations."

FIGURE 1.1   An overview of the concepts of pathology, impairment, functional limitation and disability.

PATHOLOGY >>	IMPAIRMENT >>	FUNCTIONAL LIMITATION> >	DISABILITY
Interruption of or interference of normal bodily processes or structures	Loss and/or abnormality of mental, emotional, physiological, or anatomical structure or function. Includes all losses or abnormalities, not just those attributable to active pathology; also includes pain	Restriction of lack of ability to perform an activity in the manner or within the range considered normal that results from impairment.	Inability or limitation in performing socially defined activities and roles expected within a social and physical environment.
LEVEL OF REFERENCE Cells and tissue	Organ and organ systems	Organism—action or activity performance (consistent with the purpose or function of the organ system.	Society—task performance within the social and cultural context.
EXAMPLE Denvevated muscle in arm due to trauma	Atrophy of muscle	Cannot pull arm	Change of job; can no longer swim recreationally.

.Source: Pope & Tarlov, 1991, 7.

There are two types of **Contextual Factors:**

"**Environmental Factors**" make up the physical, social and attitudinal environment in which people live and conduct their lives.

"**Personal Factors**" are features of the individual that are not part of a health condition or functional state but influence functioning. (World Health Organization, *International Classification of Functioning, Disability and Health,* 2001, 25)

These definitions are woven into the matrix found in Table 1.2. This matrix recognizes that physical body components, culturally influenced desired activities and the permissiveness of the physical and social environment are all components in understanding the factors involved in defining disability.

TABLE 1.2   AN OVERVIEW OF ICF.

Components	Part 1: Functioning and Disability		Part 2: Contextual Factors	
	Body Functions and Structures	Activities and Participation	Environmental Factors	Personal Factors
Domains	Body functions Body structures	Life areas (tasks, actions)	External influences on functioning and disability	Internal influences on functioning and disability
Constructs	Change in body function (physiological) Change in body structures (anatomical)	Capacity Executing tasks in a standard environment / Performance Executing tasks in the current environment	Facilitating or hindering impact of the physical, social and attitudinal world	Impact of the attributes of the person
Positive aspect	Functional and structural integration	Activities participation	Facilitators	Not applicable
	Functioning			
Negative aspect	Impairment	Activity limitation Participation restriction	Barriers/Hindrances	Not applicable
	Disability			

Source: World Health Organization, *International Classification of Functioning, Disability and Health*, 2001, p. 11. The definitions on pages 24-25 and this table has been reprinted with the permission of the World Health Organization (WHO), and all rights are reserved by the Organization.

The approach found in Table 1.2 also gives attention to "personal factors" such as personality, initiative, sociability, maturity and energy levels that will be influential in determining participation levels in a variety of work and non-work activities.

Table 1.3 Activities and Participation : Information Matrix

Learning and applying knowledge	Watching, listening, writing, calculating, solving simple problems, solving complex problems, making decisions, learning, applying knowledge
General tasks and demands	Understanding simple tasks, doing complex tasks, doing multiple tasks, dealing with stress
Communi-cation	Receiving verbal, nonverbal and written communication; producing a variety of communications; complex discussions
Mobility	Changing positions, carrying, walking, moving equipment, driving vehicles
Self-care	Bathing, dressing, choosing appropriate clothes, taking care of one's health
Domestic life	Cooking, domestic housework, using appliances, taking care of appliances, pets, plants, helping others
Interpersonal Interactions and relationships	Showing warmth, physical support, following social rules, relating to strangers, developing relations with family members, authorities
Major life areas	Participation in education at various levels, working, carrying out economic transactions
Community, social and civic life	Engaging in communal institutions: health care, religion, social relations, recreation, ceremonies, neighbors, citizenship acts

**The original table had two "qualifiers" in each of the nine domains where "performance" was distinguished from "capacity."
Source: Adapted and modified by illustration with permission from WHO, *International Classification of Functioning, Disability and Health.* 2001.

The classification scheme of disabilities in the ICF is quite complex. It lists nine categories or "domains" of disability each of which can be coded with many more concrete disabilities under two qualifiers entitled "performance" and "capacity".   "Performance" is what a person can actually do using personal assistants and assistive devices in a barrier free environment.   On the other hand "capacity" is a "construct" that "aims to indicate the highest probable level of functioning that a person may reach in a given domain at a given moment" without such conditions.   The gap between performance and capacity allows for a measurement of the importance of environment for a given person. The social model component in this classification schema is seen in the following statement from the ICF explication: "The gap between capacity and performance reflects the difference between the impacts of current and uniform environments, and thus provides a useful guide as to what can be done to the environment of the individual to improve performance."   The classification scheme is presented in Table 1.3.   *(WHO, International Classification of Disability and Health Functioning,* 2001, p. 15).

COUNTING DISABILITIES

Just as there are different ways to define disability there are significantly different methods to count disability and measure its severity that follow in general ways from the definition of disability that is used.   Two major agencies of the U.S. government have historically used four different definitions of disability and somewhat different methods of collecting data on disabilities that result in significantly different counts on the amount of disability and/or the number of persons with disabilities.   While precise information would be useful for health care planning, policy and program development and for determining equipment and service needs, it is not available. At the same time, these different definitions provide windows into different aspects of disability such as how many have their activities of daily living limited or how many need assistance or how many are limited in the kinds and amounts of work they can do or the nature of the origins of their disabilities.   The two major federal agencies which collect information on disability are the Census Bureau and the Department of Health and Human Services.   Table 1.4 lays out the four major data gathering devices that the federal government uses to collect data on disabilities.   The Census Bureau has three primary sources for collecting information on disability: (Disability, Census Bureau Data on Disability, 2001)

1.   The most extensive and preferred data source is the SIPP—the **Survey of Income and Program Participation** that periodically collects information by surveying a panel of households repeatedly

every four months for two years on a small sample of households. However, the small sample size, sample attrition over time and problems inherent in asking questions about complex forms of disabilities and their severity limit the accuracy of even this most thorough form of collecting data on disabilities among children and adults (McNeil, 2000)

2. The decennial census collects only a limited amount of information on disability from a fraction of the population that receives the longer census form that focuses primarily around work activity and has not used the same set of questions over time which limits the comparability of the data over time.

3. The third Census Bureau data set is the CPS—**Current Population Survey** that asks people each month for a year if they are out of the labor force or if they experience limits in the kind or amount of **work** they can do by reason of a disability or a health problem. The Department of Health and Human Services also uses a survey method of collecting data by means of the NHIS and the NHIS-D—The National Health Interview Survey on Disability begun in 1994. This collects information about housing, use of long-term care services, social activities, work history/employment, use of assistive technologies, vocational rehabilitation, transportation, health insurance, health opinions and behaviors, self-direction, family structures, community services, living arrangements and conditions and impairments. (National Health Interview Survey on Disability, 1995). Both the NHIS and the NHIS-D survey are more medically oriented than the SIPP approaches.   Their essential approach is to define disability as a **limitation of activity caused by chronic health conditions or a disability.** ("Section 1.   Prevalence of Disabilities". 2001)

A limitation of all the methods of collecting information about disabilities is that they involve surveying households which exclude over 2 millions Americans located in prisons, nursing homes and institutions for those with mental illness or mental retardation many of whom would be considered disabled. Furthermore, since these involve survey methods of asking adult people questions, they often start with the age group above 15! One of these methods is the Survey of Income and Program Participation (SIPP) carried out periodically. It defines disability in terms of **specific functional activities** that are further broken down by (1) ADLs—Activities of Daily Living, (2) IADLs—Instrumental Activities of Daily Living, (3) the use of special aids, (4)

Table 1.4 Major approaches taken by the U.S. Federal Government in Defining and Measuring Disability

Title of Survey	NHIS—National Health Interview Survey carried out by DHHS	SIPP—Survey of Income and Program Participation carried out by Census Bureau	Decennial Census	CPS—Current Population Survey carried out by Census Bureau
Sample size	1999—Interviewed 37,573 households to get information on 97,050 adults and 12,901 children under age 18	Each of 4 panels of 14,000 to 36,7000 households are interviewed over a 2.5 to 4 year period every four months	Whole population gets short form; a sample gets long form that contains questions about disability	A monthly representative sample of about 60,000 house-holds focused on income and work for people 16 years of age and older.
Definition of Disability	Focuses on chronic (lasting 3 mos or +) health conditions and disabilities that give rise to activity limitations. Has 3 measures of disability: >Activity limitation in major activity. >Need for personal assistance in IADLs. >Work limitation	Most complex: asks about: (1) Function limitations (2)ADLs (3)IADLs (4)Use of assistive tech. (5)Work disability (6)Mental functioning (7)Disabling conditions among 0-17 age group (8)Receipt of SSDI, SSI, TANF, WIC	Every 10 years gathers limited data about disability in relation to work, mobility, self-care. Defines disability as a long-lasting physical, mental, or emotional condition that limit activities in ADL, IADL, or work.	Each month asks questions about who has health conditions or disabilities that keeps them from working, forced them into retirement or new work and whether they receive Medicare, SSI (if under 65), or veteran's disability compensation.

Number of disabled in year given	39.1 million in 1994	19.4% or 49 million in 1991-92. 19.7% or 52.6 million in 1997	From 12 monthly CPS samples: % disabled: Ages 5-20 6.7% Ages 21-64 14.1 Age 65 & + 40.9 Total 23.4 N = 59.5 million	% working in 1998: M disabled 32.3 F disabled 28.5 M not disabled 89.1 F not disabled 75.8
Limitations	>Small sample size. >Not good on estimating mental illness or mental retardation. >Excludes institutional population	>Small sample size. >Not good on estimating mental illness or mental retardation. >Excludes institutional population	>Questions don't remain same each census. >Limited number of questions.	>Limited number of questions. > Excludes institutional population.

Sources: Jans and Stoddard, 1999. *Chartbook on Women and Disability in the United States. An Info Use Report.* Washington D.C.: U.S. Department of Education, National Institute on Disability and Rehabilitation Research,1999; "Disability Affects One-Fifth of all Americans", 1997; "Overview of the Survey of Income and Program Participation", 1998; McNeil, 2001; "Americans with Disabilities", 1994, Table 2; "Americans with Disabilities", 1997, Table 5.

the presence of certain conditions related to mental functioning, and (4) work.

The various definitions of disability typically produce numbers to show that 15% to about 22% of the U.S. population has a disability. However, many of the persons who have some limitation in activity would not consider themselves to be disabled because the severity of their activity limitation is not very great. According to the most inclusive definition of disability, in 1997 about 1 in 5 or 19.6% of the entire non-institutional population of 267,665,000 have a disability—making those with disabilities the largest minority group in the country. In 1997, about 52,596,000 people experienced disabilities using the SIPP data. However, if we count those with a **severe disability**—defined as a person who is unable to perform one or more activities, or who uses an assistive device to get around, or who needs assistance from another person to perform basic activities then about 33 million Americans or12.3% of the population has a severe disability. If we define severity in a more limited fashion to those who require personal assistance to carry out everyday activities, then about 9 million Americans have disabilities. ("Disability. 2001)

Table 1.5 shows detail on one of the two most comprehensive ways to measure disability undertaken in the United States for adults. Unfortunately, it does not include in its sample of interviewees some of the most disabled in the United States—those in a variety of institutions like nursing homes, prisons, and institutions for those with mental illnesses or mental retardation. At the same time the two right hand columns shows the number of persons who meet particular definitions of that type of disability and who meet the "severe" form of it.

THE DEMOGRAPHY OF DISABILITY

While counting the numbers of people with disabilities and knowing how these vary by number of risk factors or social characteristics may not seem very relevant to persons concerned with rights, such data can be important for assessing economic and social disparities between those with and without disabilities. Such information can also be informative in policy planning decisions in estimating the future costs of welfare benefits, determining the need for special education teachers, vocational counselors, hearing aids, wheelchairs, rehabilitation hospital beds and training programs for occupational therapists and so on. Table 1.6 lists some correlates – variables that are statistically correlated with disabilities. This table

TABLE 1.5 COMPONENTS IN THE MEASUREMENT OF DISABILITY USED IN THE SURVEY OF INCOME AND PROGRAM PARTICIPATION FOR ADULTS 18 AND OVER AND NUMBERS OF THEM IN MILLIONS WITH ANY AND SEVERE DISABILITIES IN 1991.

Component of Disability	Any Disability	**Severe Disability
1. **Functional Activities:** (can you) (1) lift and carry a 10 pound weight, (2) walk 3 city blocks (3) see the words and letters in ordinary newsprint (4) hear what is said in normal conversation with another person (5) have one's speech understood (6) climb a flight of stairs	34	15
2. **ADLs—ACTIVITIES OF DAILY LIVING** (1) getting in and out of bed (2) bathing (3) getting around inside home (4) dressing (5) using toilet (6) eating	8	3.9
3. **IADLs—Instrumental Activities of Daily Living** (1) going outside home to shop/see doctor (2) doing light housework (3) keeping track of money and paying bills (4) using telephone (5) preparing meals	12	9
4. **Used Assistive Devices:** (1) wheelchairs (2) canes or crutches for 6 months or longer	1.5 4.0	1.5 4.0
5. **Had a mental or emotional disability or mental retardation.**	6.9	6.9
6. **Had a condition that limited the kind or amount of work they could do.** (Aged 16-67)	19.5	
7. **Had a condition that made it difficult to do housework.** (Over age 16).	18.1	
Totals*	49.0	24.0

Totals do not add to 100 because many individuals have multiple types of disabilities as measured in the seven components listed above.

Source: Adapted from "Americans with Disabilities", 1994, p.1

> ** What is a severe disability? "Adults aged 15 and over were classified as having a severe disability if they used a wheelchair or had used another special aid for 6 months or longer, were *unable* to perform one or more functional activities or *needed assistance* with and ADL or IADL, were *prevented* from working at a job or doing housework, or had a selected condition including autism, cerebral palsy, Alzheimer's disease, senility or dementia, or mental retardation. " ("Americans with Disabilities", 1994, 1)

clearly shows some factors that are closely connected to disability either as causal influences or as consequences of disability. Or, as in the case of poverty, disability may be both a causal agent for some and a result for others and both for many.

The biggest risk factor associated with disability is age. As table 1.7 shows, the risk of disability increases substantially with age, particularly the risk of severe disability. The risk of a severe disability increases thirty fold from the youngest to the oldest age category in comparison to under a six-fold increase for all disabilities. But the consequences of disability are very substantial, especially as the severity of the disability increases.   Perhaps the most important consequence is the increase in poverty among those with disabilities of working age. The rate of poverty for all adults of working age in 1995 was 10.2% but this rose to 30% for those with any activity limitation and to 38.3% among those unable to work due to a

Table 1.7. Percentage with Disabilities by Age, October 1994-January 1995

AGE	ANY DISABILITY	SEVERE DISABILITY
O-14 Years	9.1	1.1
15-64 Years	18.7	8.7
65 Years & Over	52.9	33.4

Source: "Disabilities Affect One-Fifth of All Americans" Census Brief, 1997.

Table 1.6 Some Correlates of Disability

CORRE-LATE VAR-IABLE	DIRECTION OF RELATIONSHIP
Age	Age is the strongest predictor of disability. Only 6.2% of children in 1988 had any limitation in activity compared to 58.7% of those 85 and over. There is a noticeable increase with age of having limitations in Activities of Daily Living, limitations in Instrumental Activities of Daily Living and needing assistance with either one of these and having more bed disability days.
Work	Compared to able persons, about 6% fewer of those with non-severe disabilities were working in 1994-95 while about 54% fewer of those with severe disabilities were working.
Social Activities	Persons with disabilities reported the following percentage differences compared to non-disabled people in 1998: 13% more had daily transportation problems; 27% fewer went to restaurants weekly; 12% fewer socialized with friends, neighbors or relatives weekly; 28% less reported they were satisfied with their lives and about 23% fewer reported doing each of the following things annually—going to a movie, a live music performance or a sporting event.
Physician Contacts	As the severity of disabilities increase the number of physician contacts increase. In 1989 persons 18-64 who were unable to perform major activities were seeing doctors about five times as often as persons without limitations in major activities. Persons with health insurance coverage saw physicians more frequently than those without insurance.
Average Length of Stay LOS) and Hospital Dis-charges	As the severity of disabilities increased as measured by the degree of work activity or by the degree of activity limitation or by the increased need for help, persons with disabilities were not only more likely to have longer average lengths of stays in hospitals but to be more frequently admitted to them than persons without disabilities.

Race	Both black men and women in comparison to whites have proportionally more limitations in activity, more bed disability days, more restricted activity days, more physician visits and more hospital discharges.
Medical Expend- itures	In 1987 persons with disabilities accounted for 17% of the population but 47% of medical expenditures. While some disabilities have medically based origins, many more have negative health consequences.
Income	Persons with disabilities have substantially lower incomes than the able, often because they have lower rates of participation in the labor force, lower employment levels, and lower levels of pay.
Sources of Medical Expend- itures	Persons with disabilities have about two to three times more of their expenses for hospitalization, physician services, other professional services and drugs paid for by Medicare and/or Medicaid than do people without disabilities.
Poverty and Special Education	Almost exactly twice the percentage of children below the poverty line as above it were either receiving or needed special education in 1992.
Sex	A higher percent of males than females experience disabling conditions and injuries throughout the life cycle except after age 85 when females have more activity limitations.
Age and the Need for Personal Assistance	Only 0.3% of the population aged 15-24 need help with one or more Activities of Daily Living but in a rising curvilinear pattern, this climbs to 22.9% of those age 85 and over needing assistance.

Sources: Trupin and Rice, 1995; Max, Rice and Trupin, 1996; LaPlante, Rice and Wenger, 1995; Trupin, Rice and Max, 1995; Wenger, Kaye and LaPlante, 1996; Kennedy, LaPlante and Kaye, 1997; Trupin and Yelin, 1999; Jans and Stoddard, 1999.

disability. The cause of much of this poverty is unemployment—either due to disability-related work limitations or employment discrimination against those with disabilities, a history of a disability or a perceived disability. Table 1.8 presents data that shows that the percentage of those employed with various kinds of disability is substantially lower than those without a disability. The employment level is lower in all cases for those with greater severity of a given kind of disability.

In comparison to an employment rate of 78.2% for those without impairments, the employment rate was much lower but highest for persons with hearing and then vision limitations and lowest for persons with mobility limitations due to wheelchair use, use of other mobility

Table 1.8   Numbers and percentages of persons aged 21-64 who are employed by kind and severity of disability in 1997 (From Survey of Income and Program Participation)

KIND OF DISABILITY	NUMBER	Number and Percent employed with not severe disability	Number and Percent employed with a severe disability
Difficulty seeing	3,484,000	N = 2,997,000 % = 44.1	N = 487,000 % = 30.6
Difficulty hearing	3,416,000	N = 3,189,000 % = 63.4	N = 227,000 % = 48.5
Difficulty with speech	1,276,000	N = 1,025,000 % = 40.1	N = 252,000 % = 24.1
Difficulty walking	9,129,000	N = 5,222,000 % = 42.4	N = 3,907,000 % = 22.5
Difficulty with stairs	9,420,000	N = 7,095,000 % = 40.1	N = 2,325,000 % = 19.2
Difficulty lifting	7,232,000	N = 3,935,000 % = 38.2	N = 3,297,000 % = 20.1
Use of a wheelchair	874,000		% = 21.9
Use of cane, crutches or walker	1,484,000		% = 24.8
NO DISABILITY	152,886,000	78.2	

Source: Table 1, "Data on Disability and Employment," 1997.

assistive devices, and difficulty lifting, walking or climbing stairs. The SIPP data for 1997 showed interesting information on **"disability domains"** that enables disability researchers to get some grasp of the different kinds of disabilities and how they overlap in varying degrees among persons. It is important to understand the components of three domains shown in Table 1.9. The **communication domain** included those who had limitations in reading, hearing and speaking. The **mental domain** included those with limitations in counting and handling money, had learning disabilities or were mentally retarded, had Alzheimer's disease or dementia, or emotional or mental illnesses. The **physical domain** was the broadest category that covered using a wheelchair, cane, crutches or a walker to get around, being unable to carry 10 pounds or get into or out of a bed or chair, walk, climb stairs or grasp an object. ("Americans with Disabilities," 1994) This broad category includes some people who might not define themselves as disabled. As indicated by Table 1.9, 58.3% of all those with disabilities have a disability in one domain, while 28.3% have disabilities in two domains and 10.3% have disabilities in three domains while 4.4% have not had their type of disability identified. If we sum up the disabilities in each of the three domains, we find that 80.3% have physical disabilities alone or in combination with other disabilities, while 32.8% have communication disabilities alone or in combination with other disabilities, while 30.3% have mental disabilities alone or in combination with other disabilities.

Information about children under 15 shows they are much less likely to have disabilities than adults. Yet sizeable numbers of children have disabilities that interfere with play, movement, learning, and self care. In 1997, 2% of U.S. children under 3 years of age or 233,000 were categorized as disabled by the SIPP interview process. For those aged 3 , 4 or 5, the rate increased to 3.4% meaning 410,000 children had disabilities. Once they enter the school age years, 6 through 14, the rate triples to over 1 out of 9 children or 11.2% have a disability and of these 4.8% are regarded as severe. Some 4,018,000children in this age group were labeled with one or more disabilities the most common of which were learning disabilities. ("Americans with Disabilities": 1997 –Table 5)

The data from the year 2000 decennial census will not be available until sometime in 2002. The most recent data on the extent of disability comes from the "2000 Supplementary Survey" carried out that year and based on about a random sample of 700,000 persons.

Table 1.9 Numbers and Percentages of Persons Age 15 and Older with Disabilities by Disability Domain in 1977.

DISABILITY DOMAINS	NUMBER IN 000s	PERCENT OF TOTAL U.S. POPULA-TION	PERCENT OF ALL PERSONS WITH DISABILITIES
DISABILITY IN ONE DOMAIN	27,952	13.4	58.3
Communication	2,940	1.4	6.1
Physical	21,077	10.1	44.0
Mental	3,935	1.9	8.2
DISABILITIES IN TWO DOMAINS	13,582	6.5	28.3
Communication & Physical	7,544	3.6	15.7
Communication & Mental	727	.3	1.5
Physical & Mental	5,312	2.6	11.1
DISABILITIES IN THREE DOMAINS	4,294	2.1	10.3
DOMAIN(S) NOT IDENTIFIED	2,107	1.0	4.4
TOTALS	47,935	23.0	*100.5

*Adds to more than 100 due to rounding error.

Source: Adapted and Modified from "Americans with Disabilities": 199 –Table 2.

From this sampling procedure, estimates are made on the extent of disability in the United States for the non-institutional population—persons not in mental hospitals, nursing homes, institutions for students, prisoners and those with mental retardation. For the population ages 5 to 20, the estimate of persons with disabilities was 4,245,070—6.7% of all persons in that age group. For persons, 21 through 64, there were 22,189,889 with disabilities for a rate of 14.1%. For this age group, 48.7% of those with disabilities were employed in comparison to a rate of 78.8% for persons without disabilities. And for those aged 65 and over, 13,524,057 were estimated to be disabled for a disability rate of 40.9% (Census 2000 Supplementary Survey Summary Tables.) America has a growing rate of disability mainly due to an aging population. One disability statistics center points out that there are a number of myths concerning disability. Following is a listing of some of those myths and the correct facts:

Myth: Disability is an unusual, pathological condition.

Fact: Disability is a normal part of life, experienced by almost everyone, particularly when they get older.

Myth: Disability affects other people's families.

Fact: Nearly one-third (29.2%) of American families include at least one member with a disability. Disability affects nearly all families at one time or another.

Myth: Disability is mostly a problem for older people.

Fact: 68.4% of people limited in activity are under age 65; 57.6% are of working age and 10.8% are under 18.

Myth: Disabilities begin at birth or in early childhood.

Fact: Most people with disabilities have no disability for much of their lives. Only one-fifth (21%) of people with disabilities acquired their disability before age 20, while roughly half (53%) have onset after 40.

Myth: Most people with disabilities use wheelchairs, or are blind or deaf.

Fact: Most disabilities are much less apparent. Heart disease and back problems are the two most common causes of activity limitation affecting 7.9 and 7.7 millions Americans, respectively.

Myth: Disability is primarily a health issue.

Fact: 58.9% of non-elderly adults with disabilities rate their health as good to excellent. In many cases, disability is the result of a past health problem or an injury; such disabilities often do not necessitate continuing medical attention. (Demographics, 1996, 5. Emphasis in the original).

SUMMARY

Defining and counting disabilities is contested for a number of reasons. Perhaps the most contested aspect comes from disparate medical and social perspectives. While the medical perspective argues that disability can be defined in measurable ways since disabilities exist in individuals in detectable forms, the pure social model argues that both the definition of social disability and the person-environment context of interaction are the sources of disability and since these are changeable then disability cannot be exhaustively defined or measured since these are historically and environmentally dependent. These two models are valuable in pointing to different elements that need to be attended to—the location of disabling conditions in both the individual and the environment and the need to understand their interaction in an ever-changing historical contexts. Other perspectives on disability point out the disability is a complex and multidimensional concept that has been conceptualized in terms of physical, psychological, and physiological components, degrees of severity, presenting itself in an infinite variety of combinations, and involving a variety of others who are confronted by it: legislators developing policies about prevention and treatment, parents, friends and professionals who relate in complex ways to persons with disabilities and the very complex yet highly individualized experience of disabling processes within and without the self.

An explication of the social model is undertaken to enable the reader to understand it in contrast to the historically and professionally dominant model of disability. This explication following Paul Higgins shows that historically disability has been framed in mainly negative ways as flawed, abnormal, and sick so that disability is not only manufactured by injurious processes but also by social definitions provided by professionals and a growing disability business. This sector of the economy constructs disability identities, services them with the services it has defined they need and with the policies the able have constructed to serve and manage those who are defined as incapable of doing it themselves.

We have also argued that a new model of disability is emerging within the auspices of the World Health Organization. This model takes into account the points of both the medical and social models in arguing for an interactive model that neither loses sight of the human body or the social context of disability.

Even for medical professionals, sociological epidemiologists and welfare policy theorists, the defining and counting of disability even within an expanded sensitivity to the role of the built and social environment is not an easy task. The U.S. government continues to use a variety of definitions and measurement techniques that understandably show substantial variations in the amount and severity of disability in the United States. These definitions are not developed simply to determine medical or education or vocational rehabilitation needs but to determine the key types of functional limits people experience, how many need assistance with one or more Activities of Daily Living or Instrumental Activities of Daily Living and how many are not working. Some definitions are more directed at the impact of disability on employment, some on just mobility, and some on the chronic conditions or impairments that lead to disability as well as policies that undermine independence in living. While the measurement of disability is complex and multidimensional, it may need to be so because measurement serves many purposes.

CHAPTER 2
A BRIEF HISTORY OF THE DISABILITY RIGHTS MOVEMENT

ISSUES IN THIS CHAPTER

In this chapter we will focus on six issues related to the historical development of the disability rights movement. First we focus on what social movements are and why they arise. Social movements are about change that involves groups who advocate for change from the current system of beliefs and/or practices to another system that is believed by advocates to be better. Secondly, we will analyze types of advocates to better understand the diversity of stakeholders who advocate for changes or sometimes for the status quo. Third, we will do an analysis of the early disability rights movement and find that it was made up of advocates for categories of people with one type of disability such as visual impairment or mental illness. Fourth, we will describe the emergence of the cross-disability rights movement in the 1970s as the movement saw its most rapid growth during this time. Beginning slowly in the 1970s and coalescing more fully by about 1990 there began what Oberschall (1993, 383) calls "convergence" in the disability rights movement that involved a coming together of persons with different kinds of disabilities reflecting some "uniformity of attitudes, dispositions and behavior." Fifth, we will note the effects of electronic communication on the disability rights movement. Sixth, we will look at the major "product" of advocacy—legislation that is designed to change some oppression or discrimination. In this case we will focus on national legislation.

SOCIAL MOVEMENTS: ORIGINS AND EVOLUTION

Much of the time people pursue their goals or seek solutions to their hardships or the denial of their rights as individuals. However, when groups of such people work together to benefit some category or group of people we have the makings of a social movement. Sociologists use the term "social movement" to "refer to organized collective activities to bring about or resist some fundamental changes in an existing group or society" (Schaefer, 2001, 565). Some sociologists add that there must be large numbers of people involved to truly make it a social movement (Henslin, 1999).

Social movements can be classified as falling into three major types: (1) **personal transformation movements** aimed at changing individuals as was the case with the hippie movement or the "New Age" movement of the 1990s, (2) **social change movements** aimed at changing some aspect of society either through a **reform movement** that seeks evolutionary change within or through existing social institutions or a **radical movement** that seeks fundamental change in a society—often through political revolution, and (3) **reactionary movements** that resist changes going on or want to reinstate the values and behaviors of an earlier social order (Andersen and Taylor, 2000). The disability rights movement is primarily an example of a **reform movement** that seeks change in how those with disabilities are viewed and treated in a society. Social movements are typically spurred on by a sense of relative deprivation—that existing social arrangements for some group or category of persons--like those in wheelchairs or the parents of children with mental retardation--are not fair or right in comparison to persons without those impairments. Older social movements that occurred in the first half of the 1900s tended to be class-based movements oriented to gaining greater equity in income. But "new" social movements typical since the 1960s have focused much more on issues of "rights". These "rights" issues have involved the denial of equal opportunities for education, jobs, public access to places and services. Such social movements seek greater autonomy and self-determination for members. Movement members often develop strong identities with the goals of the organizations they join. Disability rights organizations usually have multiple objectives they want to see accomplished. These movements are normative in nature—claiming that the grievances of the deprived group pose fundamental threats to the founding values of a society. These movements want to correct what they believe are social injustices.

Sociological research reveals that social movements go through stages as they grow and mature over time (Tilly, 1978, Oberschall. 1993, Henslin, 1999, Renzetti & Curran, 2000). The first stage involves **initial unrest and agitation.** During this stage a few people are upset about some condition or form of discrimination or mistreatment they perceive. In the disability rights movement focal concerns have been segregation of those with disabilities in institutions, lack of access to education, jobs and/or services on an egalitarian basis. To be successful movements must have members who want strongly to change such conditions. Typically one or more leaders emerge to crystallize the issue(s) and give direction as to what needs to be done and how those things need to be done. Many potential movements die at this stage if leadership and agendas do not clearly emerge. The second stage, **resource mobilization,** is perhaps most critical if social movements are to endure and achieve success. Mobilizing resources involves raising money, developing an organization to give continuity and leadership to the movement, recruiting members, and developing one or more techniques of promoting the message of the movement from boycotts, mass media campaigns and lobbying, to education, sit-ins, marches and rallies. Without an organizational base an incipient social movement may die. The third stage of **organization** involves developing a division of labor among the paid/unpaid staff and volunteers, developing and then implementing ongoing policies to guide the organization to better define its goals and operating procedures. As the organization matures over time, often years or decades, the initial excitement and commitment associated with the early rise of the organization begins to wane. In the fourth stage, **institutionalization,** a bureaucracy emerges to guide the organization. This stage is seen in the formalization of a hierarchy, control usually located in a paid staff, the waning of the initial excitement that powered the early organization, perhaps a sense that many of the original goals have been reached, the acceptance of many of its policies and leadership in other parts or society and perhaps a focus on maintaining the organization for its own sake. The last stage, **organization decline and/or resurgence,** reflects the finding that some organizations decline as the original membership departs and the original goals have been wholly or partially met or their attainment seems impossible. For example, in the Table 2.2 listing of civil-rights related organizations at the national level, seven are listed which have closed down for one reason or another. The organization may have lost its base of support with changing times, and/or the demise of its original leadership and/or the emergence of new social issues which antiquate the movement. On the other hand, a variety of events or processes may lead to the organization's resurgence such as new leadership, a redefined and/or expanded mission, a challenging event or threat that requires renewed efforts to meet their original or redefined goals. (Tarrow, 1994; Henslin, 1999; Schaefer, 2001)

DEFINITIONS OF ADVOCACY AND SELF-ADVOCACY

One of the noticeable developments since World War II has been the growth of the advocacy movement and particularly the self-advocacy movement among those persons with a variety of disabilities. Self-advocacy is a subset of advocacy and in a historical sense has been the most recent development of the disability rights movement.

It is fairly certain the concept of advocacy had its roots in the British legal system where barristers or advocates were persons who were to plead in another's behalf. This pleading involved a professional relationship between a client and an advocate who was familiar with legal systems and procedures and the art of legal argument. Advocates today certainly do not need to be lawyers.   Advocacy has many variations including who is doing it, how it is done, over what time period, the resources that are generated, the purposes of the advocacy, the relationship between the advocate and advocatee, and the outcome of the process.

"*Advocacy* is the process of doing something for or speaking in behalf of some person or cause" (Stroman, 1989,182). For example, one of the functions of the International League of Societies for Persons with Mental Handicaps has been to frame statements about the "rights" of those with mental handicaps and push for the adoption of those statements by various bodies such as the United Nations or various national governments. In 1968 this league adopted a statement on such rights entitled "From Charity to Rights" which was powerfully worded, and, under the initiative of France, was adopted by the United Nations Assembly in 1971 as a "Declaration of the General and Special Rights of the Mentally Retarded" (Dybwad, 1990, 33).

"Self-advocacy is speaking for oneself, making one's needs known, and asserting one's rights" (Stroman, 1989, 192).   Self-advocacy emerged later than advocacy by others (professionals, family members and friends) in the disability rights movement. This is due to the stigma and often presumed lower incompetence of those with disabilities. However, this presumed lower competence varied greatly by the nature of the disability. For example, self-advocacy appeared first among those with physical handicaps where there was a general societal presumption of mental and social competency. In contrast, the presumed incompetence has been most pervasive about those with mental handicaps—perhaps most for those with mental retardation and followed by those with mental illness. Paul Williams and Bonnie Shoultz in *We Can Speak for Ourselves* (1982) present evidence that the self-advocacy movement among those with mental retardation began first with leisure clubs among the mentally handicapped in Sweden in the 1960s. A tradition grew in that country that these leisure clubs of the mentally handicapped could run their own meetings, make their own decisions and elect their own officers with some initial assistance from parents or professionals. These ideas were shared with other leisure clubs out of which grew regional conferences and later a national convention in 1968 in Sweden. A similar national conference was held in Great Britain in 1972. At this time there were about twenty "support groups" among the mentally retarded in Oregon. From these groups, two professionals and three persons with mental retardation attended a 1973 conference in British Columbia organized by professionals to investigate basic ideas about self-advocacy. The five attendees came back enthused with ideas about self-advocacy and shared these ideas with the twenty-some support groups in Oregon. They got a representative from each of these support groups plus some representatives from the Fairview Hospital and Training Center (an institution for those with mental retardation) to assist in planning a state convention. After many months of planning, the first convention was held in 1974 in Otter Crest, Oregon under the title "People First". During one of the 1973 planning sessions for this first state convention, the delegates were looking for a name for their new organization. One member said, "We are tired of being seen first as handicapped or retarded or disabled. We want to be seen as people first." (Williams & Shoultz, 1982, 54). "People First" was the name that won the vote. At the first state meeting in Oregon, 200 people were expected but 560 showed up.

Since 1974, the "People First" self-advocacy movement has spread across the country. By 1978, statewide conventions had been held in six other states and provinces. In 1980, over 1000 attended the "People First International" held in Portland Oregon. By 1980 there were at least 70 state or local groups and by 1986 there were 20 state chapters of People First International. (Williams and Shoultz, 1982). By 2001 there were 500 People First Chapters in the United States and 43 in other countries with a world wide membership of over 17,000. The Alaska chapter states simply that, "The People First movement promotes self-advocacy, independent living, and civil rights for people experiencing disabilities." ("Self-Advocacy has . . .", 2001, 1). The Salem, Oregon chapter describes People First as "developmentally disabled people joining together to learn how to speak for ourselves. We want others to know that we are PEOPLE FIRST, and that our disabilities come second. We form chapters at places where we work or live. We have local chapters in our cities and those chapters join together to make state chapters." ("People First of Oregon, 2001, 1).

VARIATIONS IN ADVOCACY

Advocacy involves a number of variations that are important in fully understanding its richness. The following are some dimensions of advocacy which illustrate that advocacy takes on a multiple dimensions.
(1) INFORMAL-NATURAL ADVOCATES. This is advocacy undertaken by family members and friends—parents speaking out for their children, children advocating for their older or disabled parents, spouses for each other, more distant family members or friends providing supports and looking out for a person with an impairment. While technically advocating for the needs or rights of another person, such advocacy may also or even primarily serve the needs of the advocate by relieving them of stress, giving them financial support or help in a variety of ways. The coming together of a number of like-minded advocates to form an organization to collectively pursue common goals may lead to the fourth type of advocacy listed below.
(2) SELF-ADVOCATES. A person who looks out or speaks out for their own self is a self-advocate. The potential for self-advocacy may depend substantially on the nature and severity of a disability as well as how others perceive the disabled person and their willingness to give them independence and support.
(3) PAID SERVICE PROVIDER ADVOCATES. Such advocates work for service providers that make them employees of some government agency, a non-profit or a for profit agency. As part of their job they are to advocate for the rights or needs of the individuals they serve. The potential problem here is that the culture of their employing organization or its regulations weigh heavily on the advocacy they provide rather than just the "needs" or "rights" of the person for whom they are advocating. Neufield (1979) makes a distinction between

Internal and external advocates. An **internal advocate** is one who is an employee of the very organization they may advocate against. For example, some hospitals or other organizations employ ombudspersons to look after the rights of their customers who may be endangered or neglected by other employees of that same organization. In contrast, an **external advocate,** is not an employee of the agency that he or she is advocating against. They would be the type of advocate described in the next paragraph—a rights organization advocate

(4) RIGHTS ORGANIZATION ADVOCATES. Such advocates typically have an organizational base from which they operate which will define in variable detail, the mission of the organization, the goals they are to pursue, and the methods they are to follow. Occasionally, civil rights groups may get co-opted by governmental or provider organizations for which they provide advice, research, outcome studies or the like which fit in with their mission statement. Most advocacy groups have substantial independence if they depend on member dues and gifts for their advocacy activities.

(5) SOCIETAL ADVOCATES. Such advocates are paid government employees who have the responsibility of framing legislation and regulations on behalf of persons with disabilities as well as looking at the integrity of implementation of legislation. For example, the Developmentally Disabled Assistance and Bill of Rights Act of 1975 created a network of state-operated Protection and Advocacy agencies to investigate allegations of abuse or neglect of persons with disabilities. Legislators have acted on behalf of citizens with disabilities by framing legislation to not only provide dollar and/or service resources to persons with disabilities but also to determine the adequacy of that effort as it is implemented. While this type of advocacy may overlap to some degree with PAID SERVICE PROVIDER ADVOCATES, it provides an important analytical distinction about the ownership of advocacy.

EARLY NATIONAL DISABILITY RIGHTS GROUPS

The development of disability-related organizations that claim to be national in scope and membership is a clear indicator of the development of the disability rights movement. While it would be interesting to look at local or state organizations that have been initiated to promote the interests or rights of those with disabilities, that task is beyond the scope of this book. Pelka (1997) has made what appears to be a fairly thorough investigation of early disability rights groups that became national in scope. Table 2.1 lists the starting dates,

names and mission of national organizations started before 1970 which
he identified.

TABLE 2.1 Starting Dates and Mission of National Disability Rights
Groups Started Before 1970.

START DATE	ORGANIZATION NAME	MISSION
1880	NAD—National Association of the Deaf	This is the oldest disability rights organization that is still active. According to Pelka (1997, 212) this organization's charter said the organization's goal was "to bring the deaf of different sections of the United States in close contact and to deliberate on the needs of the deaf as a class. We have interests peculiar to ourselves which can only be taken care of by ourselves."
1907	National Fraternal Society of the Deaf	This organization began as a mutual benefit insurance organization because other insurance companies either would not provide insurance to or charged exorbitant rates to deaf persons. It now has multiple service goals.
1920	DAV—Disabled American Veterans	Local self-help groups of disabled veterans after World War I came together to advocate for benefits and services for the war-disabled. It still runs more than 60 offices to help veterans get the information and services they need.
1921	AFB—American Foundation for the Blind	This organization was developed to be a clearing house for information and advocacy related to blindness and still serves those purposes.

1940	AFPH—American Federation of the Physically Handicapped This organization dissolved in 1958.	This organization was probably the first cross-disability rights organization to advocate primarily for hiring the handicapped. It argued for rehabilitation and job opportunities rather than pity and welfare handouts.
1940	NFB—National Federation of the Blind	The first totally self-advocacy organization created by the blind for themselves and remains the largest organization of the blind that advocates for the equal rights.
1945	BVA—Blinded Veterans Association	Advocates for and links veterans blinded during or since military service with rehabilitation training, services and other benefits.
1946 1951	National Mental Health Foundation NMHA—National Mental Health Association	Conscientious objectors during World War II who worked in state asylums formed this organization to gather information on and expose the horrible conditions in asylums. It merged with another organization to form NMHA which provides information to the general public on mental illness.
1947	PVA—Paralyzed Veterans Association	This organization of 17,000 has worked with other disability rights groups to advocate for disability rights and some of its chapters were instrumental in early experiments in independent living.
1948	NSCIA—National Spinal Cord Injury Association	Originally founded under a different name it first focused on activism to gain access for persons with spinal cord injuries but now focuses mainly on providing services as well as promoting and funding research on curing spinal cord injuries.

1949	UCPA—United Cerebral Palsy Association	Formed by parent groups to educate the public and providers on the nature of this disorder and advocate for better health care, education and other services and legislation to enlarge the rights and opportunities of persons with this disability.
1950	The Arc	Formed by parents of children with mental retardation, this organization has undergone several name changes as it as advocated for deinstitutionalization, education, research, social supports, prevention and other services for those with cognitive disabilities.
1957	LPA—Little People of America	This organization promotes the rights of people 4'10" or under in stature.
1958	NAPH—National Association of the Physically Handicapped	This organization replaced the American Federation of the Physically Handicapped and it seeks to improve the physical, social and economic welfare of the persons with physical impairments.
1961	ACB—American Council for the Blind	A group that broke away from the National Federation of the Blind for greater independence has many state chapters and 19 special interest affiliates such a groups for blind lawyers, and guide dog users. The Washington office provides lobbying and information clearinghouse services.
1964	LDA—Learning Disabilities Association of America	This association of persons with learning disabilities, their families and concerned professionals advocates for legislation and services on their behalf through 600 state and local chapters.

One important conclusion can be drawn from an analysis of the information contained in Table 2.1. All the organizations except two listed in this table focused on only one specific kind of disability such as visual impairments, physical impairments, mental retardation, or spinal cord injuries. The first exception was the Disabled American Veterans formed in 1920 which advocated for all veterans with any form of impairment even though the major focus was on those with physical disabilities. The second exception to this was the American Federation for the Physically Handicapped formed in 1940. Rather than focusing on the needs of one disability group, it focused on national campaigns to improve employment opportunities for those with any kind of disability despite its name which mentions only the physically handicapped. It successfully lobbied for legislation that in 1945 started the "National Employ the Physically Handicapped Week."(Pelka, 1997, 14). These campaigns brought together business leaders, disability advocates and government officials. The President's Committee on Employment of the Physically Handicapped began operating in 1952. AFPH also successfully lobbied for the Vocational Rehabilitation Act of 1954 and the amendments to the Social Security act which created Social Security Disability Insurance nationally in 1956.

Another conclusion comes from comparing the organizations listed in Table 2.1 to those in Table 2.2. About 80% of the organizations listed in Table 2.2 were created in a 30 year period starting in 1970. Only about 20% (17 organizations) of the national organizations were created in the whole ninety year period between 1880 to 1970. It was after the successes of the civil rights groups for racial and ethnic minorities that there was an explosion of interest and a copying of the philosophy and tactics of those groups by disability rights groups. The greatest number of national organizations and university and government related research/advocacy or clearinghouse agencies were founded in the 1970s. Perhaps the most creative burst of energy in the disability rights movement was that which occurred in the 1970s with over twenty national groups formed to investigate and advocate for the rights of those with disabilities. It was during the 1970s also that two out of the three most important pieces of legislation were passed that are the pillars of the disability rights legislative base. Those three acts are the Vocational Rehabilitation Act of 1973, the Individuals with Disabilities Education Act of 1975(IDEA), and the Americans with Disabilities Act of 1990 (ADA).

TABLE 2.2 ALPHABETICAL LISTING OF SELECTED NATIONAL DISABILITY ORGANIZATIONS.

ACRO-NYMN	START DATE	END DATE	NAME OF ORGANIZATION / WEB-ADDRESS	PRIMARY DISABILITY CATEGORY SERVED	FOCUS OF ORGANIZATION
AAMR	1876		American Association on Mental Retardation / *www.aamr.org*	Cognitive	Membership organization for research, education and advocacy.
AAUAP			American Association of University Affiliated Programs / *www.aauap.org*	Developmental disabilities	Association of universities that run research/service programs for persons with disabilities.
ADC	1978		Adaptive Environments Center / *www.adaptenv.org*	Physical	Architectural standards
ADD			Administration on Developmental Disabilities / *www.acf.dhhs.gov/programs/add*	Developmental disabilities	Government agency that funds many programs.
ATA	1987		Alliance for Technology Access / *www.ataccess.org*	Multiple	Technology information/services

AAPD	1995		American Association of People with Disabilities *www.aapd.org*	Multiple	Advocacy/service
AADB	1975		American Association of Deaf-Blind *www.tr.wao.adu/dblink/aadb.htm*	Sensory	Advocacy/service organization
ACCD	1975	1983	American Association of Citizens with Disabilities	Multiple	Advocacy/service
ACB	1958		American Council of the Blind *www.acb.org*	Sensory	Has 19 affiliates—advocacy/service
ADAPT	1978		American Disabled for Attendant Programs Today *www.adapt.org*	Physical	Advocacy organization for rights and services
AFPH	1940	1958	American Federation of the Physically Handicapped	Physical	Advocacy/service
AFB	1921		American Foundation for the Blind. *www.afb.org*	Blind	Advocacy/service
The Arc	1950		Formerly National Association for Retarded Citizens. *www.thearc.org*	Cognitive	Professional and membership
TASH	1974		The Association for Persons with Severe Handicaps. *www.tash.org*	Cognitive-Multiple	Advocacy group.

	Year	Organization	Category	Description
ALDA	1987	Association of Late-Deafened Adults. www.alda.org	Sensory	Advocacy/service group.
ANCOR	1970	American Network of Community Options and Resources. www.ancor.org	Cognitive	A trade association of agencies providing services to persons with developmental disabilities.
ASA	1965	Autism Society of American www.autism-society.org	Autism	Advocacy/service organization
BVA	1945	Blinded Veterans Association www.bva.org	Sensory	Advocacy/service organization
CIL	1972	Center for Independent Living www.wcil.org	Physical	Advocacy/service
CCD	1973	Consortium for Citizens with Disabilities www.c-c-d.org	Multiple	Advocacy collaborative for over 100 U.S. organizations.
CEC	1973	Council for Exceptional Children www.ced.sped.org	Cognitive	Educational advocacy
		Center on Self-Determination www.cdrd.ohsu.edu/self-determination	Multiple	Collaborative consultation
CDDC		Consortium of Developmental Disabilities Councils www.cddc.com	Multiple	Advocacy consortium of 16 state CDCs

	Year	Name / Website	Disability	Description
CUD	1989	Center for Universal Design *www.design.ncsu.edu*	Physical	University based Architectural design
CHP	1971	Center on Human Policy *www.socweb.syr.edu/thechp*	Multiple	University based policy research
CCDB	1991	Chicago Center for Disability Research	Physical	University research
COTT	1990	Committee of Ten Thousand *www.cott.org*	Hemophiliacs	Advocacy/service
DWU	1985	Deaf Women United *www.dwu.org*	Deaf	Service/advocacy
	1972	Deafpride *www.zak.co.il/deaf-info/old/deafman-pride.html*	Deaf	Advocacy organization
DR		Disability Resources *www.disabilityresources.org*	Multiple	A non-profit web site on disability information
DREDF	1979	Disability Rights Education and Defense Fund *www.dredf.org*	Multiple	Advocacy, training, research
DAV	1920	Disabled American Veterans *www.dav.org*	Physical	Advocacy/service
DIA	1970	Disabled in Action *www.disabledinaction.org*	Physical	Advocacy/service
DPI	1981	Disabled Peoples International *www.dpi.org*	Multiple	International advocacy & information

Abbrev.	Year	Organization	Physical	Service
DS/USA	1967	Disabled Sports USA *www.dsusa.org*	Multiple	Sporting events
		Family Voices *www.familyvoices.org*	Multiple	Advocates for children with special health care needs.
FFCMH	1988	Federation of Families for Children's Mental Health. *www.ffcmh.org*	Mentally Ill	Advocacy group by parents for their children.
HOW	1970	Handicapped Organized Women. Refocused in 1988 as Learning How	Physically disabled women	Advocacy/service
HSRI		Human Services Research Institute *www.hsri.org*	Multiple	Research/information centered. Operates National Center for Family Support.
IAC	1993	Institute on Disability Culture *www.dimenet.com/disculture*	Multiple	Disability history/culture
ICDRI	1998	International Center for Disability Resources on the Internet *www.icdri.org*	Multiple	Collects and disseminates information on disability issues.
	2001 / 1995	Justice for All *www.jfanow.org*	Multiple	Web site focused on current issues.

			Learning disabilities.	Advocacy/service
LDA	1964	Learning Disabilities Association of America www.ldanatl.org		
LPA	1957	Little People of America www.LPAonline.org	Midgets and dwarfs	Self-advocacy and service organization
MPLF	1971	Mental Patients' Liberation Front www.communityworks.com	Mentally Ill	Self-advocacy
MIUSA	1981	Mobility International USA www.miusa.org	Physical	International exchanges.
NAMI	1979	National Alliance for the Mentally Ill www.nami.org	Mentally Ill	Advocacy group
MHF2	1999	Mothers From Hell 2 www.mothersfromhell2.org	Cognitive +	Advocacy group run by mothers
MUMS		Mothers United for Mutual Support www.netnet.net/mums/whatis.htm	Cognitive +	Mutual Support group for mothers and caregivers.
NARPA	1980	National Association for Rights, Protection and Advocacy. www.connix.com	Mentally Ill	Advocacy/service

			Deaf	Advocacy/service
NAD	1880	National Association of the Deaf *www.nad.ord*	Deaf	Advocacy/service
NADDC		National Association of Developmental Disabilities Councils *www.naddc.org*	Multiple	Government related association of state disability councils
NAPH	1958	National Association of the Physically Handicapped— replaced an earlier organization. *www.naph.net*	Physically disabled	Advocacy/service organization
NARIC		National Rehabilitation Information Center *www.naric.com*	Multiple	Government
NBDA	1982	National Black Deaf Advocates *www.nbda.org*	Deaf	Advocacy
	1980	National Center for Law and the Handicapped	Multiple	University based rights advocacy
NCD	1978	National Council on Disability *www.ncd.gov*	Multiple	Government
NCIL	1982	National Council on Independent Living *www.ncil.org*	Multiple	Government

NCLD	1977	National Center for Learning Disabilities *www.ncld.org*	Learning disabilities	Advocacy/service
		The National Center for Self-Determination *www.self-determination.org*	Multiple	Located at Oregon Health & Science University.
	1992	National Empowerment Center *www.power2u.org*	Mentally ill	
NFB	1940	National Federation of the Blind *www.nfb.org*	Blind	Advocacy/service
	1907	National Fraternal Society of the Deaf/Deaf Insurance. *www.nfsd.com*	Deaf	Service/advocacy
	1984 1996	National Legal Center for the Medically Dependent and Disabled—A government agency up to 1996 *www.med.upenn.edu*	Multiple	Focus on right-to-die legislation.
NIDDR		National Institute on Disability and Rehabilitation Research *www.ed.gov/offices*	Multiple	Government agency providing money for service and research

NMHA	1909		National Mental Health Association www.nmha.org	Mentally ill	Advocacy/service
NMHF	1946	1951	National Mental Health Foundation www.mentalhealth.org	Mentally ill	Service/advocacy
NOD	1982		National Organization on Disability www.nod.org	Multiple	Advocacy and service program
NPND			National Parent Network on Disabilities www.npnd.org	Multiple	Advocacy group for parents of children with disabilities.
NSCIA	1948		National Spinal Cord Injury Association www.erols.com/nscia/	Physically Impaired	Service/advocacy
OSERS			Office of Special Education and Rehabilitative Services www.ed.gov/offices/OSERS	Multiple	Government agency
PVA	1947		Paralyzed Veterans of America www.pva.org	Physically impaired	Self-advocacy and service
	1974		People First, People First International www.peoplefirst.org.uk	Mental retardation	Self-advocacy

	1952	President's Committee on Employment of People with Disabilities *www.dol.gov/dol/odep*	Multiple	Government supported employment advocacy
PCMR	1961	President's Committee on Mental Retardation *www.acf.dhhs.gov/programs/PC MR*	Mental Retardation	Government supported advocacy and research
NAPS	1985	National Association of *Psychiatric Survivors* *www.nasmphd.org*	Mental illness	Service/advocacy
RAD	1977	Rainbow Alliance of the Deaf *www.rad.org*	Gay and lesbian deaf	Service/advocacy
Ri	1922	Rehabilitation International *www.rehab-international.org*	Multiple	Works with 200 organizations in 90 countries and with the United Nations.
SABE	1991	Self Advocates Becoming Empowered *www.sabe.usa.org*	Mentally retarded	Self-advocacy
SHHH	1979	Self Help for Hard of Hearing People *www.shhh.org*	Deaf	Self-advocacy and services

SDS	1986	Society for Disabilities Studies *www.uic.edu/org/sds/links.html*	Multiple	Research oriented organization.
UCPA	1946	United Cerebral Palsy Association *www.ucpa.org*	Cerebral Palsy	Advocacy/service
	1975	Western Law Center for Disability Rights *www.Wlcdr.everybody.org*	Multiple	Legal rights information/advocacy
VOR		Voice of the Retarded *www.vo4.net*	Cognitive	Conservative advocacy for a range of residential services
WAPD		World Association of Persons with Disabilities *www.wapd.org*	Multiple	Information sharing
	1977	White House Conference on Handicapped Disability *www.ncd.gov/newsroom/news/r9 9-269.html*	Multiple	Government sponsored research and advocacy
WID	1983	World Institute on Disability *www.wid.org*	Multiple	Membership organization with information sharing.

(Note: this list does not include most disability specific organizations that serve only one very specific disability such as dyslexia. It focuses primarily on U.S. national organizations or U.S.-based international organizations. Information on these organizations is sometimes difficult to obtain or not easily summarized on the mission, funding source(s), nature of membership, scope of persons with disabilities served and organizational goals. For further information of these organizations go to their website. Five categories of disabilities are used here: **mental illness, cognitive, sensory** (vision and hearing impairments), **physical and multiple** for covering more than one disability category.)

A third conclusion that can be drawn from the information contained in Tables 2.1 and 2.2 is that the 1970s was the period in which the cross-disability rights groups fully emerged. As Pelka (1997, 81-2) observes,

> Until the 1970s, most disability-related organizations focused on representing or providing services to persons with a specific disability. This was true both for consumer-controlled advocacy groups such the American Council of the Blind or the National Association for the Deaf, for services organizations such as the National Multiple Sclerosis Society, and for parents' organizations such as United Cerebral Palsy Associations. This 'ghettoization' made it difficult to work toward common goals. It means that many disabled people shared the same stereotypes about people with differing disabilities as mainstream society. Furthermore, people with multiple disabilities, for instance, blind wheelchair users, had difficulty obtaining services and participating in disability specific organizations.

The first organization founded to develop cross-disability awareness, sensitivity and undertake cross-disability advocacy projects was the American Coalition of Citizens with Disabilities (ACCD) formed in 1974(Pelka, 1997). Another cross-disability organization that was focused principally around disability rights training and legal advocacy was the Disability Rights Education and Defense Fund founded in 1979. It not only involved cross generations of members--parents and their children with disabilities, but also people with a variety of disabilities as well as professionals and lay persons in the agency. It provides training and technical assistances to persons with disabilities, their parents, lawyers, service providers and legislators. Its mission includes lobbying for law and policy reforms, advocacy on behalf of individual clients and litigation ("How Does DREDF Carry Out Its Mission?" 2001).

A fourth conclusion drawn from a comparison of the information in Tables 2.1 and 2.2 is that the variety of types of organizations which emerged was also new. We see government-based, university-based, and citizen-based groups being created to serve both general and specific purposes. For example, The President's Committee on Mental Retardation, which was first appointed in 1961 by President Kennedy, has periodically met to investigate and make recommendations about national policy regarding mental retardation. This panel brought together both representatives from the parent's movement and professionals in the field to survey existing knowledge and programs in the field and make recommendations. Its 1962 report, *A Proposed Program for National Action To Combat Mental Retardation,* made 112 recommendations. This resulted in a very significant act the following year—The Mental

Retardation Facilities and Community Mental Health Centers Construction Act. (Pelka, 1997)

VARIATIONS IN ADVOCACY ORGANIZATIONS

James I. Charlton in *Nothing About Us Without Us: Disability Oppression and Empowerment* (1998) develops a classification of ten types of disability organizations that provides insight into the multiple targets, constituencies, and sizes of disability related organizations. This classification system helps students of the disability rights movement better understand the very diverse functions of such organizations in the larger picture of the disability rights movement which is changing the lives of millions of people with disabilities. Charlton's classification system is as follows:

1. LOCAL SELF-HELP GROUPS. Such groups could range from small rural to large urban organizations that serve limited geographical areas in a country. Such limited organizations or chapters often provide a range of services such as mutual support, peer counseling, financial aid, cooperative work projects, and information sharing programs for their immediate members. Since the disability rights movement (DRM) is an international movement, such groups help hundreds of thousands of individuals deal with the oppression and deprivation that people experience around the world in their own communities. For example, Charlton (1998) points out there are more than 175 income producing self-help projects in South Africa--most associated with the national organization called Disabled People South Africa.

2. LOCAL ADVOCACY AND PROGRAM CENTERS. The most important and most frequent type of such organizations are local CILS—Centers for Independent Living, which are nonresidential information and advocacy centers. The advocacy they engage in may be for individual persons or systemically for issues that confront many such persons in their geographic service area such as housing needs, attendant services, transportation or job discrimination. For example, Access Living of Metropolitan Chicago, founded in 1979, is a nonprofit organization with 40 staff members and a budget over $1.8 million annually that advocates for all the issues and concerns of people with disabilities from domestic abuse, housing and job discrimination to health care issues. Its funding is complex with revenues coming from individual and business gifts and funds from city, state and federal governments for providing a ranges of services to its constituents.

3. LOCAL SINGLE ISSUE ADVOCACY GROUPS. Such groups focus on advocacy rather than providing a range of services as do such organizations listed above as Local Advocacy and Program Centers. These single issue advocacy groups tend to come and go rather quickly if the issues for which they advocate get solved. They may advocate for such changes as improved transportation access, public awareness, information and referral services, curb cuts, housing services, or policy changes in service organizations.

4. PUBLIC POLICY GROUPS. These groups may be variously called centers, institutes, information clearing houses, programs, or funds and operate some array of services that relate to disability policy issues. Often they are principally operated by people without disabilities and have a paid staff. They may do research, write position papers, take on evaluation projects, testify at public meetings or legislative hearings, develop web sites with links to other disability groups, provide individual or group training and a wide array of other services. They may be government bodies, government-appointed study commissions, foundation-funded programs, academic policy and service programs and/or quasi-public bodies. They are a central part of the disability rights movement and give that complex movement much of its rationale for existing. Dozens of groups are emerging here. One of these is the Center for Self-Determination with a staff of five that deals with emerging issues related to "self-determination" such as Medicaid waivers, brokering and independent support coordination, the use of new fiscal intermediaries in individual service administration, and a complex communications program on new developments. ("About Us", 2001).

5. SINGLE ISSUE NATIONAL ADVOCACY GROUPS. These groups focus on one issue at a time. For example, ADAPT—Americans Disabled for Attendant Programs Today, created in 1983, was the offshoot of a demonstration held in Denver in 1978 to protest the lack of accessible bus transportation for wheelchair users by Atlantis Community, Inc, a disability cooperative and independent living center. In 1983 some of the same activists held another demonstration to protest a lack of accessible bus transportation and formed an organization called ADAPT—Americans Disabled for Accessible Public Transportation. Over the next 7 years this group organized dozens of demonstrations to protest inaccessible public transportation and support the passage of Americans with Disabilities Act in 1990 with its provisions for accessible public transportation. When they accomplished that, they next went on to another single issue campaign—to get personal assistance services.

that would enable persons with disabilities to live in their own homes rather than in institutions like nursing homes or facilities for those with mental retardation. They kept their original acronym, ADAPT, but changed the APT part of their acronym from Accessible Public Transportation to Attendant Programs Today. (Pelka, 1997; Charlton, 1998)

6. **NATIONAL MEMBERSHIP ORGANIZATIONS.** Such organizations in the United States usually have both state and local chapters as well as a national organization through which members can participate in various forms of advocacy and other programs. Most organizations are relatively democratic but sometimes they develop national bureaucracies that may be somewhat resistant to change over time. For example, DPI—Disabled Peoples/International was formed in Thailand in 1983 to promote a cross disability network of some 110 organizations from around the world involving greater efforts of advocacy for rehabilitation in third world countries. There is also a national branch in many countries—for example Disabled Peoples International—Thailand. The national program in Thailand also has many local chapters that are focused around self-help activities. (Charlton, 1998) The Arc in the United States is an example of a large membership organization with a state office in every state and hundreds of local chapters. Their web site describes this group as "The national organization of and for people with mental retardation and developmental disabilities and their families"(The Arc, 2001).

7. **NATIONAL COALITIONS/FEDERATIONS OF GROUPS.** As the number of disability rights organizations rapidly increased in the United States, networks and collaborative activities were established to unify their advocacy efforts on a national basis. One of the extensive developments in the 1970s in the United States was the rapid expansion of independent living centers to promote independent life styles. As they grew in number, many activists believed they needed one association to advocate on their behalf, share information across this developing movement and provide technical assistance to centers or other groups involved in the disability rights movement. Thus, NCIL—National Council on Independent Living, was formed in 1981 to engage in these activities as well as advocate for new legislation. It played a role in the passage of several key pieces of legislation: The Civil Rights Restoration Act of 1987, the Fair Housing Amendments Act of 1988, and the 1990 Americans with Disabilities Act. (Pelka, 1997, Charlton, 1998)

8. **NATIONAL SINGLE DISABILITY ORGANIZATIONS.** These organizations represent the older and traditional approach of

professionals serving people with one disability. Some "disability activists would consider most of these groups to be outside the DRM because they are not controlled by people with disabilities, they are often deferential to government or philanthropic organizations, and they tend to be apolitical"(Charlton, 1998, 145). They tend to follow the medical model of disabilities and focus on raising money for a group that needs charity or for research on cures or prevention. The American Association on Mental Retardation, which is composed mainly of professionals who work in academic or provider settings, would be a good example of such an organization in this country.

9. REGIONAL ORGANIZATIONS. Regional organizations are federations of groups serving a delimited geographical area. Thus NAMI-PA—the National Alliance of the Mentally Ill in Pennsylvania is a state chapter that is a federation of many local chapters serving cities or counties or clusters of counties in that state.

10. INTERNATIONAL ORGANIZATIONS. The disability rights movement is a growing movement. While disability rights activities have been advocating for many decades in the United States, their emergence has been more recent in many other countries—especially third world countries where the scope of disability is often very great. These international organizations may have large or small agendas. For example, Mobility International based in Eugene Oregon focuses on enabling disabled activists to visit other countries to review their services and policies, while ADD, Action on Disability and Development, headquartered in Great Britain, had established contacts with 152 countries by 1998 with thousands of people reading their newsletter and contacting the organization. Perhaps one of the most extensive and effective of the international organizations is Disabled Peoples' International with more than 70 countries having DPI chapters and which was influential in formulating the UN's *World Program of Action Concerning Disabled Persons* in 1982 and in getting the UN to adopt an international awareness campaign in 1992-93 called the Decade of Disabled Persons. (Charlton, 1998) A more recent international organization is the World Association of Persons with disAbilities that has an extensive web-site that can be accessed in six languages. It provides many opportunities for international communication with its chat rooms, lists of resources, newsletter, chapters and affiliates, opportunities for volunteers, bulletin board, speaker's bureau, assistive device lab and other resources and services. ("Voices of Positive Ability", July 23, 2001)

THE EXPLOSION OF DISABILITY RIGHTS IN THE 1970s

As mentioned earlier, the disability rights movement really exploded in the 1970s. We see this in several forms: (1) There were numerous demonstrations around the country protesting a lack of accessible busing, protesting various forms of discrimination against people with disabilities and strongly advocating for the regulations defining discrimination under the 1973 Vocational Rehabilitation Act. (2) There was a rapid increase in the number of organizations getting involved in the disability rights movement. And they were effectively organizing to recruit and sensitize members to discrimination and to alert the media to the many forms of stereotyping and discrimination that persons with disabilities faced. Furthermore, there was a growth of a cross-disability awareness that if all the various disability groups pulled together either through single disability organizations or through multi-disability groups they would collectively have more power. (3) There was passage in this decade of two of the three pillars of the Disability Rights legislation ever passed in the U.S.—the 1973 Rehabilitation Act and the Individuals with Disabilities Education Act of 1975.

In 1982 a group of disability rights activists met in East Lansing, Michigan under the sponsorship of the Institute for Educational Leadership and the Mott Foundation. For five days they met to review from where the disability rights movement had come and where it was going. Robert Funk (1984, 15-16) summarized the conference attendee's beliefs this way:

> The independent living/disability rights movement is rooted in the 1960's, though many of the essential policy and programmatic innovations which defined the formal structure we see today did not appear until well into the following decade. During the sixties, disabled people were profoundly influenced by the social and political upheaval which they witnessed. They identified with the struggles of other disenfranchised groups to achieve integration and meaningful equality of opportunity. They learned the tactics of litigation and the art of civil disobedience from other civil rights activists. They absorbed reform ideas from many sources— consumerism, self-help, demedicalization, and de-institutionalization.

> One of the distinguishing marks of the 1960's politics shared by many who swelled the ranks of the disability rights and independent living movements was an emphasis on personal transformation—changes of consciousness—preceding and underpinning social activism. Disabled

people had to achieve a dramatically new and positive valuation of themselves as a group as a pre-condition to effective organizing in pursuit of specific programs and policies. A critical aspect of this process of rethinking disability was discarding psycho- logically the sectarianism which had long fragmented disabled people into so many subgroups—the blind, spinal cord injured, retarded, post-polio, etc. From these experiences, many disabled individuals emerged for the first time with a sense of themselves as members of a unique and valuable community, a sense supported by their comprehensive view that they had the rights—hitherto denied—to participate as fully equal members of American society.

One remarkable fact, viewed in retrospect, was the large number of disabled individuals, many of whom were substantially isolated, prepared to act along similar lines. The implication of their new politicized perspective on disability issues was that real reform could be assured only by the development of a broad-based coalition of disabled people throughout the United States who demanded both fundamental national policy reforms and community based support services that would permit them to break the tradition of dependency and institutionalization and live as part of the social and economic community.

One of the first activist organizations that developed chapters in four other eastern cities without every developing a national office was the DIA—Disabled in Action. It was started by Judith Neumann in 1970 in New York City. It was a direct action and grassroots group that may have been one of the first to engage in street demonstrations to gain publicity for its policy stances. For example, it demonstrated against President Nixon's veto in 1972 of the Act that would be eventually passed the next year—the Rehabilitation Act of 1973. These protests included a demonstration at the Lincoln Memorial and in cooperation with a group of disabled Vietnam veterans occupied Nixon's New York reelection campaign headquarters. In 1976 and 1977 the DIA was the first group to protest the charity approach to raising money for disability services by picketing the United Cerebral Palsy Associations' telethon for raising money for crippled children. Since then the New York and Philadelphia chapters of this group have filed lawsuits and led demonstrations for making public bus services accessible, making poling cites accessible, and demonstrating against wheelchair inaccessible Greyhound Bus Company buses. Judith Heumann became an activist because as a wheelchair user she had to stage a long battle and finally a lawsuit in New York City in order to gain a teaching position in a public school. (Fleischer and Zames, 2001; Shapiro, 1993).

Many of the national organizations promoting the rights and independence of individuals with disabilities had the their beginnings in local efforts. A good case in point is what is called the "Independent Living Movement" which had several roots and which, in turn, spawned several nation-wide organizations. In the fall of 1963 Edward V. Roberts, who was later to be called the "father of the independent living movement", got permission to enter the University of California at Berkeley after completing two years at San Mateo Community College. He had contracted polio at age 14 in 1953 and was a "respiratory quadriplegic"—he was paralyzed from the neck down and needed a respirator by day and an iron lung by night to breathe. He needed money to attend Berkeley, but the California Department of Rehabilitation turned down his request for financial assistance seeing him as an "infeasible" client being unlikely to ever work. Along with several others, he went to the local press and got publicity that led the rehabilitation official to reverse the agency's earlier position and grant him financial assistance. Officials at Berkeley were also reluctant to admit him because of the University's lack of access and concern for his health. Because there were no personal assistants yet, he was allowed to stay in Cowell Hospital located on the Campus. His brother Ron provided him personal assistance. Within a few years other students with severe physical disabilities were admitted to Berkeley and some of them formed the "Rolling Quads"—a group all in wheelchairs that was dedicated to making the campus and nearby community physically accessible. Roberts completed his master's degree in political science by 1966 and continued further graduate work at Berkeley. In 1969 he went to Washington, D.C. where he along with some of his Rolling Quad friends were asked to develop a program to reduce the college drop-out rate of students with disabilities. The package of services they developed was labeled—PDSP—Physically Disabled Students' Program that included wheelchair repair, personal assistance services, emergency attendants, and help in getting any available financial assistance. As Pelka, (1997, 61), points out,

> The Cowell residents outlined three basic principles on which the PDSP would operate: (1) that the experts on disability are the people with disabilities; (2) that the needs of the people with disabilities can best be met by a comprehensive, or holistic, program, rather than by fragmented programs at different agencies and offices, and (3) that people with disabilities should be integrated into the community. These principles would become the heart of the independent living philosophy.

A few years later in 1972, Roberts moved back to Berkley to become the first executive director of the Center for Independent Living which was created on the principles of PDSP and with a $50,000 grant from the federal Rehabilitation Services Administration. The CIL struggled for several years but meantime a very similar group operating on about the same principles was also emerging in Huston and over the next decade went through a number of name changes but emphasized the viability that providing a variety of self-directed services can enable severely disabled persons to live in the community outside of institutions. (Pelka, 1997)   Since the founding of these two centers hundreds of other independent living centers have been developed all over the country with each providing services as are needed by the constituents in that area.

As a follow-up on the development of Centers for Independent Living, in 1982 the National Council on Independent Living (NCIL) was formed as an association of CILs to provide its members with technical assistance, support other disabilities rights organizations, advocate for greater federal funding of but greater local control in CILs, organize conferences on the principles and operations of CILs, and advocate on other related issues.   As a nonprofit organization, NCIL follows its own principles by having 20 of its 22 member governing board be people with disabilities.

At a national conference on CILs in 1982, the participants affirmed that the movement for independent living centers was founded on three propositions and three operational principles.   The three propositions were: (1) Consumer sovereignty—that the disabled persons who used the services of the center, not professionals, should ultimately determine how services were to be organized; (2) Self-reliance—disabled persons must rely mainly on their skills to gain the rights and benefits to which are legally entitled; and (3) Political and Economic Rights—persons with disabilities should be entitled to pursue their own interests in these two arenas.   The three operational principles that follow closely from these propositions are that: (1) Disabled people should design, manage and evaluate the organizations that serve them; (2) Services for the Disabled should be community based and community responsive; and (3) Two kinds of services should be offered to the disabled in their community— advocacy and a range of services to individuals that enhance independence, empowerment and self-determination (Funk, 1984).

The energetic Edward Roberts was instrumental in helping found several other organizations to promote the interests and rights of the disabled. DPI—Disabled People's International was organized in 1981 in Singapore in order to promote the disability rights movement worldwide. In 1983 with the help of two other disability rights activist,

Judith Neumann and Joan Leon, Roberts used the prize money he had won from being a MacArthur fellow to help found WID—World Institute on Disability. This organization has been both a forum and an information sharing center on the disability rights movement and CILs in particular for the international center.

One of the critical ideas about the independent living movement is that it stands for the conceptualization of disability as a social rather than a medical model. In the medical model, a person with a physical disability would often be kept for a long time in a rehabilitation hospital where they would undergo rehabilitation to minimize the physical impact of the disability and learn to adjust to a discriminating world. In contrast, the social model emphasizes altering the social and physical environment so that it is less stigmatizing and less restrictive than the way the world has often been for those with disabilities. Fleischer and Zames (2001, 46-7) contrast these two models this way: "The purpose of the rehabilitation prototype is to enable the person with the disability to be as physically and economically self-sufficient as possible. The objective of the independent living construct is to fully integrate the person with the disability fully into the social, economic and political fabric of the community." The first model sees the person as a patient or client under the supervision of a professional, the second as a "consumer" who is making the decisions about his own needs and desires. One of the results of the independent living movement was to critique the medical/rehabilitation model which focused on changing the person and replace it with ideas of being self-determining rather than professionally determined.

One of the most critical incidents in the disability rights movement was its response to the failure of the Department of Health, Education and Welfare to publish regulations on how to implement Section 504 of the Rehabilitation Act of 1973. The Carter administration had been dragging its feet in finishing these regulations. Section 504 of the 1973 act was one simple sentence that was to become one of the most significant building blocks of the rights of persons with disabilities. It read, "No otherwise qualified handicapped individual in the United States, as defined in section 7(6), shall, solely by reason of his handicap, be excluded from participation in, be denied the benefits of, or be subjected to discrimination under any program or activity receiving Federal financial assistance." (Pelka, 1997, 278). But by 1977, the regulations to implement this law had not been released even though one lawsuit resulted in Judge John Smith of the U.S. District Court for the District of Columbia issuing an order in July of 1976 requiring that HEW develop and publish these regulations with deliberate speed. But by early spring of 1977, HEW Secretary Joseph Califano had not released the regulations. Soon after Carter came into office, members of the American Coalition of Citizens with Disabilities (ACCD) began meeting with Califano and his staff about these regulations. But nothing happened. Finally, after about two months of delay, Frank Bowe, the deaf executive director of ACCD wrote a letter on March 18, 1977 to Califano about ACCD's frustration with the delay in issuing the regulations and warning that ACCD would take action if the Section 504 regulations were not signed by April 4, 1977. They were not signed by that date. The ACCD was organized to react and they did starting the next day on April 5. They held demonstrations at most of the ten regional headquarters of HEW as well as at the Federal HEW office. In several locations they had sit-ins including HEW headquarters in Washington where they lasted 28 hours before exiting after being denied food or access to phones by Califano. But the most dramatic sit-in that drew much public sympathy was the one at the San Francisco HEW office led by Judith Heumann. It lasted for 25 days with about one-half of the initial protesters remaining in the HEW office building the full time. On April 28, Califano signed and released Sections 504 regulations to the great relief of protestors and the great joy at what they had accomplished. It was these regulations that required new buildings built with federal money had to be accessible and that existing buildings should be accessible in three years. These regulations said schools and universities receiving federal funds needed to be physically and socially accessible and that prevented employers from discriminating against people with disabilities. (Fleischer and Zames, 2001; Shapiro, 1994; Pelka, 1997).

THE LEGISLATIVE RESPONSE TO THE DISABILITY RIGHTS MOVEMENT.

The following paragraph shows the historical record of what the U.S. Congress has done in legislating for those with a range of disabilities. While several significant acts were created after World War I and II, and one act in the 1950s and two in the 1960s, over 80% of the federal legislation impacting on those with disabilities is a product of about 30 years from 1970 to 2000. This was when the disability rights movement was very active with perhaps its greatest burst of energy in the 1970s following the civil rights revolution of the 1960s. While some of the legislation has had less impact than others, the total impact has been tremendous to those both within and without the Disability Rights Movement. It has been highly reformative in providing the same rights to persons with as without disabilities. And it is this author's opinion that much of this legislation would not have occurred had it not been for those thousands of individuals who provided leadership and membership support in the disability rights movement. It is the author's opinion that the three most important pieces of legislation for opening up opportunities for those with disabilities were the Rehabilitation Act of 1973, the Individuals with Disabilities Education Act of 1975 (renamed this later), and the American with Disabilities Act of 1990 which is often cited as "ADA".

There follows a listing of federal disability legislation organized around three pieces of information on each bill that was passed: date, title of the legislation, and the key provision(s) of the legislation

> 1918; *Vocational Rehabilitation Act*—amended many times with 1943 amendments important. This legislation provided money to the states and federal agencies to provide a range of rehabilitation services to veterans. The 1943 amendments, the LaFollette-Barden Act, established the Federal Office of Vocational Rehabilitation

> 1920; *Federal Civilian Vocational Rehabilitation Act.* This legislation extended the above act to civilians with disabilities.

> 1946; *National Mental Health Act.* Created National Institute of Mental Health (NIMH) that promotes training and research on mental illness/health.

> 1956; *Amendments to Social Security Act initiating "Social Security Disability Insurance*—SSDI. Defined disability as inability to work in a significant way and provided federal disability payments to those medically determined to be unable to engage in substantial work activity. Eligibility and monthly payments were based on length of covered years and payments into the social security system.   In 1972 SSDI recipients became eligible for Medicare benefits.

> 1963; *Mental Retardation Facilities and Community Mental Health Centers Act.*   The goals of this legislation was toprovide facilities and programs to provide community-based programs for those with mental illness and mental retardation in order to hasten deinstitutionalization for those with these disorders.

> 1968; *Architectural Barriers Act.* Required that all building leasedor constructed or altered or financed by the federal government (except buildings used by the military) after 1969 be accessible to people with disabilities. Also set standards for accessibility. Little enforcement of this law until later.

> 1970; *Urban Mass Transportation Act.* Created national policy to make mass transportation facilities accessible to elderly and handicapped. But lacked specific enforcement mechanisms.

> 1972; *Amendments to Social Security Act creating SSI— Supplemental Security Income.* Created means tested (income and assets test) program of federal payments starting January 1, 1974 to those with disabilities under age 22 who had never been eligible for work. Such persons were also made eligible for the Federal/State Medicaid program of medical services for the poor.

> 1973; *Rehabilitation Act of 1973*---as amended later in 1974, 1978, 1986, 1992. Granted money (I) to states and agencies to run rehabilitation pro-grams to prepare people for work, (II) for research/demonstration programs, (III) to states and agencies for a variety of rehabilitation services, (IV) for research related to the act, and (V) created the "Bill of Rights" for Americans with disabilities by creating a new definition of disability, requiring affirmative action programs by contractors having federal contracts more than $2,500, establishing a Architectural and Transportation Barriers Compliance Board, extended grants to tribal authorities and required state advisory councils with a majority membership from those with disabilities.

> 1974; *Federal-Aid Highway Act Amendments of 1974.* All federally funded highway projects were to be planned, designed, constructed and operated to allow use by elderly and disabled. Led to many curb cuts.

> 1975; *Developmentally Disabled Assistance and Bill of Rights Act.* Required federal and state governments to withhold money from state institutions for the developmentally disabled if they did not provide appropriate treatment, medical care, or diet. Required such institutions to provide reasonable visitation hours and no physical restrains unless necessary. Also established a network of Protection and Advocacy (P &

A) organizations to advocate for the rights of those with disabilities.

> 1975; *Education for Handicapped Children Act was renamed in 1990 as "IDEA"*— Individuals with Disabilities Education Act. Prior to this act many children with disabilities were excluded from public education. This act required a free, appropriate, essentially integrated (in the least restrictive environment) public education for all children with disabilities. It required schools to provide current training for teachers working with the disabled and procedural requirements in developing "Individualized Education Programs" for each child.

> 1978; *Amendments to the 1973 Rehabilitation Act.* Added Title VII to the 1973 act called "Comprehensive Services for Independent Living" which financially supported centers for independent living to provide housing referral, transportation, attendant care, peer counseling and other services.

> 1980; *Civil Rights of Institutionalized Persons Act.* This act empowered the Justice Department to investigate cases where persons with mental illness or developmental disabilities civil rights were being abused in institutions for them.

> 1982; *Telecommunications for the Disabled Act.* This law required that by 1985 most phones serving the public be accessible to those with hearing impairments. Also, states were allowed to subsidize the availability of TDDs— telecommunications devices for the deaf.

> 1984; *Voting Accessibility for the Elderly and Handicapped Act.* A weak act without penalties that require federal registration and polling places to be physically accessible to persons with sensory disabilities or mobility limitations.

> 1984; *The Social Security Reform Act.* This act required that the Social Security Administration continue benefits to terminated SSDI beneficiaries until they had exhausted all levels of appeal because many formerly disabled persons with SSDI benefits had been terminated without a hearing or medical investigation early in the Reagan administration.

> 1984; *Child Abuse Prevention and Treatment Act.* Because some disabled infants were being euthanized, this law requires

that since all states run child abuse prevention programs that are federally funded that those states must operate a child-abuse reporting system to detect such abuses.

> 1986; *Protection and Advocacy for Mentally Ill Individuals Act.* This law requires the same rights and Protection and Advocacy organizations for the mentally ill living in a variety of institutions as did the 1975 Developmentally Disabled Assistance and Bill of Rights Act.

> 1986; *Employment Opportunities for Disabled Americans Act.* This act removed many of the disincentives of SSI and SSDI recipients from going to work by allowing them to keep their Medicaid and Medicare benefits plus some of their earnings that had formerly been denied them.

> 1986; *Air Carrier Access Act.* This act states that discrimination is not only prohibited in agencies receiving federal funds but also in **private** agencies serving the general public such as airlines.

> 1987; *Civil Rights Restoration Act.* This law overturned a Supreme Court decision that narrowly interpreted which agencies could receive federal funding under various civil and disability rights acts.

> 1988; *The Technology Related Assistance for Individuals with Disabilities Act of 1988 as amended.* This act provided federal money to the states to assist in developing several types of programs to make people with disabilities more aware of technology, to make it more accessible, to coordinate their efforts with other agencies and to be more "consumer responsive" in order to enhance independence for persons with disabilities.

> 1988; *Fair Housing Amendments Act.* Added people with disabilities to the list of persons protected from housing discrimination under the Civil Rights Act of 1968.

> 1990; *Ryan White Comprehensive AIDS Resources Emergency (CARE) Act.* In response to the growing Aids epidemic which was overwhelming the medical resources of some communities, this act gave funds to those communities to develop comprehensive care programs, early intervention programs, confidentiality regulations and evaluation of the assessment of such programs.

> 1990; *Americans with Disabilities Act (ADA).* This major legislation (I) prohibits employers with 15 or more employees

from discriminating against qualified individuals with disabilities by requiring them to make reasonable accommodations to such persons; (II) prohibits discrimination or access barriers in public services provided by federal, state or local governments or public mass transportation; (III) prohibits discrimination against persons with disabilities in public places such as restaurants, theatres, department stores, and parks; (IV) requires that phone companies make available to TDD users a relay system whereby they can connect to non-TDD users and requires the close-captioning of federally funded TV programs; and (V) among its miscellaneous provisions are those excluding from coverage transvestites, transsexuals, current users of illegal drugs, pedophiles, pyromaniacs, compulsive gamblers, kleptomaniacs, voyeurs and several other disorders.

> 1995; *Community Attendant Service Act.* Authorizes money to the states to design customer-centered programs to provide attendant care services to persons who need them in order to live in the community rather than in institutions.

> 1996; *Telecommunications Act.* This act requires manufacturers of telecommunications equipment and providers of such services to ensure equipment and services such as cell phones, pagers, call waiting and operator services are accessible to persons with disabilities.

> 1996; *Mental Health Parity Act.* Starting 1-1-1998, employers with 50 or more employees who previously offered coverage of mental health services (excluding chemical abuse/ dependence) were to offer comparable dollar annual and lifetime limits on a parity with medical and surgical benefits unless the costs of such coverage increased total costs by 1% or more.

> 1998; *Assistive Technology Act.* Provides grants to the states to maintain and strengthen comprehensive statewide programs of technology- related assistance to individuals with disabilities of all ages that enable them to access and use telecommunications.

> 1999; *Ticket to Work and Work Incentive Improvement Act.* This act improves access to training and placement services for those with disabilities and extends Medicare coverage for SSDI beneficiaries up to 8.5 years if they have lost cash

assistance because of returning to work; also gives states the right to extend Medicaid coverage for certain persons with disabilities. It also funds demonstration Medicaid services to workers with disabilities who without those medical services might become further disabled. Sources: Pelka, 1997; "A guide to disability rights laws, 6-27-2000; "Medicaid", 2000; Bloom, 1984.

THE ELECTRONIC COMMUNICATIONS REVOLUTION

One of the significant developments of the 1990s is the explosion of opportunities that the internet revolution has supplied to people with disabilities. Persons with disabilities have historically been more susceptible to social isolation than those without disabilities. But the development of the internet has opened up communication channels about many things of interest to persons with disabilities or those who relate to them as parents, friends and professionals: advocacy organizations, service organizations, chat rooms, support groups, new policies and programs, new service providers, new assistive devices, and access to a huge amount of information on a variety of disabilities. The new technology has vastly improved communication among those with disabilities and those who serve them through an array of organizations. Table 2.2 provides the web sites of those organizations that have them and many of those web sites provide links to many other related web sites. The communications revolution has been important in (1) reducing the isolation of many people with disabilities, and in (2) internationalizing the disability rights movement, and (3) in permitting the communication that is so central to effective advocacy. The legislation listed in Table 2.3 passed in 1988, 1990, 1996 and 1998 documents the importance of promoting the communication that is critical to disability rights movement. This legislation has: (1) greatly improved access to technology, particularly telecommunications technology, (2) promoted the removal of physical access barriers at all three levels of government institutions and many other public places, and (3) prohibited discrimination at all three levels of government and among employers having 15 or more employees.

SUMMARY

This chapter has focused on the reforms that the disability rights movement (DRM) has wanted to achieve and the federal legislative responses to that movement. The DRM has been a reform movement pushed by those with disabilities and their supporters to achieve the civil rights that other Americans have. A large number of disability organizations have been initiated, mainly since 1970, to promote the civil rights of the largest minority group in the country now in the vicinity of 50 million people. These organizations have organized resources along multiple dimensions identified as informal advocates, self-advocacy, paid provider advocates, rights organizations advocates, and societal advocates to help achieve their aims. Up to 1970, much of the legislative response had been to provide vocational rehabilitation for those with physical disabilities. But starting around 1970, the DRM became (1) much more active as indicated by the number of new national organizations founded to push for the rights of those with disabilities, (2) more cross-disability oriented meaning that many of the new organizations were trying to represent people with different types of disabilities in order to be more effective as they represented larger numbers of people with very similar concerns, and more inclusive by including many types of organizations and agencies dealing with advocacy issues such as professional, academic and governmentally based groups that are included among the ten types of advocacy organizations discussed.

The 1970s saw an explosion of civil rights activities for those with disabilities. This involved the development of many new DRM organizations, membership recruitment, lobbying, public education, demonstrations and growing inclusion of those with disabilities in the legislative process. Two of the three major pillars of the disability rights laws were passed in the 1970s: the Rehabilitation Act of 1973, and IDEA in 1975 which was to transform public education. The legislative response to the DRM continued into the 1980s and 1990s. The 1980s saw legislation that confirmed or extended the disability rights legislation of the 1970s. For example, the Civil Rights of Institutionalized Persons Act of 1980 extended to persons with developmental disabilities confined to institutions the right to have abuses of them investigated. Then 1986 legislation extended the same rights to those with mental illness living in institutions. The 1990s started with the passage of the very significant ADA for which hundreds of various DRM organizations had been lobbying. The growing electronic communications revolution has shrunk the isolation of many of those with impairments. The 1995 Community Attendant Services Act gave support to the growing demand for "self-determination"-- the disability rights principal focus in the 1990s to be discussed more fully in Chapter 7.

CHAPTER 3
THE DISABLED AS A MINORITY GROUP

ISSUES IN THIS CHAPTER

One of the dominant sociological frames of reference and analytical tools has been the minority and majority group concepts. The first issue we will address in this chapter is to look at the meaning of a minority group and then do a comparative analysis to determine if those with disabilities fit the minority group concept as it was first developed and applied to racial and ethnic minorities. A second focus will be to investigate two of the key and interactive determinants of minority status—how minorities are viewed (attitudes) and treated (behavior). A third focus will be to look at a schemata of the range of forms that unequal treatment takes in the course in human history, but more particularly at the end of the 20th century. A fourth focus will be to look at processes of how the relatively powerless status of those are treated as a minority changes over time and the range of outcomes that occur.

THE MINORITY GROUP CONCEPT

Like many concepts in sociology, the concept of a minority group is evolving over time so that its first use has been modified multiple times and each user of the concept is free to define it the way they find useful or the way they believe it best reflects distinctions that people use in classifying and categorizing others in everyday social life. Some now prefer to substitute "dominant" and "subordinate" concepts for majority and minority distinctions for several reasons. One is that a minority group is not always a numerical minority and thereby the so called majority is not always the majority as best exemplified by the population of South Africa. In South Africa, black Africans make up about 80% of the population but have had much less power than the numerical minority of whites. The second and more important reason is that a key distinction between the two groups is a power differential that leads to unequal treatment. However, the public is much more aware of the concept of minority than they would be of "subordinate" group. Thus, we will use the concept of minority group even though the concept of a subordinate group carries more meaning socially than the concept of minority which is much better established in the realm of public discourse.

The first use of the term "minority group" incorporated a modifier and came from Europe in the form of "national minorities" to refer to a group of people living in a new country and which was not their original homeland and who constituted less than half of the population of their adopted country. The one word "minority" was coined in America by Donald Young in his 1932 book, *The American Minority Peoples.* He used the term as it had been used in Europe and then the United States to refer to national minorities not living in their original homeland. In 1945, Louis Wirth extended the definition to include three components: (1) physical or cultural identifiability, (2) unequal treatment, and (3) self-awareness of being treated differently. (Stroman, 1982). Wirth's (1945, 347) definition is:

> We may define a minority as a group of people who, because of their physical or cultural characteristics, are singled out from others in the society in which they live for differential and unequal treatment and who therefore regard themselves as objects of collective discrimination.

It is noteworthy in this definition that it is socially interactive—people are singled out by the dominant group for some distinguishing physical or cultural features, the dominant group behaves differentially toward them, and then the minority group becomes aware they are treated differently. In 1958, two anthropologists, Charles Wagley and Marvin Harris developed a more particular definition of minorities by inductively determining what commonalities all so-called minority groups shared in the new world. Their definition includes five distinguishing characteristics the last of which involves only a high probability of being present. Their definition (p.10) states:

> (1) minorities are subordinate segments of complex state societies;
> (2) minorities have special physical or cultural traits which are held in low self esteem by the dominant segments of the society; (3)

minorities are self-conscious units bound together by the special traits which their members share and by the special disabilities roup.these bring; (4) membership in a minority is transmitted by a rule of descent which is capable of affiliating succeeding generations even in the absence of readily apparent physical or cultural traits; (5) minority peoples, by choice or necessity, tend to marry within the group

As the minority group concept has been applied to groups other than racial, religious, and nationality groups, several modifications have been made to the above definition. First, the subordinate status is defined as stemming from discrimination or differential treatment, not necessarily smaller numbers. Second, the involuntary inheritance feature is sometimes questioned with religious groups since people may change their religious orientation without changing their more unalterable racial or ethnic traits. Thirdly, the endogamous tendency of marriage within the group (which thereby establishes a pattern of descent) does not apply to women, homosexuals, and for many groups is losing its applicability as patterns of identity, discrimination and inclusion change and as within-group marriage patterns diminish.

Table 3.1 lists the five characteristics of a minority group and provides a quick review of some of the issues of whether those with disabilities are a minority group. The most compelling argument is that they have been stigmatized and treated differently over the centuries of world history as well as in the course of U.S. history. We shall document forms and patterns of that inhumane and unjust treatment later in this chapter as well as in several subsequent chapters. However, the pattern of treatment has not been uniform among all groups with the most exclusionary and segregating patterns of treatment reserved for the deaf and blind and those with emotional and intellectual disabilities. Those with physical disabilities, whether related to injuries or diseases, have generally fared better.

One of the problematic areas is the degree to which those with disabilities are physically visible or culturally identifiable. Race, essentially a social construct now, at one time in American history was taken as a biological construct and assumed to be principally based on skin color with other surface features like nose and lip size, the presence of eyefolds, hair and eye color assisting in that identification. However, racial classification in the United States was always principally a social designation rather than a technical determination of

Table 3.1   Issues in the Applicability of the Minority Group Label to Persons with Disabilities.

Minority Status Element	Applicability to persons with mental and physical disabilities.
1. Experience discrimination and less power	The range of exclusions, patterns of discrimination, and diminished elements of social, political and economic power all apply.
2. Display distinguishing physical and/or cultural characteristics	This element is somewhat problematic—mainly because of the huge variability in the severity, nature and definitions of differences seen as disabling. Some have visible physical impairments or noticeable "differences" in their behavior while others have invisible impairments. The deaf have a clear culture while many others with disabilities do not have clear cultural differences except as stimulated by their responses to stigma, labeling, exclusions and discrimination.
3. Have involuntary membership in minority group that is passed on by rule of descent	While involuntary, many disabilities are acquired by disease, injury or aging but some may contain varying degrees of genetic inheritance. Disabling conditions can sometimes be overcome by "treatment". Many disabilities reveal unique trajectories in how they increase or diminish over time but are infrequently inherited.
4. Have group identity as minority group member who is perceived and treated as different.	Identities are problematic since there is so much variation that ranges from no group identity among severely retarded to a high identity of disabled people active in self-advocacy groups. Also, many do not globalize their identity as disabled but as having a bad back, a learning disability, arthritis or bipolar disorder. Only a particular disabling condition may give some an identity while others may gain an identity if they experience labeling, discrimination and perhaps in fighting these
5. Practice endogamy	There are higher rates of marriage among persons with similar types of disabilities prompted by more frequent contacts by being grouped together for treatment, housing, recreation and their shared identities.

the predominance of one racial strain over another. And with successive waves of immigration and biological amalgamation much of the U.S. population is composed of increasingly diverse admixtures of biological and social inheritance. Race has become increasingly questioned as a meaningful biological classification device. The situation is even more difficult with regard to those with disabilities. The tremendous diversity of disabilities along with the difficulty in defining disability in operational terms makes it quite difficult to come to either scientific or public ways of easily identifying all persons with disabilities. Some have obviously visible physical impairments while others have invisible physical or mental impairments. Some are born with disabilities and their trajectory of dealing with them as well as the range of responses may be quite different than those who acquire disabilities due to injury, illness and aging. For some, disabilities remain constant while others may move into and out of varying degrees of severity of the disability or even be "cured" of them. Some, particularly the deaf and the blind to a less degree, may develop some subcultural traits that help identify them while others lack any distinctive cultural practices that may set them apart in their own mind or the minds of others. Perhaps it would be safe to say that persons with the most severe forms of mental and physical disabilities are more identifiable either through their visible differences in appearances or behavior.

The third element, membership by involuntary inheritance, is not problematic with regard to voluntariness. However, some may acquire injuries by participating in voluntarily risky behavior such as automobile racing or sky diving. However, they undoubtedly assessed the risks as "low". On occasion, some people do intentionally injure themselves. We would have to invoke a special exception mechanism to inheritance to include them. In contrast the degree to which disabilities are genetically inherited as opposed to being acquired shows huge variability. And many disabilities may have synergistically interrelated biological and social origins that defy easy classification into either biological inheritance or social acquisition. The involuntary component of this identified element of a minority group is probably more important than the means by which one became a disabled. Whether a disability is inherited or acquired does not seem to change the fact that it is a involuntary condition

The fourth element is developing an identity as a disabled person. Some with minor limitations in instrumental activities of daily living would not would not classify themselves as among the disabled. Some

Some who cannot swim, ski, walk a half mile, or lift 10 pounds may not think of themselves as disabled if those activities are not important them—or not important to them at a particular point of their life such as when they are older. The scientific measurement of the variable of identity may not be adequately classified as simply present or absent but require a continuum of shades of identity from nonexistent, to very weak to very strong on a 10 point scale. Some may regard their disability as an opportunity to grow spiritually and not as a stigma while others may resent the new limitations and the socially isolating responses it brings. Some may find that their identity is fulfilled by joining in the disability rights movement to advocate for more services or against job discrimination while others do not have any interest in participating in any aspect of the movement. Some may identify with people with just their type of disability be it muscular dystrophy, Lou Gehrig's disease, or obsessive compulsive behaviors while others may identify with persons who have any type of disability. While there can be many variations in how researchers could detect and measure identity, according to survey evidence, 74% of persons with a disability report they have a sense of "common" identity (Fine & Asch, 1988). The one group that appears to have the strongest sense of identity is a subset of those with severe hearing impairments—those deaf from birth or an early age who have been immersed in a British or American sign language environment, had deaf parents and/or went to a school for the deaf, who in turn defined themselves as deaf. They conceive of themselves as a **linguistic** minority which is a subset of cultural minority which is excluded from the dominant culture because they lack oralism—fluency in the spoken language of the dominant group. On the other hand, they want to maintain their separate schools because they use the only language in which most feel comfortable. They want to resist any assimilation that would force them to loose their sign language for it provides their best means of communication (Barnes and Mercer, 2001).

In 2000, a Harris survey asked people with disabilities to identify levels of identity with the disabled. They found that only 16% of those with "slight" disabilities in comparison to 30% of those with severe disabilities had a **"very strong sense of identity with others in the disabled population"** (emphasis added). On the other hand, a larger percentage, 47% (up from 40% in 1986) had a weaker **"somewhat"** or **"strong"** identity with the disabled community. ("Sense of Common Identity Among People with Disabilities", 2001)

The last element, higher marriage within the group, remains a research question to a certain degree. But a general sociological insight is that people tend to marry persons with whom they have more contact and with whom they share some interests and with whom they have about equal social statuses. It is known that persons with specific kinds of disabilities may be more frequently in contact with each other through educational identification and segregation, rehabilitation programs, residential programs, and recreational programs. Some may come together in disability rights groups. General social expectations about who would be the best or "most appropriate partners" for them may constrain their choices in the direction of choosing partners with shared characteristics.

While some of the elements of classifying all persons with disabilities as belonging to a minority are problematic, the most important element, experiencing less power and discrimination is widely evidenced historically. And this is most evident among those with the severest mental and physical disabilities. Over time, researchers and government agencies concerned with measuring and counting disability have increasingly defined disability in more inclusive ways so that between 20 and 25% of the U.S. population may be defined as disabled with only about half or less of those having a "severe" disability. It is particularly to this more delimited group that the concept of a minority is most applicable. That is because they are more visible, experience greater stigma and discrimination, share in an identity because of their visibility and treatment and perhaps because of their participation in a self-advocacy group.

THE MODEL OF STIGMA AND DISCRIMINATION BEING MUTUALLY REINFORCING

The dominant model of the role of stereotypes and discrimination is that they are mutually reinforcing according to the view of many sociologists. However, many citizens seem to think that people's beliefs and ideas and attitudes toward others shape how they act toward them with little thought being given to how the overt discriminatory words and actions of others shapes belief systems, stereotypes, and attitudes. But in fact, the behaviors of others that treat people differently because of their disabilities helps shape both attitudes and patterns of treatment. (Stroman, 1982; Renzetti and Curran, 2000).

The images of persons with disabilities as portrayed in the mass media, novels, radio and in studies of public attitudes show an almost exclusively negative attitudes.   While sometimes people with disabilities are shown as normal, most images depict persons with disabilities as sharing one of more of these images: as tragic figures, as abnormal, as deviant, as needing wonder cures, as unemployed, poor, pitiable, pathetic, sinister, evil, cripples, freaks, sexually incompetent or unfulfilled, objects of humor or ridicule, and mentally incompetent. (Barnes and Mercer, 2001; Barnes, 1992; Zola, 1985).   Stereotypes vary somewhat by the very nature of the disability—e.g. persons with mental illness are more likely to be seen as dangerous while persons with cognitive disabilities are more likely to be seen as pitiable and incompetent. One of the key ideas in the creation of a minority status is that a minority group does not define itself—it is defined by the dominant group which marginalizes the role of disabled people in society. Their disability becomes their "master status" rather than their occupation, role as a parent or children or some other voluntarily chosen behavior which sets them apart.   The very meaning of subordination is that minority group members have less control over their lives than do superordinate group members who have more power, status and resources to define itself and the "other"—those who are different because of their disability.

THE FORMS OF DISCRIMINATION AGAINST THE DISABLED MINORITY.

The original sociological conceptualizations of minorities was developed to explain intergroup **processes** and **outcomes** between racial and/or ethnic cultural groups.   The key elements of this dominant/minority model was that the dominant group had more power, it used that power to discriminate against minority groups defined as inferior by their differentness as determined by race and/or culture and/or national origin, and as a result of that discrimination or differential treatment the minority group did not share equally as a group in the desirable values in social life: health, jobs, education, income, or status.

Table 3.2 lists the ways minority group theorists have conceptualized the **processes and outcomes** of how the two groups interact—driven primarily by the greater social and economic power of the dominant group which is almost always a numerically larger group

group than the subordinate group. It should be noted that the processes and outcomes listed in Table 3.2 move from the morally worst at the top of the table to a egalitarian form at the bottom. While all the processes except pluralism involve discrimination or unequal treatment, discrimination in this model is reserved for less severe forms of dominance. Discrimination is "the denial of opportunities and equal rights to individuals and groups based on some type of arbitrary bias." (Schaefer, 2001, 264). It should be pointed out that in complex and large societies with multiple minority groups many of these processes may be occurring simultaneously even though one process or outcome may be a more accurate description for some minorities than others or for some time periods than others.

APPLICABLILITY OF THE MINORITY GROUP MODEL OF PROCESSES AND OUTCOMES TO THOSE WITH DISABILITIES

How applicable is the minority group model first developed for racial and ethnic groups to those with disabilities? We will explore each of the processes and/or outcomes to see if they are applicable to the disabled and to see if we can locate historical examples of them. While the model posits that the dominant group holds negative attitudes toward the minority group which rationalizes the discriminatory treatment of them, the racial and ethic model points out that minorities are often initiated by processes of population migrations, territorial annexation and colonialism. These three origins of racial and ethnic groups coming into contact with one another are not applicable to the disabled as a minority. However, the concept of an **internal colonizer**, where the dominant group of able people control the minority population of people with disabilities is applicable to the operation of the medical model where the providers of institutional care such as education, housing, health care and rehabilitation services dominate those with disabilities. (Schaeffer, 2000)

EXTERMINATION. Ravaud and Stiker (2001) refer to extermination as "exclusion" and point out that exclusion can occur through two processes they call "elimination" and "abandonment". In elimination, life is taken from a person or group—this is genocide— the killing of a group of persons because of their race, ethnicity, beliefs or disabilities. As part of the genocide in Nazi Germany

Table 3.2. Processes and Outcomes of Minority and Dominant Group
Interactions

PROCESS/ OUTCOME	DESCRIPTION OF THE PROCESS/OUTCOME
EXTER- MINATION	The minority group is eliminated by killing living members of it and/or preventing their reproduction
SLAVERY	Members of the dominant group "own" members of the minority group who are given few if any "rights".
EXPUL- SION	The dominant group forces the minority group out of the territory or nation state the dominant group believes it owns.
SECES- SION	The minority group withdraws to another territory where it is less threatened or it becomes the dominant group there.
SEGREGA- TION	The two groups are physically separated. This may be due solely or partly to the dominant group. It may involve **degrees** of segregation in various areas of life: residential, educational, work, politics, worship, recreation, health care, familial.
UNEQUAL TREAT- MENT: DISCRIMI- NATION	Discrimination is differential and unfair treatment of an individual because of his group membership. It is a denial of equal opportunities or equal rights in comparisons to the opportunities or rights of the dominant group.
FUSION: >Biological Amalga- mation >Cultural Blending	Fusion describes both a process and a outcome when two or more groups are blended together to form a new group. This blending may occur by miscegenation or intermarriage of the two groups (biological amalgamation) and/or a cultural blending of their cultures to form a new culture. This is often called the **melting pot** theory about the blending of cultural of biological elements of two or more groups
ASSIMILA- TION	This is both a process and an outcome by which the minority group as a whole or individual minority group members become like the dominant group by adopting its culture and characteristics and being accepted by the dominant group as one of them.
PLURAL- ISM	This "ideal" outcomes sees dominant and minority groups continuing to exist along side each other but with equal opportunities, equal rights and mutual respect.

approximately 200,000 persons with disabilities (particularly "those with mental illness or congenital malformation") were killed. (Ravaud and Stiker, 2001, 502). Elimination was apparently practiced in some earlier societies on a small scale where malformed children were let to die in the natural environment. They were not cared for or fed. While direct action was not taken to kill them, they were let to die. In today's society, some children who are grossly malformed at birth or persons suffering from irrecoverable brain death may be left to die by withdrawing feeding tubes. Or orders to not resuscitate persons with disabilities can be made. Because of the cultural judgments that we sometimes hear that "I'd rather be dead than crippled" or have some other disabling condition, one organization was formed in 1996 called "Not Dead Yet". This organization protests the low value put on the life of people with disabilities, the move toward assisted suicides, and allowing "defective" children to die. (Fleischer and Zames, 2001). Other variations of extermination exists. One is where prenatal tests indicate that the child would be born with substantial birth defects. Some parents may elect to terminate the pregnancy on the assumption that the child would have a low "quality of life" and/or require an "excessive" amount of care which they feel unprepared to give. Elimination can occur another way—not by elimination of persons directly but by the elimination of persons with disabilities from procreating on the assumption they can eliminate one or more disabling conditions by genetic control. During the period of 1900 to about 1930, tens of thousands of persons in institutions for persons with mental retardation were sterilized. In addition, thousands of others diagnosed as mentally retarded were prohibited from marrying in order to avoid procreation on the assumption that intelligence was inherited. And most of those living in institutions for the mentally retarded were residentially segregated by sex in order to avoid mixing of the sexes and possible procreative activities that might occur if they lived and/or worked together. (Stroman, 1989).   The historical evidence shows that extermination in several forms has been practiced in the past and still is evidenced in more passive forms today against some persons with disability.

SLAVERY. There appears to be no evidence of ownership of persons with disabilities as slaves simply because of their disabilities. However, throughout history, the "characterization of disabled people in mainstream culture has stressed their significant 'abnormalities'. These are variously used as sources of "entertainment" or to induce and confirm the fears and abhorrence of them in the nondisabled population." Barnes and Mercer, 2001, 517). Garland (1995, 46) reports that many affluent Greek and Roman households kept a "sprinkling of dwarfs, mutes, cretins, eunuchs and hunchbacks, whose principle duty appears to have been to undergo degrading and painful humiliation in order to provide amusement at dinner parties and other festive occasions."

> Evidence of society's fascination with perceived bodily abnormalities persisted throughout the Middle Ages. Many royal courts in Europe retained people of short stature as "court jesters" or kept a complement of "fools" including people with cognitive impairments and learning disabilities, as well as others who feigned "idiocy" to provide amusement. It was also a common practice for people with perceived "deformities" to be put on display at village fairs on market days, festivals, and holidays. (Barnes & Mercer, 2001, 518).

Freak shows existed through much of recorded history to the early part of the 20th century in both Europe and America where persons with alleged mental, physical and behavioral deviations were put on display at circuses, fairs and carnivals. While they were not slaves, they were treated as defectives and perhaps this was one of the few forms of work they were allowed to perform because of how they were regarded by society. It was a clear form of exploitation and degradation that parents and/or entertainment employers promoted.

EXPULSION AND SECESSION.   In the history of dominant and minority ethnic and racial groups there have been many examples of expulsion. The U.S. treatment of Indians provides a good example of this when Indians were repeatedly pushed west as European migrants to American kept moving the frontier west. In 1830 the Indian Removal Act required all Indians living east of the Mississippi to move west of it—primarily to "Indian" Territory---land that settlers didn't want--yet. Thus the Indians were expelled from their homeland territories to new areas unfamiliar to them. Later, Indians would be expelled to even more desolate areas to be called Indian reservations to be held in perpetual trust for them by the federal government. (Kelley, 1990). But nothing comparable has occurred with any group of disabled persons.   And while some African Americans have espoused moving back to Africa to escape slavery and their subsequent oppression following slavery, few have done so although the nation of Liberia was founded by African Americans moving to Africa in a secessionist move around the turn of the century. (Schaefer, 2000). However, no comparable movement of the disabled returning to a homeland from which they had been moved against their will exists. Thus, these responses are only applicable to ethnic and racial minorities and not persons with disabilities.

SEGREGATION. In the next three chapters we will look in more detail than in this chapter at the pattern of segregating those with disabilities. This pattern went beyond the residential segregation of racial and ethnic groups each living in distinct geographic subareas within a city, township or county. Rather, this segregation was into residential institutions that were "total institutions"—places where people lived 24 hours a day and often for long periods of time. Some of these institutions started out as residential schools where persons who were deaf or blind or who were developmentally disabled would spend about nine months a year in them for training or education to return home to their families in the summer time and sometimes other vacations or holidays in the 19th century. But as the early optimistic hopes fell of being able to educate persons with such disabilities to levels high enough to function as others, "inmates" or "students" began to accumulate in them and the size of such institutions grew. Over time they became long-term care custodial institutions as their educational or rehabilitation function became secondary goals for which they were often under-funded. Much the same can be said for residential hospitals for those with mental illness. Often they started out with the goal of rehabilitating people to return to their home communities. This certainly did occur for some of the patients. But others, the most severely mentally ill, accumulated in such institutions. This resulted in more institutions being built and others enlarged as greater numbers of patients stayed for long periods of time. Lerner (1982) reports that in 1890 there were 8.4 residents per 100,000 population in institutions for the feeble-minded. But by 1923 there were 39.3 residents per 100,000 in institutions for the feeble-minded—a 368% increase in 33 years. In 1890 there were 118.2 patients per 100,000 population in insane asylums, but by 1923 there were 241.7 patients per 100,000 population—an increase of 104%.

The numbers of persons maintained in public mental hospitals peaked in 1955 at 535,540 while the peak institutionalization of those with mental retardation occurred in 1967 at 194,657. These were rarely voluntary placements by the persons involved. Nearly all those with mental retardation were placed with the help of parents—often upon the recommendation of their physician and others. Many of the patients in mental hospitals were put there involuntarily as they were seen as a threat either to themselves or others and mental hospitals afforded a location for "treatment".

Many of the institutions built for either the feeble minded or insane up to 1950 had been built in rural locations where land was cheap, but more importantly, to aid in the functioning of such institutions by either keeping the inmates in a protected environment or one that protected the rest of the population by excluding easy access to the able population. A number of rationales have existed for the separate residential locations for persons with either mental illness or mental retardation. These rationales have waxed and waned over time as cultural definitions of the dangerousness and needs of those with mental illness or retardation have been reformulated. But as we shall see, the primary rationale in the last century was to provide a more appropriate place for education of the retarded or rehabilitation of the insane—segregated from criminals, the destitute poor and from each other. In these institutions more specialized training for the retarded or rehabilitation for the insane could occur than if such persons remained in the community or were mixed together with each other and with the poor and criminal where the function of the almshouse, jail or prison was confinement and community safety rather than inmate education or rehabilitation. Other rationales for total residential segregation were developed. One of these was that the security of those incarcerated could be greatly increased if other elements of the population could not take advantage of persons in their weakened mental states. Another rationale was that such populations have been incarcerated to protect the security of the outside population from their dangerous criminal activities. Furthermore, their reproduction and potential contribution to the intellectual and moral decline of civilization could be better controlled if they were sequestered in institutions where their sexual activities could be monitored and controlled. Also, institutions in remote rural areas were less expensive to build and maintain and permitted many of their residents to engage in farming under close supervision to help defray the costs of their institutional care. (Stroman, 1989; Grob, 1994; Rochefort, 1997).

UNEQUAL TREATMENT: DISCRIMINATION. The more severe forms of unequal treatment described in previous paragraphs are declining around the globe although segregation for purposes of rehabilitation, training and education still exist but are declining as more community-based programs promote more residential integration and social inclusion of those with disabilities. However, a variety of forms of unequal treatment or discrimination exist. They may come in two forms called interpersonal and institutional discrimination.   **Interpersonal discrimination** proceeds from the beliefs and practices of individuals when they are acting on their own and not performing some worker role as part of the policy of an institution or organization.   However, **institutional discrimination,** involves the denial of rights or unequal treatment by individuals in social structures such as banks, hospitals, universities, government, realtors, manufacturing firms, law firms, etc.   Such practices are often systematically shared within various institutional sectors and are often rather hard to detect and eradicate because they are part of traditional or built-in institutional arrangements and policies about who is admitted, trained, excluded, and how they are treated in subtle ways. (Renzetti & Curran, 2000).

Discrimination comes in many forms and institutional areas against those with disabilities.   In this section of the book we do not intend to provide an exhaustive cataloguing of all forms of discrimination but rather to **illustrate** some examples of discrimination within various institutional sectors.   We start with one of the most important areas—work—inasmuch as work provides people a strong identity and the means of learning a livelihood from poverty level to high affluence.   In turns this **master status** helps fix their identity in the social order by the kind of work they do and the amount of prestige and other resources that come from that work.

EMPLOYMENT DISCRIMINATION.   About 10% of those 16 to 64 have a disability.   A comparison of employment or unemployment rates of those with and without disabilities need to be read cautiously for to be considered unemployed by the U.S. Department of Labor a person needs to be registered as looking for a job through the U.S. Job Service and be out of a job.   However, some people with disabilities who are neither working or registered to work are not counted as unemployed because they are not part of the official "labor force". But there are substantial differences in job holding among those with and without disabilities.   The information in Table 3.3 reveals a substantial difference in employment of those with and without disabilities and how the severity of disabilities impacts on both employment and earnings.   The information for this table was collected by means of a poll carried out by Harris in 2000.

The information in Table 3.3 shows that 49% more people without than with disabilities of working age (18-64) are working. However, in that age group, there is less of a gap if we compare employment rates between able and disabled groups who report they are able to work—a difference of 25%.   Younger persons with disabilities in comparison to older persons with disabilities are more

Table 3.3   A comparison of the nondisabled to the disabled in working, work preferences, income levels and poverty in 2000. (Figures are in percent)

BASIS OF COMPARISON	No Disability	Disability	% Gap
People age 18-64 working full or part time.	81	32	49
People age18-64 who say they are able to work and are working	81	56	25
People age 18-29 who say they are able to work and are working	81	66	15
Respondent reports that jobs they have require them to use their full talents and abilities	48	40	8
Percent of college grads who are unemployed	14	55	41
Percent age 18-64 living in poverty	10	29	19
Percent age 18-29 living in poverty	10	19	9
Unemployed people who prefer to be unemployed	60	33	27

Percent who want to work by severity of disability:
    Very severe
    Somewhat severe
    Moderate severity
    Slight severity
		73
		70
		60
		51	

Have household incomes of $15,000 or less by severity of disability:
    Severe
    Slight
	10	33
		15	

Earn over $50,000 a year by severity of disability:
    Severe
    Slight
	39	15
		33	

Source: "Employment Rates of People with Disabilities". 2001. National Organization on Disability (*http://www.nod.org*) pp.1-3.

likely to be working and less likely to be in poverty although nearly twice the proportion are in poverty for the 18-29 age group if they are disabled. There is a surprisingly large gap among college graduates where 55% of college graduates with a disability are unemployed compared to 14% of the nondisabled. This table also shows that the severity of disability substantially increases a persons chance to be in poverty as well as substantially decreasing chances of making $50,000 or more a year. People with disabilities report and file claims on employment discrimination in all its many forms: not getting a job interview, being passed over for jobs when they are equally qualified, working fewer hours, not getting equal opportunities for training or promotions, and making less pay than similarly qualified workers. All of this leaves the working disabled at lower economic rungs on average (2001; Fleischer and Zames, 2001). The Harris poll carried out by the National Organization on Disability in 2001 found that persons with disabilities perceived they were often discriminated against because of their disability: 51% said they had been refused a job because of a disability, 40% report being denied a workplace accommodation, 32% report being given less responsibility than coworkers, 29% report being paid less than workers in similar jobs with similar skills, 28% believed they had been refused a job promotion; 22% were refused a job interview. On the other hand, the ADA and a good economy have improved employment for persons with disabilities who are able to work. In 1986, just 46% of people with disabilities capable of work were working, but 14 years later in 2000, this percentage had increased to 56%. ("Employment Rates of People with Disabilities", 2001).

One of the very important factors that impacts on lowered employment of persons with disabilities is their deficit in educational achievement.   Table 3.4 compares persons with and without disabilities in terms of educational achievement. Gains are being made here but a deficit still exists. In 1986, 61% of persons with disabilities were graduating from high school. By 2001 this had increased to 78% but lagged 13% points behind those without disabilities. However, the percentage of those with disabilities graduating from college dropped from 30% in 1986 to 26% in 2000. ("Education Levels of People with Disabilities, 2001).

HOUSING DISCRIMINATION.   The deinstitutionalization of many persons with mental retardation, mental illness or physical disability, involved their transference to some type of residence in

Table 3.4. Educational Achievements of Persons with and without Disabilities, 2000.

EDUCATIONAL LEVEL	NO DISABILITY	DISABILITY
Percent without a high school diploma	9	22
Percent who had graduated from college	23	12
Percent who had completed high school	90	
Slight disability		83
Severe disability		67
Percent who had completed high school	23	
Slight disability		16
Severe disability		7

Source: "Educational Levels of People with Disabilities" 2001. National Organization on Disability, (*http://www.nod.org*) p.1.

normal residential communities.   However, they sometimes faced housing discrimination once placed outside of asylums, schools or hospitals.   The zoning regulations in many communities have been used to try to exclude group homes which house small groups of persons with disabilities.   While the courts have usually found that such practices are discriminatory, the very fact that operators of group homes have had to wage court battles to get open access to communities is noteworthy and a clear indicator of the stereotypes that such persons are dangerous or will somehow lower the quality of neighborhoods. (Stroman, 1989).

Many persons with disabilities who do not work, particularly the mentally ill, find a deficit of housing available for them.   A combination of factors: unemployment, low income, the rising costs of housing, a shortage of low-cost or low rent housing contribute to the extensive homelessness of those with mental illness.   While the estimates of homelessness have ranged from about 250,000 to 2,000,000, perhaps around one third of the homeless have a history of psychiatric illness.   While perhaps some of the homelessness of the mentally ill can be attributed to landlords refusing to rent to them, most of it is not due to discrimination but the correlates of poverty itself. (Rochefort, 1997)

Another form of discrimination in housing appears to flow from a pattern of construction that has historically taken little thought for those who get around on wheels and sticks instead of two legs. Either there is too little housing built for those with activity limitations or the units in a given community are grouped together. "Design apartheid" or "*social polizarization*" occurs because "specially adapted housing tends to be built in clusters and because state or local authority housing for rent tends also to be marshaled in estates in particular quarters of towns and (inner) cities, the upshot is a segregation of various groups or classes within a population." (Drake, 2001, 421-422). While no index of residential segregation has been designed to test the residential segregation of those with disabilities as it has for racial and ethnic minorities, anecdotal data suggests that such segregations exists.

One of the developments in the Center for Independent Living Movement has been to promote the principles of "adaptable design" as contained in the Fair Housing Amendments Act of 1988 to apply to new housing. These principles were developed collaboratively by architects and the disability community in the 1980s. "Adaptable design incorporates certain fixed access features but allows others to be added to existing structures as they are needed" (Fleischer and Zames, 2001, 45). These features allow people to remain in their own homes even as their disabilities change following individual trajectories of aging, rehabilitation, and/or growing disability.

HEALTH CARE. Discrimination in the area of health care takes place in essentially two ways—at the level of patients interacting with health care providers and at the policy level where guidelines, practices and professional ideologies are developed for various classifications of patients with disabilities. This area is particularly important to the disabled because, on average, they experience substantially more health problems than the rest of the population. This is so for several reasons. First, some disabilities flow from diseases or inherited biological conditions. Second, disabilities flow from injuries that have an impact on the body and/or brain. Third, those with some forms of disabilities—particularly intellectual disabilities—are more likely to have multiple disabilities some of which require medical attention and which may interfere with healthy exercise practices. And fourth, many persons with disabilities find vigorous exercising of the body more difficult or impossible which tends to undermine good health. People who spend much of their time in wheelchairs or lying in bed and unable to move by themselves, for example, not only are unable to exercise their heart, lungs and limbs but may develop pressure sores on heels and buttocks from lying in the same positions for long periods of time. Their greater need for more medical care however is undermined by a weaker position in the economy and polity to either purchase or negotiate that care.

At the level of the delivery of medical services persons with disabilities have often complained about the quality of care they got because physicians and others often did not believe what they told them, did not understand disability, shared in the patronizing and/or stigmatizing attitudes of the larger society, and were unaware of the special needs of and services for those with disabilities. French and Swain (2001) in their exploration of the relationships between disabled people and health and welfare professionals cite a number of examples of poor treatment:

>One woman reported that between the onset of symptoms such as dizziness, an inability to walk on occasion, bowel and bladder problems, double vision and numbness in her legs and the diagnosis of multiple sclerosis five years later that she had been told she had a "housewife syndrome" and needed to occupy herself with her children so she'd feel better.

>Numerous people with disabilities reported being prodded and displayed before groups of medical students as examples of tragedies or for them to guess what was "wrong" with a particular patient.

>Female children with disabilities have reported negative experiences of "public stripping" in hospitals where they may be paraded in front of medical students undressed, photographed naked, been exposed to insensitive questioning as if they were medical specimens without feelings.

>Patients in rehabilitation settings often report a lack of empathy for them when they are wrestling with how to cope with new disabilities.

>Patients are sometimes not told the whole story about their condition but it will be shared with other members of the family. There is sometimes an assumption they cannot handle the truth or are mentally incompetent to understand it.

French and Swain (2001, 751) conclude:

> Ultimately, it can be argued, the relationships between professionals and disabled people is a reflection of the social structures, ideologies, and power relations that disable people with impairments. Disabled people are generating the impetus for fundamental change, but the focus for change is professional structures, policies, practices, and ideologies.

Power relations and structures are, by their nature, deeply ingrained, and cosmetic changes mask lack of fundamental change. The challenge for professionals is that, from the experiences of disabled people, they have been part of the disablement of people with impairments. Central to a changing relationship is the changing paradigm from a medical model to a social model of disability and, with this, possibilities for professionals to work for and with disabled people in confronting the barriers of institutional discrimination.

At the policy level of health care French and Swain (2001, 736) argue that medical and welfare professionals are seen as "the agents or representatives of the state, or . . . the economic and political elite. Of particular importance to professional-disabled people relations is the maintenance of the status quo by pathologizing and individualizing problems that have been socially and economically created." Medical professionals in this context are often invested with almost the sole power to determine what the "needs" of a disabled person are and what resources will be made available to them—not only medically, but also in domains having little to do with medicine—education, employment, and housing.

Perhaps the most intrusive, violating, and invalidating experiences for disabled people emanate from the policies, practices and interventions that are justified and rationalized by a personal tragedy view of disability and impairment. The tragedy is to be avoided, eradicated, or nondisabled "normalized" by all possible means. Such negative presumptions about impairment and disability are so common that the abortion of impaired fetuses is barely challenged. There is considerable and growing pressure on women to undergo prenatal screening and to terminate pregnancies in which impairment has been detected. . . The erroneous idea that disabled people cannot be happy or enjoy an adequate quality of life lies at the heart of this response. The disabled person's problems are perceived to result from impairment rather than the failure of society to meet that person's needs in terms of appropriate human help and accessibility. There is an assumption that disabled people want to be "normal." However, disabled people who know themselves that disability is a major part of their identity rarely voice this. Disabled people are subjected to many disabling expectations, for example, to be "independent" and "normal," as well as to "adjust" and "accept" their situation. It is these expectations that are disabling, rather than the impairment itself. (French and Swain, 2001, 737.)

The medial care system is seen as discriminatory in another way. There are few people with disabilities working in the health care system as it has tended to exclude persons who are defined as having limitations. While medical professionals may see many people with disabilities as patients they are trained in the medical model that locates problems in individuals and not the system. They see few fellow workers with disabilities which helps maintain cultural attitudes that people with disabilities are not expected to go into the health care field. According to Ian Basnett (2001) who became a quadriplegic after earning his medical degree, physicians get little training in the social model of disability. They think of curing such individuals. "To most physicians, the possibility that they are acting as agents of social control and oppression, however passively, is abhorrent and likely to produce an abreaction." (Basnett, 2001, 452).

TRANSPORTATION. Access to public transportation is only one aspect of the entire "access" issue of fundamental concern to the disability movement. While only a small percentage of all persons with disabilities are wheelchair or walker users, perhaps no other issue so visibly shows the problem of access and is as easily understood in the public mind. Without access to buses, trains, cars, and airplanes, mobility for wheelchair and walker users is greatly constrained. The lack of public mobility to be able to go to work, school, vote, shopping, church, health care and recreation is immediately understood by most to be so encompassing that its effects are overwhelmingly drastic. Protesting the lack of access to the most widespread form of public transportation in U.S. cities, buses, has been one of the key methods that disability advocates have used to bring attention to their demand for access to the world beyond their homes. Several examples of the role of protests in improving bus transportation will help make the related points that lack of access to bus transportation was critical to acquiring equal opportunity, it had long existed as a denial of equal opportunity, and the most effective way to get results was to stage protests to which media representatives were invited in order to put pressure on public officials.

Fleischer and Zames (2001, 56) point out that in *Disabled in Action of Pennsylvania v. Coleman (E.D., Pa. 1976)* "a coalition of thirteen disability and senior citizen organizations sued three federal transportation agencies to require that the federal government would mandate the wheelchair accessible Transbus." Up to this point, the very limited bus services for the disabled had been provided by paratransit buses (small buses equipped for persons with disabilities and used solely by them) or in a few regular buses that had been retrofitted with wheelchair lifts.   However, disability advocates believed the universally designed Transbus approach was best because its low floor and wide-door could be used by all in the same way and if all (able and disabled alike) used it, repairs would be more regularly made than had been the case with retrofitted buses. Demonstrations were held in multiple cities on July 12, 1978 to push for the Transbus approach to be financially supported by the Department of Transportation.   Wheechair users blocked the street in front of the United Nations on that date.   While the decision on the federal support of the Transbus was delayed in the 1980s, it has become the dominant bus type in the 1990s.

Multiple groups in New York City have filed suits and staged demonstrations to get accessible bus service consistently available to wheelchair users.   The Eastern Paralyzed Veterans Association and Disabled in Action of Metropolitan New York have filed suits and staged demonstrations to get reliable bus services for people with disabilities in 1979 and the early 1980s in their city.   Other cities have seen similar demonstrations.   However, the right to accessible public transit has followed a circuitous route with some cities providing lift buses, others paratransit systems and still other the more integrating Transbus approach favored by disability advocates. (Fleischer & Zames, 2001).

ADAPT—Americans Disabled for Accessible Public Transit— was formed in 1983 to train and lead people to engage in direct action protest.   "In eight years, there had been several hundred arrests of ADAPT members in civil disobedience protests around the country. The group disrupted every national convention of the American Public Transit Association (APTA), the association of public bus systems.   By offering themselves up to mass arrests, they forced each city, from St. Louis to San Antonio, to consider the injustice of excluding disabled people from using buses." (Shapiro, 1993, 128). An Atlantic activist Mark Johnson acutely described the importance of public transportation for the disabled: "Black people fought for the right to ride in the front of the bus.   We're fighting for the right to get on the bus." (Quoted in Shapiro, 1993, 128).   Much of the battle over access to full equality under the non-discrimination clause of Section 504 of the 1973 Rehabilitation Act had to do with the long fight to achieve access to public transportation.   It was not only a highly visible and understandable right, but one critical for social participation in many areas of life.

While section 504 of the Rehabilitation Act forbids discrimination against persons with disabilities in programs receiving federal funding, organizations representing those with disabilities have often had to file suit against offending agencies or programs if they were to extend the rights of those with disabilities. In 1986 a decision by the U.S. Supreme Court in *Department of Transportation v. Paralyzed Veterans of America*, said while airports had to be accessible, private carriers did not. Up to that time, many air carriers had a pattern of sometimes discriminating against persons in wheelchairs by not serving them at all or by requiring them to be accompanied by a personal attendant whether needed or not and to have to pay for them. In response to this decision then, the 1986 Air Carrier Access Act was passed within four months of this Supreme Court's decision that prohibited discrimination not just by agencies receiving federal funding but by private businesses serving the general public. This law anticipated the 1990 ADA by no longer requiring the use of federal funds by a business to be found guilty of discrimination. According to Pelka (1997, 5-6), the rapid progress of this bill, with the support of Senator Robert Dole and attorneys from the Paralyzed Veterans Association, "was seen as a sign of the growing influence and sophistication of the disability rights lobby in Washington." In late 1999, Continental Airlines was charged by the Department of Transportation with discriminating against disabled passengers and was faced with a $250,000 fine for giving inadequate assistance to wheelchair-using passengers during 1997 and 1998. The Department found in Continental records, 13 instances of stranding passengers with disabilities aboard their planes or in terminals and around another hundred cases of the negligent handling of people in or needing wheelchairs. ("Continental Charged with Discrimination Against Disabled", 2001)

ACCESSIBLITY. One of the great concerns of persons with mobility limitations has been physical accessibility to the places they want to go. In testimony to Congress in 1989 when the American with Disabilities Act was being considered, nineteen year old Lisa Carl testified that in the previous year she had been excluded from a movie theater in Tacoma, Washington because the movie theater owner refused to sell her a ticket arguing he didn't have to let her in. Lisa was in a wheelchair. Lisa Carl testified that she did not cry on the outside but she cried inside because she only wanted to watch a movie like other people. Her testimony was for the ADA that would provide the same protections from discrimination against people with disabilities that have been provided decades earlier to racial and ethic minorities in the 1964 Civil Rights Act. In a 1986 Lou Harris and Associates poll, disabled persons were asked why they remained so separate and didn't go out as much as nondisabled people. Just "59% explained that they were afraid to go out. They were fearful of being mistreated, as Carl had been at the movies. And 40 percent said their access to public places was restricted by physical barriers, meaning building and streets, while 49 percent said transit systems were inaccessible." (Shapiro, 1993, 106) Shapiro goes on to state that at that time—in the late 1980s, "No other groups of citizens was so insulated from the American mainstream." (Shapiro, 1993, 106). While racial and ethnic minorities had been protected from segregation in public places 25 years earlier, many persons with disabilities are still segregated by physical and attitudinal barriers.

Disability rights activists knew that the passage of the 1990 Americans with Disabilities Act bill would give them great protection if it was passed even though it had been watered down from some of its earlier versions. In March of 1990, about three months before the ADA was signed into law by President George Bush, ADAPT organized a "Wheels of Justice" campaign in Washington to lobby and demonstrate for the bill. While the 475 protestors at the White House, many in wheelchairs, and the 250 protestors at the Capital, were small in number compared to many demonstrations, they got national attention with speeches from disability rights activists demanding their rights to access. (Pelka, 1997; Shapiro, 1993).

Shapiro (1993, 142-143) tells the following story and interprets its significance for the drive for access led by various components of the disability rights movement.

The postmaster in a small town was told that he would have to make his post office building accessible to people in wheelchairs. There were twenty formidable steps leading to the only public entrance, and the revolving door there was too narrow for even the smallest wheelchair. The postmaster objected to any renovation for disabled patrons. He sputtered in protest, "I've been here for thirty five years and in all that time I've yet to see a single customer come in here in a wheelchair."

For disabled people, there is more at stake in such exclusion than just the right to buy postage stamps. Segregation—whether the results of stairs or attitudes—creates harmful myths and stereotypes. Worse, it sets up a self-fulfilling prophecy for failure. That disabled people are invisible or separated, Americans like the postmaster have long assumed, is proof that they do not need inclusion or are not even capable or worthy of it.

Shapiro goes on to discuss what sociologists have long argued about minorities—they are assumed to be inferior because they are few models of success among them. But why is this the case they ask. They answer that personal and institutional discriminatory practices of the dominant group make the minority a dependent caste due to a lack of opportunities. They are defined as inferior and then the dominant group acts to make that status come true. By being excluded they are less likely to be seen as active and engaged.

One of the positive features of the 1990 Americans with Disabilities Act was that it was both regulatory and empowering in the sense that while some parts of the law opened up the environment by regulations for the physically disabled—it is also empowering by requiring advocates who see particular instances of access discrimination to file complaints and lawsuits which means that advocates are empowered to monitor compliance with the law. (Fleischer & Zames, 2001). Litvak and Enders make an important point about improving access in the environment by modifying it. Such changes often help others and meet certain universal needs. Curb cuts not only help wheelchair users but also those using handcarts, wheelbarrows, baby strollers, bikes, and skateboarders.

One of the indicators of inclusion is the comparison of rates of voting between those with disabilities to those without. Many voting places remain inaccessible to persons with physical or sensory disabilities. In 1984 Congress passed the Voting Accessibility for the Elderly and Handicapped Act. While this law required that federal registration and polling locations be accessible to persons with sensory or physical disabilities, it is a weak law that lacks enforcement mechanisms. As shown in table 3.5, 10% fewer people with disabilities vote than others. One recently uncovered anachronism is that 44 states have constitutions that bar persons with "mental disabilities" from voting. This places them under psychological guardianship that could keep them from voting even though some of them may be registered to vote. According to Kay Schriner, somewhere between 500,000 and 1,250,000 may be banned from voting booths if these statutes are enforced. She points out that the only other group of people who cannot vote are convicted felons. Schriner's research found that some of the earliest state constitutions drafted and ratified in the 1700s forbade the "idiot and insane" from voting on the assumption this would guarantee that voting would be done by informed and competent voters. And many later states adopted these statutes, as late as 1945 in Missouri and Alaska and Hawaii in 1959. However, few states have removed these exclusionary and defunct laws that bar some persons from voting based on outdated values and misperceptions about the capabilities of people with mental disabilities. ("Voting Laws Discriminate Against Mentally Disabled", 2001).

ACCESS TO SUPPORT SYSTEMS. One of the critical and ongoing social issues facing those with disabilities is whether they will have adequate access to the range of supports that will enable them to have as much control over their lives as possible. Litvak and Enders (2001) define disability-specific "support systems" as composed of three interactive elements—assistive technology (AT), personal assistance services (PAS) and adaptive strategies (AS) all of which are set within a social and cultural context. Assistive technology was defined in a rather constraining way by the 1988 Technology-Related Assistance for Individuals with Disabilities Act as "any item, piece of equipment, or product system, whether acquired commercially off the shelf, modified, or customized, that is used to increase, maintain, or improve functional capabilities of individuals with disabilities." (Quoted in Litvak and Enders, 2001, 716). This is a constraining definition for it may limit federal payment to devices that are "medically necessary" or designed only for those with disabilities rather than following a **universal design definition** of "the design of products and environments to be usable by all people, to the greatest extent possible, without the need for adaptation or specialized design". Examples of assistive technology include van lifts, augmentative communication devices, lowered workbenches and kitchen countertops, powered wheelchairs, and typing splints. An expanding array of assistive technology devices are coming onto the market from sip and puff controls on power wheelchairs to foam collars on pens that allow persons with limited dexterity to write. Personal assistance services include service animals or personal assistants who provide a person with a service they are unable to do on their own such as picking up things, hearing alarms or doorbells, seeing things for people with visual impairments and helping them with activities of daily living from toileting to transferring from bed to a wheelchair. Adaptive strategies, the third component of the support system involves the ways things are done, the techniques and skills used to cooperate with others and use of tools and personal assistance services. (Pelka, 1997; Litvak and Enders, 2001).

A number of laws have been passed to try to improve assistive technology and the availability of both it and personal assistants to people with a range of disabilities. The 1982 Telecommunications for the Disabled Act required that most phones serving the public be accessible to those with hearing impairments and that telephones be hearing-aid compatible. This act also provided for federal subsidies to the states if they would buy the more expensive hearing aid compatible phones for individuals who needed them as well as subsidies for telecommunications devices for the deaf (TTYs). Federal subsidies were also provided for phones compatible with artificial larynxes, breath activated telephones and telebraille machines for the deaf-blind. The Technology Related Assistance for Individuals with Disabilities Act of 1988 was passed because many persons with disabilities were unaware of assistive technology that could aid them and/or they could not afford such technology. Also there was insufficient cooperation and coordination among agencies funding the development and acquisition of assistive technology. This act allowed states some variability in programs to increase public awareness of technology, how to make it more available, and how to make technology developers more responsive to the end users of that technology. The 1990 Americans with Disabilities Act's Title IV required that telephone and telecommunications companies make TDDs (telecommunication devices for the deaf—commonly called TTYs) available to the deaf so they could communicate with hearing people. This involves TTYs users being able to access a relay system which in turn transmits a message by a regular phone to a hearing person. This act also required the closed captioning of federally funded television programming. (Pelka, 1997). The 1996 Telecommunications Act required telecommunications equipment manufactures and service providers to provide equipment and services that enabled persons with sensory impairments to be able to use cell phones, pagers, call-waiting and operator services. The 1998 Telecommunications Act provided grants to the states to maintain and strengthen comprehensive statewide programs of telecommunications assistance to persons with disabilities. Substantial gains are being made in opening up communication channels for those with disabilities. (Seelman, 2001; Fleischer and Zames, 2001; Blasiotti, Westbrook and Kobayashi, 2001). Despite federal legislation to reduce the communications gaps a "digital divide" still remains and is large between persons with and without disabilities. In 2000, just 28% of the disabled reported access to the internet either at home or at their work compared to 57% of the nondisabled as shown in Table 3.5.

Access to appropriate services is still a problem for many persons with disabilities.   One area of great concern is the inappropriate treatment of many persons with mental illness who are incarcerated in prisons and jails. According to a 1999 U.S. Department of Justice study, about 283,000 persons with severe mental illness are incarcerated in prisons every day.   The National Alliance for the Mentally Ill (NAMI) contends that this 16% of the nation's census in jails and prisons should not be located in such places but should be in treatment programs.   They estimate that only 30% of the 70,000 patients in public psychiatric hospitals are forensic patients.   They argue that this form of discriminatory treatment by imprisonment is frightening to people with severe disabilities and needs to be replaced by mental health courts that divert mental patients out of the criminal justice system and into the mental health system. (NAMI, 2001, "The Criminalization of People with Mental Illness").   The premier advocacy group for persons with mental illness (NAMI) also argues that the Vocational Rehabilitation programs have served persons with physical disability and mental retardation more effectively than it has persons with severe mental disorders.   Noble, Honberg, Hall and Flynn (1997, 3) argue they "have evidence that the federal-state vocational rehabilitation system has, for the most part, been an abject failure as a viable source of vocational rehabilitation services for people with severe mental illnesses." Others point out that even some psychiatric treatment facilities inappropriately use seclusion and restraint practices that result in unnecessary deaths, injuries and suffering. (Hash, 1999).

Access to appropriate services is a common problem as many people who need support services or institutional care are on waiting lists. ADAPT has contended since 1990 that 25% of Medicaid long term care funds should be redirected away from nursing homes to attendant or personal care services. ("Real Homes Not Nursing Homes", 2001) Already about one-third of the disabled use a personal assistant and somewhere between 32 and 45% use assistive technology. However, the number of persons in institutions could be lowered if the appropriate services were offered in the community. Perhaps the key question about the use of PAS is who will control the employment and pay of attendant services. (Litvak and Enders, 2001). That question will be the critical issue that will be addressed in Chapter 7.

Table 3.5 The Inclusion Gap, 2000

Label of Gap	Responses to Question Asked	Persons Without Disabilities	Persons With Disabilities
Community Participation Gap	Percent of persons who say they are completely uninvolved in their communities	21	35
Transportation Gap	Percent who say they have a problem with inadequate transportation	10	30
Political Participation Gap	Percent of voting age who voted	51	41
Healthcare Gap	Percent who say they postpone medical care because they can't afford it	12	28
Religious Participation Gap	Percent who say they attend religious services at least once a month	65	47
Technology Gap	Percent who say they have access to internet at home or work	57	28
Education Gap	Percent who fail to complete high school.	9	22

Sources: "What is the Community Participation Gap?"; "What is the Transportation Gap?"; "What is the Political Participation Gap?"; "What is The Healthcare Gap?"; "What is the Religious Participation Gap?"; "What is the Technology Gap?"; "What is the Education Gap?" National Organization on Disability. *http://www.nod.org.* 2001.

INDICATORS OF INCLUSION & EXCLUSION. Periodically the National Organizations on Disabilities contracts with Lou Harris and Associates to do a national survey of people with and without disabilities to discover the "gap" that separates the two about integration or inclusion into social life. Table 3.6 points out some of their findings for the year 2000. The biggest gap remains in technology—a 29% shortfall in those with access to the internet at home or at work by those with disabilities. More than twice the percentage of those with disabilities report postponing medical care because they can't afford it. And 20% more of those with disabilities have problems with transportation. The smallest differences between those with and without disabilities are in voting and then in graduating from high school.

CRIME VICTIMIZATION. One of the indicators of minority status is a higher rate of crime victimization than is true for the dominant group. This is found to be particularly true for those whose disabilities make them easier targets for crime and abuse because of their physical or mental limitations. "Research consistently finds that people with substantial disabilities suffer from violent and other major crime at rates four to ten times higher than that of the general population. Estimates are that around 5 million disabled people are victims of serious crime annually in the United States." One estimate in California was that only 4.5% of the crimes committed against those with disabilities are reported to authorities, compared to a 44% reporting rate for the general population. "Several studies suggest that 80 to 85 percent of criminal abuse of residents in institutions is never reported to authorities." ("Disabled Most Likely to be Victims of Serious Crime", 2001, 1-2).

One small study of victimization in California found that 80% of the women and 54% of the men with mental retardation had been abused at least one time. One study of intellectually disabled women found a high rate of repeat victimization—nearly half of the women who had been sexually assaulted had been assaulted ten or more times. (Sobsey, Lucaride and Mansell, 1995). A variety of factors account for the underreporting of such crimes including isolation and communication difficulties, lack of training of crime investigators for dealing with this population, lower rates of police follow-up, prosecution, and conviction, and continuing stereotypes of persons with disabilities that contribute to higher rates of victimization.

A more recent study of 40,000 children in Omaha schools from 1995 to 1996 found that children with disabilities suffered a rate of abuse 3.44 times greater than children without disabilities, and children with behavior disorders suffered a relative rate of physical abuse 7.3 times that of non-disabled children. The relative rates for sexual assault was 5.5 times greater, for neglect 6.7 times higher, and for emotional abuse 7 times higher. These findings are consistent with other studies that uncover that children and adults with psychiatric disabilities suffer some of the highest rates of crime and criminal abuse among people with disabilities. ("Disabled Most Likely to be Victims of Serious Crime," 2001, 2).

FUSION. This process or outcome, while applicable to some types of minorities like racial or ethnic minorities, is not really applicable to those with disabilities, or gender or sexual orientation minorities. This is so because disability, insofar as it is located in the person rather than the environment, is often an acquired characteristic that cannot be extinguished by marriage between those with and without disabilities. But able persons who are married to disabled persons are intuitively believed to be more understanding of and less discriminatory toward them. And cultural blending may be difficult to conceptualize for those with hearing disabilities unless both hearing and deaf people were to use sign language and oral language with equal facility. While this is theoretically possible, it is doubtful that even most hearing people would learn sign language to be able to communicate with an extremely sparse population of deaf people. Apart from the deaf who clearly are a cultural or linguistic minority, many doubt that other persons with a disability have a singular encompassing culture that could be fused with the dominant culture to produce a new hybrid culture.

ASSIMILATION. Many with disabilities, because of their perceived differentness and/or lack of functionality, would like not to be disabled. But many persons who have always had a disability or acquired it do learn to accept their situation. The assimilation process could involve several types of responses. First, it could involve **hiding** or not revealing those disabilities that are not observable. In this way those with disabilities could "pass" as able if their disability is not discovered. Second, those with less severe disabilities may **disclaim their importance** in their daily lives seeing them as insignificant or of little significance. Over 80% of people with less severe disabilities say they do not have a "strong" identification with others with disabilities. ("Sense of Community Identity Among People with Disabilities", 2001). Disability is relative to age, sex and social expectations. Thus, with ageing, many people lose some functionality but see it as **normal for a person of their age.** Third, many people **use assistive technology to minimize the effects** of some disability whether it is drugs to control depression or attention deficit hyperactive disorder or a variety of tools to improve mobility.

A review of the 1994 National Health Survey Data shows that an estimated 4.8 million Americans use canes, 1.8 million use walkers, 1.6 million use wheelchairs, 1.7 million use back braces while 4.2 million use hearing aides. ("How many Americans use wheelchairs and other assistive devices or technologies?" 2001). A fourth response is to **cure** the disability or to **remove** it or, sometimes to **prevent** its occurrence in the first place. Thus, a variety of preventive programs exist to reduce the extensive disability that comes from accidents (Pope and Tarlov, 1991). Hip and knee replacement and a variety of other surgeries are used to restore people to earlier levels of functioning to such a degree they are not considered disabled. Thus, it is clear that a variety of programs, technologies, and treatment interventions including vocational rehabilitation programs exist to assimilate people back to better functioning levels than before the interventions were begun.

PLURALISM. While some people with disabilities can be returned to a level of functioning no longer perceived as disabling or seriously disabling, many cannot. Those whose condition is not alterable would like to see themselves treated as just part of the variety of human nature without stereotyped value judgments of inferiority, dependency, incapability, sickness, tragedies, suffering or whatever terms are applied to them. The pluralism model that recognizes different identities, cultures, and ways of life without evaluating them as clearly inferior or superior is what many people want. They want to escape the social fact of **handicaptivity.** But one of the problems with this model is how to describe and operate prevention programs to reduce or minimize the effects of injuries, disease and other disabling conditions without making persons with such impairments seem undesirable and thus stigmatizing those who do become injured. We teach children not to run in front of cars to avoid injuries; signs are posted around shallow swimming pools to not dive into them to avoid serious head and spinal core injuries; we implore children not to throw things at others for they might blind them. Teaching prevention makes value judgments that non-injury is better than injury. However, if injury does occur, then we need to accept it as a part of life that happens. Pluralism is the model of not just integration but of integration with equality. It is inclusion and social acceptance without interpersonal or institutional discrimination.

SUMMARY

Persons with disabilities are a diverse group whose visibility, self-awareness of being in a minority group, involuntary status, and practice of endogamy is variable across and within various categories of disability. At the same time the critical distinguishing features of being a minority group is that there exist cultural stereotypes about their differentness or deviance from normality or wholeness and the consequent discrimination against them. From this viewpoint, those with disabilities are a minority although those with less severe disabling conditions and less visible ones typically have a lower consciousness of being a minority and may experience less stereotyping and discrimination from the able dominant group than persons with more severe and/or more visible disabling conditions.

The most widely supported model of how minority groups are created and maintained over time suggests that stereotypes about them and a variety of forms of discrimination directed toward them are mutually reinforcing. The medical model focuses almost exclusively on the conditions in the persons which are believed to cause the disability while the social model recognizes that the maltreatments of persons with perceived disabilities may be as important or more important than the disabling condition itself. A review of processes and outcomes that create, sustain and/or change relations between racial and ethnic minorities do not always apply well to the conceptualization of the disabled as a minority. Thus, the processes of slavery, expulsion, secession and biological fusion (amalgamation) or cultural fusion have very limited applicability in describing the historic relations between those with and without disabilities. However, extermination, segregation, unequal treatment (discrimination), assimilation and pluralism are concepts well suited to describing relations between the able dominant group and the subordinate group defined as disabled by the dominant group. As we shall see in subsequent chapters, the extensive segregation of persons with disabilities into insane asylums, training schools and rehabilitation hospitals has been over a century long process that remains with us even yet. An analysis of individual and institutional discrimination against those with disabilities shows that it has been extensive and invasive of all areas of life from education and employment to residential and recreational choices and the provision of health care, transportation and access to physical locations and social circles. Access to services has been controlled by others and multiple indicators of inclusion and exclusion show that gaps exist between what people with and without disabilities can do. Crime victimization against those with disabilities runs high because of the vulnerabilities they experience. Inclusion into the mainstream of life where people are judged as normal is attempted by some who try to pass as nondisabled, minimize their disability, see their disability as normal for a person of their age and history, use assistive technology to minimize the impact of a disability or search for cures and treatments that will restore them to nondisabled statuses. But for some, particularly those with severe disabilities and their humanistic allies, the concept of pluralism—equal respect and treatment irrespective of some differences is at the heart of their ideal society. They want to live in a world where all are respected, their basic rights as persons affirmed, and the supports they need to achieve their best are available.

CHAPTER 4
WAVE I OF DEINSTITUTIONALIZATION—PERSONS WITH MENTAL ILLNESS

THE ISSUES IN THIS CHAPTER

Two major waves of deinstitutionalization have occurred in the United States. The first wave began in the mid 1950s for those persons with mental illness. The next wave began roughly 15 years later and affected those who had been designated as having development disabilities the largest subcategory of which are those with mental retardation. Both of these waves are still rolling but the size of both waves is growing smaller as a majority of those in such institutions have been released and few new persons are sent to such institutions.

In this chapter we first define institutionalization and deinstitutionalization. Then we will look at the changing numbers of persons resident in institutions for the mentally ill over time to see the growth of institutionalization and then growing deinstitutionalization. The sources for this change will be analyzed under six headings. Among those factors that contributed to it are groups that organized to protest and change the conditions found in asylums for the mentally ill. Special attention will be given to those groups to help us better understand the role of advocacy and self-advocacy in achieving the rights of citizens with mental illness.

DEFINING INSTITUTIONALIZATION AND DEINSTITUTIONALIZATION

The first definition of institutionalization we will focus on in this chapter is that persons with diagnosed and treated mental illness were at one time primarily housed in public residential mental health facilities. In other words they did not live in their own homes or apartments or on the streets or other places. These residential facilities have been called different names over the last 200 years such as asylums, hospitals, psychiatric hospitals and other names. Most have been public facilities in the sense that they are supported by tax dollars but some have been private facilities paid for by private resources. Some of those with mental illness have also been housed in jails, prisons, regular hospitals, poorhouses, nursing homes, and institutions for those with mental retardation, and correctional facilities for juvenile delinquents. (Dowdall, 1996; Grob, 1994). The pattern of where they lived and why their residential placements changed is the subject of this chapter. One way to look at institutionalization is to count the numbers of persons in such institutions at different points in time and also to calculate rates of mental illness institutionalization by dividing the number of people living in such institutions (whether voluntarily or involuntarily) by the total population. Several limitations would exist in such an analysis inasmuch as sizeable differences over time existed as to what constituted mental illness, the desirability of and "need" for treatment, the best locations and methods for treatment, and the lack of accuracy in statistics of how many people in all these residential locations were actually mentally ill rather than being in institutions for other reasons. The assumption that severely mentally ill are hospitalized or resident in just one type of institution is not valid and thus makes counting persons in such institutions to be better seen as rough estimates rather than true counts. Lerman (1982) points out that in earlier times many persons with mental illness were located in institutions other than public and private mental hospitals such as homes for the aged, jails and prisons, institutions for the mentally retarded, tuberculosis hospitals, rehabilitation and general hospitals, homes/schools for the physically handicapped, detention facilities, homes for unwed mothers, homes for dependent and neglected children and chronic disease hospitals. And some persons with "problems" that today would not labeled as mentally ill were placed in asylums for the mentally ill.

The second definition of institutionalization, mainly its effects on people housed in residential institutions, is one of the key reasons why we might be interested in the numbers housed in such facilities. If we use the assumptions found in the medical model we might be able to conclude that changing numbers of people housed in private and public facilities would indicate the mental health of the population. However, if we use the assumptions found in the social model of disability we would expect relatively less stability in the numbers of the mental ill as definitions of it and culturally appropriate interventions and their locations change over time. The second definition of institutionalization is that prolonged living in such a total institution tends to have a number of detrimental effects on residents. These effects have been variously measured and defined as enforced dependency, forced idleness, loss of independence skills and/or problem solving skills, loss of hope, lowered self-esteem, growth in their self-definitions of being ill, reduced aspirations, loss of social connection with the outside world and decreased knowledge of changes in the outside world and how to cope with it. (Cockerham, 1996; Eaton, 1974; Townsend, 1976). Halpern (1980, 6) says being "institutionalized" refers to

> patients' dependence on the hospital and to the encouragement that the hospital environment gave to the development and maintenance of maladaptive behaviors above and beyond those the patient originally brought to the hospital. In brief the hospital environment was found to have a negative effect on the health and well-being of the patient.

However, we must be careful in not making a tight causal connection here—while those living longer in mental facilities are more subject to the processes defined as institutionalization, those living longer there are also those with more severe kinds of mental illness, those with fewer social connections in the outside world that would help draw them back, and those with fewer social competence skills in the first place. Thus, longer stays in mental hospitals may be associated with institutionalization as both a cause of it as well as an effect of factors associated with the severity of mental illness, preexisting skills of the person and other variables like marital status, social class, work performance, and legal counsel. (Cockerham, 1996; Rushing 1971).

Deinstitutionalization has had two key meanings related to the concepts of institutionalization. One meaning is simply a numerical one—to depopulate facilities for those with mental disabilities. The other is to try to remove those institutional processes in public mental hospitals that were alleged to create dependency, hopelessness, learned helplessness and other maladaptive behaviors. Thus, the first meaning suggests reducing the population size of institutions by three main processes—(1) releasing many of the persons confined in them, (2) shortening the length of stays in them, and (3) reducing both first admissions and readmissions. As depopulation occurred, states closed some of their state hospitals and downsized others by closing parts of them or using them for other purposes. But the question then occurs--where would patients go if they needed treatment services? Other beds and/or supportive programs for them must be found in other places—principally in their "home" communities. But the complex process of developing services and residential programs in the local community to serve those formerly living in state hospitals and schools is not a simple transition for it involves tens of thousands of people in thousands of communities learning new skills to either work or live in new places. As we shall see, the people who were no longer staying in state mental hospitals did not all go back to their original homes. Some ended up in nursing homes, jails, local hospitals with or without psychiatric wings, board and care homes, were homeless, or lived in other special residential programs such as half-way houses and homeless shelters. The other meaning of deinstitutionalization is to remove the debilitating effects of stays in an institution by replacing "custodial" care with truly rehabilitative care. However, this is a challenge to bureaucratic organizations that typically get low priority in funding from state legislatures. Persons with emotional disabilities have been relatively powerless in the political realm in comparison to the vast majority of the population that is seen as mentally healthy.

DEINSTITUTIONALIZATION—DEPOPULATION

One of the dramatic changes in the last half of the 20th century has been both the long-term depopulation of mental hospitals—now often called psychiatric hospitals—and a large decline in the average length of stay. The shortening of the treatment period in mental hospitals and releasing some who had been there for long periods of time rather than admitting fewer patients were the main sources of depopulation in the first two decades of the deinstitutionalization movement. The depopulation of psychiatric hospitals from a peak census of 558,000 in 1955 to 60,000 in 2000 is a huge decrease in

TABLE 4.1 RESIDENT PATIENTS IN STATE AND COUNTY
HOSPITALS, 1950-1997.

YEAR	YEAR-END RESIDENT POPULATION	NUMERICAL CHANGE OVER PRIOR PERIOD	PERCENTAGE CHANGE OVER PRIOR PERIOD
1950	512,501		
1955	558,922	+46,421	+9.1
1960	535,540	-23,382	-4.2
1965	475,202	-60,338	-11.3
1970	337,619	-137,583	-29.0
1975	193,436	-144,183	-42.7
1980	132,164	-61,272	-31.7
1985	109,939	-22,225	-16.8
1990	90,572	-19,367	-17.6
1994	72,096	-18,476	-20.4
1997	56,424	-15,672	-21.7

Sources: Adapted and modified from Rochefort, 1997; Center for
Mental Health Services, *Mental Health, United States, 1998;*
"State and County Psychiatric Hospitals, Inpatient Census,
Beginning of 1998", 2001.

light of a large population growth in that 45-year period. Instead of
nearly doubling in size to match population growth, psychiatric
hospitals in 2000 only housed 11% of what they did in 1955. (Hobson
and Leonard, 2001). And as this depopulation occurred, some mental
hospitals were closed. In 1954 there were 352 county and state public
hospitals, but by 1990 this number had dropped by 22% to 273
hospitals (Cockerham, 1996). Table 4.1 shows the decline over time.

The pace of depopulation was not even, and as we shall describe
later, was influenced by the waxing and waning of multiple forces
pushing for deinstitutionalization over that period. The fifteen year
period from 1960 to 1975 saw the biggest numerical and percentage
decreases. From the 1960 to 1965, the annual census reduction in
state hospitals averaged a little over 12,000 a year but in the 1965 to
1975 decade the annual reduction in census was over 27,000 per year.
From 1975 to 1980 the annual reduction dropped back to 12,000 and
after 1985 up to 1997 it averaged around 4,000 per year.

FORCES CREATING PRESSURE FOR DEINSTITUTIONALIZATION

Forces for change reflect the social context and the language of the era in which they occur. Reform movements in the field of mental health services are not limited to the last half century but go back to efforts by Dorothea Dix in the first half of the 19th century to get those with mental illness separated from those in prisons and separated from those in workhouses as well as the moral treatment

TABLE 4.2.   Historical Reform Movements in Mental Health Treatment in The United States.

REFORM MOVEMENT	ERA	SETTING	FOCUS OF REFORM
Moral treatment	1800-1850	Asylum	Human, restorative treatment
Mental Hygiene	1890-1920	Mental hospital and clinic	Prevention, scientific orientation
Community Mental Health	1955-1970	Community mental health center	Deinstitutionalization, social integration
Community Support	1970-present	Community support	Mental illness as a social welfare problem (e.g. housing, employment)

Source: *Mental Health: Report of the Surgeon General,* 1999. p. 79.

philosophy developed in France.   Table 4.2 shows four major reform movements in the field of mental health treatment in the United States since 1800.   While this table oversimplifies movements that were more complex than presented, it does help us see some key focal points in the various reform movements before the current one that focuses first on deinstitutionalization of patients, then their integration back into home communities where a variety of "social supports" like housing, employment training, peer support, transportation, casework planning and the like will be used.

In this section we will identify six forces qualitatively associated with deinstitutionalization.   Various researchers may conceptually organize these forces in different combinations, but the following analysis points to significant forces or events that can be associated with this major change in mental health treatment practices over a period of about five decades but which had peaked by 1980 when the political climate changed with Reagan coming into office. These six forces, often interdependent and mutually supporting, were:

(1) A chorus of criticism about the operation and effectiveness of public mental hospitals.

(2) The introduction and extensive adoption of mind-altering drugs that could control many of the worst symptoms of some types of mental illness.

(3) The leadership of President Kennedy to support federal policy changes in the treatment of those with mental retardation and mental illness.

(4) The shift to community based care for mental illness made possible primarily by the 1963 Community Mental Health Centers Act.

(5) A change in public opinion and advocacy for those with mental disabilities.

(6) The desire and opportunity by the states to reduce the growing costs of operating mental hospitals.

The Criticism of Public Mental Hospitals.   The criticism of public mental hospitals came from both popular and scholarly writers, former patients and their family members, and professional advocates. Four critical developments occurred during the World War II years which raised public consciousness about the seriousness of mental illness in terms of its social and economic impacts. One of these was the provision that conscientious objectors (COs) could be assigned to alternative work assignments where there were manpower shortages. About 2,000 COs were assigned to work as attendants in some sixty mental hospitals that were understaffed during the war years. The conditions they found were alarming to some of them— decrepit buildings, substandard and inhumane care. After the war in May of 1946 some of these COs got an expose in *Life* magazine of the shocking conditions in some of the state hospitals. Later that year some of the leaders formed the National Mental Health Foundation with headquarters in the American Friends School in Philadelphia. This group was influential in changing public opinion that led to increased funding for state mental hospitals. But in the long run the growing costs of such institutions was one of the reasons state legislators wanted to control the costs for mental health services by providing less costly community based services.   In 1951 this advocacy group joined with the National Committee for Mental

Hygiene and the Psychiatric Foundation to form the National Association of Mental Association. This powerful advocacy group continues to provide services to members and general information to the public about mental illness. (Rochefort, 1997; Pelka, 1997)

A second critical development that came out of World War II was the epidemiological finding that approximately1out of 8 men considered for military service in the war was rejected on neurological or psychiatric grounds. This constituted nearly 40% of all rejections. And even after this screening, over one-third of all the men discharged for disability were let go due to neuropsychiatric problems. This evidence showed that the toll of mental illness was costly to the nation in terms of personal suffering, lost productivity and the costs of mental health services. (Rochefort, 1997)

The third significant development was the often-successful experimentation with new briefer therapies to deal with neuropsychiatric problems. The older Freudian therapies and long-term custodial care seemed inappropriate during the press of war when early intensive treatment, group therapy, sedation and even hypnosis were used to deal with mental illness. Also, greater recognition of the social origins and social contexts of mental illness occurred during and immediately after the war years. (Rochefort, 1997)

A fourth development intertwined with the three preceding developments was a change in public and congressional attitudes toward those with mental illness. Because many men with mental illness served in the military, there was a sense that they and the nation could be better served by more knowledge and better services in this area. Up to this time, mental illness had been seen as only a medical problem and had always been the province of the states. It was stigmatized and resulted in many forms of discrimination including employment discrimination. But in 1946 Congress passed the National Mental Health Act which created the National Institute of Mental Health whose funding steadily soared over the following decades to fund basic, clinical and administrative research on mental illness, plan and implement community-based mental health programs and train a variety of mental health practitioners. The creation of the National Institutes of Health was a critical development for the field of mental health as it lead to the federal funding of health research and training that it had never before supported. This signaled a change in federal priorities. In 1948 the NIMH operated on a budget of $4.5 million of which about 71% went as grants to research and training agencies. By 1962, this amount was increased by more than 23-fold to $106.2 million of which 85% was going to external investigators and training institutions. (Cockerham, 1996; Rochefort, 1997).

Following World War II, a rash of critiques from the mass media and popular and scholarly presses described the horrible conditions in and inhumane treatment of residents of some state public mental hospitals. In 1946 two high-circulation national periodicals, *Life* and *Reader's Digest*, published articles respectively with the titles, "Bedlam USA", and "The Shame of our Mental Hospitals". Ridenour (1961) says these articles triggered similar exposes in ensuing years in both many daily newspapers and other magazines. Several major newspapers had reporters regularly covering local mental hospitals. And a number of books describing the terrible conditions in hospitals followed starting with Mary Jane Ward's *The Snake Pit* in 1946, then Albert Deutsch's *The Shame of the States* in 1948, John Martin's *The Pane of Glass* in 1956 and the novel by Ken Kesey in 1962, *One Flew Over the Cuckoo's Nest.* At about the same time, sociologists, psychologists and anthropologists were studying life in hospitals and arguing that often the very nature of this incarceration not only did not lead to recovery but made recovery less likely. Stanton and Schwartz (1954) argued that some the disturbances found in patients result from the functioning of institutions. Goffman (1961) provided the sharpest critique of asylums arguing that they often induce in patients a sense of stigma and alienation and helplessness much beyond their admitting conditions which often leads to an unwillingness to leave them. In his *Eclipse of the State Mental Hospital,* Dowall (1996) argues that in contrast to some organizations, state asylums became "maximalist organizations" over time. Such long-lived maximalist organizations have high initial costs, high operating costs because they provide services 24 hours a day for 365 days a year, require extensive exterior (state) funding because they are not self-supporting and lack organizational flexibility or adaptiveness. It was this combination of factors which did not make them very amenable to out-patient, community based services, and thus their depopulation in the last part of the 20th century. Dowdall points out (1996, 1), "For more than a century, state mental hospitals have served as the central organization for the care of the mentally ill, the pivot around which public policy has turned. But in the past few decades state hospitals have been eclipsed by other organizations dealing with mental illness, by the stigma generated by mental illnesses, and the spoiled image of institutional failure." The "poor" care found in mental hospitals during and immediately after World War II was later redefined as reprehensible and damaging by the 1960s. This laid much of the foundation for either making such hospitals more human and effective or providing for mental health care in the local communities to avoid the serious problems with institutions.

The Role and Growth of Pharmacotherapies in the Treatment of Mental Illness. "The advent of chlorpromazine in 1952 and other neuroleptic drugs was so revolutionary that it was one of the major historical forces behind the deinstitutionalization movement." *(Mental Health: A Report of the Surgeon General, 1999, 68).* Since the introduction of the first "mind-altering drugs" from France and India, there have been multiple waves of research that first extended the variety of such drugs that could control many of the symptoms of mental illness, and then additional research by which medical investigators came to understand the mechanisms by which they worked. But the critical effect that these new drugs had in the 1950s and 1960s was that they blunted many of the symptoms of severe mental illness and gave professionals, patients and their families the belief that many of the mentally ill could live in the community in their own homes or apartments, half-way houses, board and care facilities, nursing homes, and other residential programs. By controlling many of the behaviors of persons with mental illness, such persons could often be released to community care programs. The initial use of these drugs was not only important in depopulating mental hospitals but opened up opportunities for community integration and community employment for some persons with mentally disabling symptoms. The evolution of drug research based on both neuroscience and molecular biology has stoked support for the medical model of psychiatric illness so that more effective therapeutic agents with fewer undesirable side effects can be targeted to more particular mental disorders. For example, antipsychotics (neuroleptics) can be targeted to schizophrenia and psychosis; antidepressants can be targeted to anxiety and depression; stimulants can be targeted to attention-deficit/hyperactivity disorder; antimamics like lithium can be targeted on mania; and antianxiety (anxiolytics) can be targeted on anxiety. *(Mental Health: A Report of the Surgeon General, 1999).*

President Kennedy's Support of Policy Changes. In 1955 The Mental Health Study Act was passed by congress authorizing the investigation of problems related to mental illness. The research proposed in this act was carried out by the Joint Commission on Mental Illness and Health. Their report to the congress came out in 1960 under the title, *Action for Mental Health.* This committee's recommendations included an expansion of community mental health services that would allow detection, early intervention, crisis intervention and intensive treatment. It also recommended simultaneously reforming the quality of care in such institutions while reducing their size. It also recommended providing federal money to the states and localities for mental health services. To change mental health care from a state responsibility to a shared federal-state responsibility was a revolutionary recommendation. (Halpern, 1980). In 1961 Kennedy appointed a special "President's Panel on Mental Retardation". He took a special interest in this issue because he had a sister with mental retardation. This Panel included professionals as well as Elizabeth M. Boggs, founder of the National Association for Retarded Children, who brought to the panel a parent's perspective. In 1962 this Panel made 112 recommendations in its report entitled, *A Proposed Program for National Action to Combat Mental Retardation.* The recommendations included suggestions for strengthened educational programs, more comprehensive community services and changes in residential programs for the retarded. On February 5, 1963 in a speech to Congress Kennedy urged the nation,

> to reduce, over a number of years, and by hundreds of thousands, the persons confined to . . . institutions; to retain in and return to the community the mentally ill and mentally retarded, and there to restore and revitalize their lives through better health programs and strengthened educational and rehabilitation services. . . ." (Quoted in Pelka, 1997, 250)

As a result of the work of both the Joint Commission on Mental Illness and Health and the President's Panel on Mental Retardation and the president's powerful leadership, two very important pieces of legislation were passed in 1963 that furthered the process of depopulating institutions for both those with mental illness and mental retardation. The first act was the Maternal and Child Health and Mental Retardation Planning Amendments which was primarily oriented to providing funds for investigating the causes and methods of preventing retardation, for surveying the need for and to plan comprehensive services for those with mental retardation, and to provide demonstration funds for the education of children with mental retardation. The second act, the Mental Retardation Facilities and Community Mental Health Centers Act, provided funding for a variety of community facilities and services for persons with mental illness and mental retardation that would enable deinstitutionalization to take place. (Pelka, 1997; Halpern, 1980). The president's leadership in charting federal intervention and funding for service realms formerly in the hands of the states was critical in opening the doors to depopulation and then providing the services in their own communities for those who formerly would have received in-patient care at state-run mental hospitals.

The Shift to Community Based Mental Health Care. As the evidence in Table 4.1 shows, the depopulation of the state hospitals was not immediate after the passage of the 1963 Community Mental Health Centers Act. Nor was this shift easy as augmented services and facilities in thousands of local communities had to be developed to be provide help to that growing number of patients who were no longer sent to a distant state hospital for an episode of care. The original goal of the 1963 act was to create about 1500 community mental health centers in the U.S. that would blanket the entire country. Each center was to serve a catchment area of about 100,000 people. However, by 1972 only 300 centers were in operation, 650 by 1977 accessible to an estimated 43 percent of the population, and by 1990 just 700 centers were in operation. The 1975 amendments to the act required that all centers were to minimally provide for at least five basic services: inpatient care, emergency care, partial hospitalization (day care programs), outpatient care, and education and consultation. Eventually with later amendments, 12 services were to be available, but funding shortages made it impossible for most centers to offer all the services in subsequent years. (Cockerham, 1996; Mechanic, 1999).

A combination of forces ideologically justified the shift to community based care. Professionals, civil rights activists, and humanitarians all saw the shift away from the dark age of custodial confinement to conveniently available local care as the right thing. The deinstitutionalization that moved slowly for the first decade starting in 1955 picked up speed as the tactics and egalitarian philosophy of the civil rights movement were adopted by the movement for the rights of the incarcerated mentally ill. The 1960s was a period of welfare expansionism that saw the introduction of both Medicare and Medicaid in 1966 that enabled many new persons to seek medical help, including mental health care, that had formerly been out of their financial reach. Also, during the period of 1965 to 1975 when public mental hospital patient censuses were decreasing by an average of 8.6% a year, we see the increased disability and welfare payments enable some patients to afford the return to home or board and care settings or expanding public housing. (Rochefort, 1997).

During the period of 1960 to 1990, many people were still being admitted to state hospitals, but the average length of stay had decreased by more than half—from 41 days in 1970 to 15 days in 1990. One of the major changes was the decrease in chronic care patients who often spent long periods of time in mental hospitals. In 1960, of the 541,625 patients in public mental hospitals, over 36% of them had been there 10 years or more while another 18% had been there from 4.9 to 10 years. By 1970 after the initial wave of mental hospital deinstutionalization, these longer term residents made up 47% rather than 54% of the residents as they did in 1960 (Cockerham, 1996; Halpern, 1980). The shift can be counted in another way—where episodes of care occur. An episode is a period of treatment from its beginning to end whether it be a day, a month of sessions or a year in a mental hospital. In 1955 there were 1.7 million patient care episodes compared to 5.5 million in 1973. However, in 1955, 77% of these episodes occurred in public mental hospitals; but by 1973, only 32 % were in public mental hospitals with the remaining 68% occurring in a variety of other settings. (Halpern, 1980).

The shift to community care has seen a diversification in where people get care for mental health needs. Mechanic (1999) refers to some of this shift as *"transinstitutionalization"*, that is transferring persons from one type of institution to another. Thus, many patients released from state public hospitals were directly or indirectly transferred to nursing homes or local hospitals partly because the federal government picked up around half the costs of staying in these facilities compared to sharing none of the costs in state mental hospitals. Today's mental health service system is so fragmented that no one guiding principle can be used to explain how it is organized. *Mental Health: A Report of the Surgeon General,* (1999, 73-74) divides our fragmented system into four *sectors*, three *settings*, two categories about *duration of care,* and two forms *of financing* as follow:

SECTORS:

Specialty Mental Health (psychologists, psychiatrists, psychiatric nurses, psychiatric social workers for example and the places where they work)

General   Medical/Primary   Care   (family   physicians,   nurse
practitioners, internists, pediatricians for example and the places
where they work)
Human   Services   (social   welfare,   religious,   educational   and
charitable personnel and the places where they work)
Voluntary Support Network (self-help groups and organizations)
SETTINGS
Home
Community (services outside home but in local community)
Institutions (for example in mental hospitals, residential treatment
centers, nursing homes typically more distant than community
services)
DURATION OF CARE
Acute (short term care—typically less than a month)
Long-term (typically over a month in residential care that is often
custodial in nature wherein supervised living predominates over
active treatment.
FINANCING
Public (either provided by government agencies or paid for by
some level of government.)
Private (either provided by private agencies or paid for by private
sources such as cash or employer-provided insurance.)

Where do people now go for care?   The answer varies by
whether a person is of school age or not.   Table 4.3 shows several
things.   One is that the most important origin of services for children
ages 9-17 using mental/addictive services is from the school while
such services are not available to adults.   More than twice the
proportion of adults use the health sector in comparison to human
service professionals.   But, equal numbers use the "general health"
sector rather than the "specialty mental health" sector which is
generally judged as a more appropriate location for mental health
care.

Another approach to the location of services is a "facilities"
approach.   Counting the number of facilities and comparing those
numbers over time is a rather crude approach to get at the use of
services for it does not show total capacity or actual use of each type
of facility's capacity.   Still it is one indicator that may show changing
patterns of care.   Table 4.4 shows the number of such facilities by
type of facility in 1990.

TABLE 4.3   Proportion of adult and child/adolescent populations (ages 9-17) using mental/addictive disorder services in one year.

SOURCE OF SERVICES	ADULTS--% *	CHILD/ADOLESCENT AGES 9-17--% **
Total Health Sector	***11%	***9%
Speciality Mental Health	6%	8%
General health	6%	3%
Human Service Professionals	5%	***17%
School Services		16%
Other Human Services	5%	3%
Voluntary Support Network	5%	---
Any of Above Services****	15%	21%

*Source: Regier et al., 1993; Kessler et al, 1996. **Source: Shafer et al., 1996.
***Subtotals do not total due to overlap.
****May total to less than categories of services as some persons use multiple services.

Table 4.4   Number of mental health organizations in the United States, 1970 and 1994

TYPE OF ORGANIZATION	N, 1970	N, 1994	PERCENT CHANGE
Nonfederal general hospitals with psychiatric services	797	1,612	+102.2
Multiservice, freestanding psychiatric outpatient, and psychiatric partial care organizations	1176	2,474	+110.4
Residential treatment centers for emotionally disturbed children	261	459	+75.9
Private psychiatric hospitals	150	430	+186.6
State and county mental hospitals	310	256	-17.4
VA medical centers with psychiatric services	115	161	+40.0
TOTAL, ALL ORGANIZATIONS	3,005	5,392	+79.4

Source: Adapted and Modified from. Center for Mental Health Services, *Mental Health, United States,* 1998. (Washington, D.C.: U.S. Government Printing Office. 1998)

The largest number of facilities in 1994 which provided psychiatric treatment were several types of organizations that included multiservice centers, freestanding psychiatric outpatient clinics and psychiatric partial care organizations. They accounted for nearly 46% of all organizations providing psychiatric care in 1994. There growth was 110.4% over the 24-year period shown in Table 4.4. There has been a large growth in the number of general hospitals with psychiatric in-patient beds. Between 1970 and 1994 the number of nonfederal hospitals with separate psychiatric departments showed a big growth—102.4%-- and many patients formerly referred to state mental hospitals were now getting services in local hospitals. Many other general hospitals without separate psychiatric departments also provide beds for persons with psychiatric disorders. Also, many nursing homes provide care to persons with either mental illness or mental retardation but are not considered mental health facilities. The biggest growth percentage wise has been the increase in private psychiatric hospitals—186.6%--from 150 in 1970 to 430 in 1994. This reflects some growth in coverage in psychiatric services in many health insurance plans but perhaps even more the profitability of private psychiatric hospitals for investors. Admissions to private psychiatric hospitals increased more than fivefold from 92,000 in 1969 to 470,000 in 1992. In 1970, beds in private psychiatric hospitals accounted for only 2.7% of all psychiatric beds; but by 1994 they accounted for 14.6% of all such beds. The most dramatic changes have been not only the reduction in the number of public mental hospitals but the even greater decrease in the number of their beds being used. But as public mental hospitals have shrunk in size as they increasingly offer a variety outpatient services in the areas in which they are located. In 1970, public mental hospitals contained 78.7% of all 24-hour in patient psychiatric beds. But by 1994 this was down to 28.2% of all psychiatric beds! (*Mental Health, United States, 1998*). Public mental hospitals and Veterans Administrations hospitals are more likely to see patients with severe and persistent forms of mental illness than are outpatient programs or general hospitals. Many long-term patients in VA hospitals and nursing homes are mentally ill older persons.

Advocacy and Changing Public Opinion Toward Persons With Mental Illness. In many ways public opinion has changed regarding mental illness and mental health services. Research involving using the same questions in the 1950s as in the 1990s shows that people have gained a greater understanding of the forms of mental illness and can better distinguish it from general anxiety and unhappiness.

However citizens in the 1990s tended to associate mental illness more with dangerousness and violence than earlier that scholars find both unwarranted and stigmatizing. (Swindle, 1997; *Mental Health, A Report of the Surgeon General*, 1999). The stigma is damaging for it inhibits many people from getting needed mental health treatment, and since it is poorly funded in comparison to physical health care, people are less likely to get mental health care or tell others about it. Old beliefs about a mind/body split and the ability of people to pull themselves out of mental illness still persist. For example, one recent survey showed that "71% believed that mental illness is caused by emotional weakness", "65% believed that mental illness is caused by bad parenting", "35% believed mental illness is caused by sinful or immoral behavior", and "43% believed that mental illness is brought on in some way by the individual" ("Did You Know?" 2001). Stigma can have powerful effects in how people think about others and how they treat them. The labeling model emphasizes that prejudiced attitudes and discriminatory behavior have reinforcing effects on each other—that negative attitudes toward those with mental illness tends to lead to discrimination and discrimination in turn leads to rationalizations of the behavior which justify it. Discrimination against those with mental illness may be conceptualized as occurring at two levels—interpersonal and institutional. The interpersonal level would involve treating people differently when one is not acting in a formalized role found in some organization such as a teacher in a school, a nurse in health care organization, a landlord who is renting property, a human resource professional who hires, fires and promotes people. In contrast, when acting in official capacities as an employee or officer of an organization and in carrying out its stated or unstated policies then we would have instances of institutional discrimination if their actions were found to be injurious and unfair by legal standards.

There are multiple indicators of stigma being associated with mental illness:

• Over half of all those with mental illness do not seek treatment because of the stigma associated with it. This tends to be heightened among young people and older people, and those living in rural areas. (*Mental Health: A Report of the Surgeon General.* 1999)

• People are less willing to pay for mental health services whether through taxes or higher premiums, especially if the severity of the disease is not seen as severe, in comparison to physical ailments. (*Mental Health: A Report of the Surgeon General*, 1999).

- While persons who commit crimes related to physical disorders would usually get treatment if they are incarcerated in jails and prisons, those with mental illness often go without treatment. The National Alliance for the Mentally Ill (NAMI) reports that a 1999 study of by the U.S. Department of Justice estimated that 16% of all persons in jails or prisons were severely mentally ill. They argue that the estimated 283,000 persons with severe mental illness in jails and prisons outnumber the 70,000 in public mental hospitals of whom only 30% are forensic patients. NAMI believes persons with mental illness should receive treatment. ("The Criminalization of People with Mental Illness", 2001).

- Persons with mental illness are less likely to be employed and promoted.   For example, "the unemployment rate among American adults with depression is 23 percent, compared to 6 percent of the general population." ("Community-Based Mental Health Services Improve Lives and Save Dollars," 2001).

- Persons with mental illness sometimes face housing discrimination. This is especially true for persons who are entering newly established group homes or half-way houses or community residential rehabilitation facilities. (Rose, 1996).

- Persons with mental illness are often portrayed in the mass media as violent. Critics argue that this leads to fear and mistrust of those with mental illness inasmuch as a typical TV watcher will see three mentally ill people shown weekly and most are shown as violent. ("Before You Label People, Look At Their Contents,", 2001) Several investigators have shown the overall risk of violence is low among those with mental illness. It is higher among those with severe mental illness, especially if they are noncompliant with their medication regimen and highest among those with dual diagnoses (both mental illness and substance abuse). "Yet the risk of violence is much less for a stranger than for a family member or person who is known to the person with mental illness. . . . *In fact, there is very little risk of violence or harm to a stranger from casual contact with an individual who has a mental disorder." (Mental Health: A Report of the Surgeon General.* 1999, 7).

The consumer and advocacy movement has evolved over time to espouse different causes and points of view. Sometime various branches of the movement have argued vehemently against opposing views within the movement as regards the use of medications, the value of institutionalization, the best ways to combat stigma and reduce discrimination, the origins of mental illness, the role of support groups, and the perceived efficacy of various therapies in successfully treating mental illness. Most consumer and family organizations offer two major forms of help: (1) information and support and (2) advocacy for services and access to them. But it is important to note here that terminology helps define contrasting positions and views of the mental health service system. Those who use the term "consumers" believe they have the power the choose or reject services they find suitable or not and like consumers of retail goods have channels of complaint to deal with poor services or inferior products. On the other hand, those who label themselves as "survivors" or "ex-patients" emphasize they have survived an oppressive system of treatment whether as in-patients or out-patients and that they were manipulated by the providers in the system rather than having choices about the services they got. (Chamberlin & Rogers, 1990).

The origins of the consumer movement began as protests in the early 1970s by former patients of public mental hospitals who were inspired by the civil rights movement in protest of the system's treatment of them. The early 1970's "mental patients' liberation movement" saw themselves as rejected and stigmatized by society and robbed of decisions regarding their own treatment and normal lives. The early movement was militant—typically against laws favoring involuntary commitment, against the use of electroconvulsive and antipsychotic medication treatments, and against coercive psychiatry. They took on such names as the Alliance for the Liberation of Mental Patients, Project Release, and the Insane Liberation Front. Their members were survivors or ex-patients of the system who organized in homes and churches to help members locate community-based services and advocate for self-determination, access to services and to reform oppressive or ineffective systems. (Frese, 1998; Chamberlin, 1990). The Mental Patients' Liberation Front was founded in 1971 by two former mental patients from Boston. One of its first projects was to publish a 56 page pamphlet advising mental patients of *Your Rights as a Mental Patient* (1975). In 1975 seven members of this advocacy group who were patients at Boston State Hospital filed a landmark suit that changed patients rights forever. In this case, *Rogers v. Okrin (1979),* the court ruled that the mental hospital could no longer continue its practice of secluding patients or drugging them against their will. Upon appeal, the First Circuit Court of Appeals ruled that patients had a right to refuse drug treatment unless they had been ruled incompetent by a judge. (Pelka, 1997). During the late 1970s and after the book, *On Our Own* in 1978, a former patient's experience of surviving the mental health system, many groups formed to press for reforms, especially the provision of community based services. One group, the National Association of Mental Patients, argued for ending all treatments in oppressive hospitals, while the more centrist Mental Health Consumers' Association wanted to see modest reforms in the system. These groups eventually disbanded. *(Mental Health: A Report of the Surgeon General, 1999)*.

Some groups that emerged were largely or solely self-help groups while others combined these services with advocacy and information and referral services. Three variations of self-help groups emerged: (1) the separatist model that eschews professional help, (2) the supportive model that allows professionals to aid in auxiliary roles such as information sharing, and the (3) partnership models where professionals share leadership roles along with members. Over time consumers have come to play a variety of roles in providing a growing range of community-based mental health services such as running and/or staffing: drop-in centers, outreach programs, housing programs, job-training programs, business programs, crisis intervention services, research roles, and case-management programs. (Long & Van Tosh, 1988; *Mental Health: A Report of the Surgeon General,* 1999)

Mental Health: A Report of the Surgeon General, 1999, outlines five ways in which the consumer/advocacy movement has contributed not only to depopulating the public mental hospital system but in having a major impact on the provision of mental health services, legislation at both the state and federal level, and on research: (1) One has been the extensive proliferation of self-help/advocacy groups that have helped thousands of consumers with mental illness learn about and cope with their illness and social responses to it. (2) A second has been its impact on mental health policy and programs so that providers are more attuned to the needs of the people they serve. Consumers have become "empowered" enough to have very substantial influences on policy and how programs are operated. (3) Consumers are now involved at the multiple levels in the planning, delivery and evaluation of mental health services as well as serving on consumer affairs and consumer protection and advocacy agencies in many states. (4) Many consumers or ex-patients are employed in the mental health system and related agencies. This opens up opportunities for other consumers to find employment in other areas. (5) Finally, consumers are participating in research as respondents, active participants, partners, and as independent researchers who are engaged in designing and executing a variety of clinical and evaluative investigations.

One important form the advocacy movement has taken is where family members of those with mental illness act on their behalf. Sometimes they may be seen as more credible than the stigmatized persons for whom they are acting. Frequently it has been parents advocating for their children, but sometimes children advocating for their parents, or husbands and wives for their spouses or other family members wanting to help a relative. The family movement has spawned many advocacy groups, but three main ones have emerged since 1979: the National Alliance for the Mentally Ill, the Federation of Families for Children's Mental Health, and the National Mental Health Association. The largest and perhaps most influential of these is NAMI—National Alliance for the Mentally Ill with chapters in all states and membership over 200,000. This group was formed in 1979 to serve the needs of families of adults with chronic mental illness. These needs have varied somewhat over time but have included preparing parents to receive home family members who had been in institutions, providing information on the nature of the many forms of mental illness and the range of services available in various states and communities, advocating for improvements in community services and educating the public about mental diseases. Several distinctive features of NAMI are (1) that it adopts a hard medical model—that mental illness is a **brain disease,** (2) that it functions to serve families who have an adult member with a severe or chronic brain disease; (3) that it advocates for more neuroscience research to develop more and better treatments of brain diseases; (4) that it wants parity of treatment and insurance coverage for persons with mental illness; and (5) that it fights the stigma associated with mental diseases by educating the public that they are brain diseases and by operating programs like the "Stigma Busters" to eradicate the stigma of mental illness wherever it occurs. By means of 7,500 "Stigma Busters", members who identify stigma in movies, TV programs, local newspapers or wherever, NAMI contacts the stigma-sponsoring organization to try to get it to change its terminology or stigmatizing presentations. ("Stigma Busting Network and Alerts", 2001; *Mental Health: A Report of the Surgeon General,* 1999).

NAMI has become a formidable organization by its grassroots organization to reduce stigma and its successful lobbying efforts to improve services, increase funding for research and gain insurance parity for mental health care. One of the great advocacy successes of NAMI was its national campaign to achieve parity of treatment of mental illness with physical illness under health insurance. Many health insurance policies prior to 1995 had a $1 million cap on medical services for physical illness but a $50,000 or lower cap on mental health services. Or policies required substantially larger deductions and larger ongoing copayments for services for mental health care than for physical health care. While NAMI did not totally reach its goal of total parity of coverage, it made great gains. The goal of the "Campaign to End Discrimination" was to reduce all forms of discrimination against those with mental illness—principally starting with health insurance. This campaign had three elements in its campaign message and three tracks in how NAMI was going to change national opinion. The overall "Campaign Message" was "Mental Illnesses Are Brain Disorders". The three supporting subthemes were (1)" *Treatment works!* But there is a lack of understanding that brain disorders can be successfully treated." (2) *"Discrimination must end!* Discrimination against people with brain disorders is widespread, more so than against those with other physical illnesses." (3) *"Discrimination against brain disorders causes an unfair economic burden!* Discrimination causes unfair financial hardship for those with brain disorders and their families." The campaign was designed to occur over several years starting in 1995-96 to reach government officials, "multipliers", "influentials" and then the general public by using three channels of communication: (1) members were to educate the public about brain disorders, (2) an anti-discrimination campaign was to be carried out by the central office to educate policy makers about the injustice of inequities between physical an mental health insurance coverage, and (3) the organization was to carry out a national campaign about the advances in science that have expanded our understanding and treatment of brain disorders. The campaign was eminently successful and achieved its goal earlier than expected when President Clinton signed into law the Mental Health Parity Act of 1996 on September 26. (Hall, 1996; Purdy, 1996).

The second major organization providing information and advocacy is one that serves families of children with mental health problems. The Federation of Families for Children's Mental Health has over 120 state organizations or chapters with representatives from across the country and Canada. While the national office focuses on advocacy issues at the national level, the state organizations and chapters provide both advocacy, information, and a range of services like a support network for the families who want to join. This organization advocates for that roughly 12% of all children—about 6 to 8 million persons, who have emotional, behavioral and mental disorders. ("Welcome to the Federation of Families for Children's Mental Health, 2001)

The oldest organization representing families and professionals is the National Mental Health Association. It has gone through several name changes since it was founded in 1909 by Clifford Beers, who wrote about his struggle with mental illness and degrading and abusive treatment in mental hospitals in *A Mind That Found Itself,* published in 1908. In 1950 the National Committee for Mental Hygiene (the 1909 organization's name) merged with the National Mental Health Foundation and the Psychiatric Foundation to form the National Association of Mental Health which was renamed the National Mental Health Association in 1979. This organization is the most comprehensive of the mental health organizations taking as it does a public health approach to mental disorder. It has multiple goals and programs to fulfill its overall mission of improving the mental health of Americans and reducing the stigma and discrimination persons with mental illness experience. In 2001 NMHA had many "minor" programs and the following eight "major" programs in operation: (1) a national public awareness campaign to improve knowledge of mental illness symptoms, increase access to services and advocate for services; (2) using the 5,000 advocates it has trained to work on a variety of state and federal advocacy projects to improve services and reduce discrimination; (3) partnering with other groups to develop model community-based care programs; (4) a children's mental health campaign to develop awareness of and services for youth with mental and emotional disorders; (5) a consumer support and empowerment program to assist consumers in organizing and advocating; (6) an information center that includes a rich web site; (7) a justice program to assist adults and youths going untreated in the criminal justice system; and (8) a federally sponsored "safe schools/healthy students action center" to work with school districts nationwide to work on youth health and safety issues. ("How Does NMHA accomplish its mission?" 2001). One of its current other endeavors is its "Stigma Watch program" that "tracks news and entertainment coverage of mental health issues for fairness and accuracy". NMHA says "Our goal is to correct and prevent stigmatizing advertising, television and radio programming, and print features." NMHA officials contact the offending party in an attempt to change their behavior. ("Stigma Watch", 2001). One of the most successful campaigns waged by NMHA along with some other advocacy groups was its efforts in the 1980s and 1990s to strengthen the role of parents in getting services for their children in the face of uncoordinated child-serving agencies that often ignored them and blamed them for their children's behavior. "NMHA, a pioneer in the mental health advocacy field, assumed a pivotal role in strengthening the child mental health movement in the 1980s and early 1990s." *(Mental Health: A Report of the Surgeon General.* 1999).

Controlling Hospitalization Costs and Shifting Costs to the Federal Government. One of the powerful political factors to help explain the shift of treatment of mentally ill persons from public state hospitals to community hospitals and other organizations was not only the growing cost of state mental hospitals to the states but federal legislation than enabled the states to shift much of the cost of caring for the mentally ill from the states to the federal government. As improvements were made to many old state mental hospital buildings, staffs enlarged, and new programs begun to improve their image and performance, per capita costs of operating such facilities escalated in the 1960s and beyond. (Dowdall, 1996) And the costs of operating such facilities had always been a state expense and remains so now. The critical piece of legislation that initiated cost shifting of about half of mental health care expenses from the states to the federal government was the 1965 amendments to the Social Security Act which created Medicare and Medicaid. Under Medicaid, the federal government pays about half of medical costs, but a higher percentage of the costs in poorer states than in higher income states (on a sliding scale), for those who were low-income persons. The original Medicaid act said states could include the cost of inpatient hospital and skilled nursing facilities for persons 65 and older in institutions for TB or mental illness. However, it explicitly excluded the same services for persons under age 65 following legislative precedents set by Congress in 1950 and 1960 that funded the forerunners of the Supplemental Security Income legislation of 1972. In 1972 the social security act was amended to allow state-Medicaid eligible persons under 21 to have federal cost sharing for services provided to them at inpatient psychiatric hospitals. What this has meant then is that after 1965 states got **no** federal fiscal help for providing inpatient care to adults, aged 21 through 64, in state mental hospitals. This policy acted as a powerful stimulus to the states to deinstitutionalize adult mental hospital patients so that around half of their costs of care in other facilities and programs would be borne by the federal government. Because some states did not like this exclusion, Congress clarified what it meant by an IMD—Institution for Medical Diseases in 1988. It defined IMDs as "a hospital, nursing facility or other institution of more than sixteen beds that is primarily engaged in providing diagnosis, treatment or care of persons with mental diseases, including medical attention, nursing care, and related services." (Quoted in Edwards, 1997, 19). This definition did allow many adults with mental illness or developmental abilities who were living in smaller institutions (16 beds or less) or group homes or home-based programs to receive federal funds in their state and thus decrease that state's cost of mental health services by shifting some to the federal government. Edwards (1997) and others, for example, Dowdall, (1996) argue that cost-shifting of mental health services to the federal government was a very powerful motive for state legislatures and governors to promote deinstitutionalization. In some cases, residents of mental institutions ended up in other institutions like general hospitals or nursing homes. Edwards (1997) believes however that this policy forces some states to try to serve some of the most severely mental ill in local institutions or nursing homes when approximately 30% of all patients do not respond well to local treatment organizations because they lack the more skilled array of services and personnel that reinvigorated state hospitals now have. According to him there may be nearly a third of mentally ill persons who are more appropriately and effectively treated in specialized mental hospitals than in more generic community programs.

SUMMARY

The first wave of depopulating state institutions of their residents began with those with mental illness. The deinstitutionalization movement has two forms—the first and minor reform was to try to change state mental hospitals away from custodial institutions that kept most patients for long periods of time, undermined the continuation of the skills with which they entered the institution and often robbed them of their dignity. This reform of maximalist institutions is hard to achieve and rarely accomplished in large measure. The second and major form of deinstitutionalizing persons in state hospitals was to reduce their censuses by admitting few new patients, keeping patients for much shorter stays, and releasing many residents to the community where they will often get outpatient care. In the United States, the number of state mental hospitals has declined significantly but their censuses have been whittled from 558,922 in 1955 to 56,424 in 1997—a startling 90% decrease even while our population was nearly doubling in size. To understand this major transformation of a large health care institution deeply embedded in our national policy from a central place of treatment to a maligned and relatively small role in treatment, we investigated six forces that in intertwined and complex ways have led to a greatly diminished role of the state mental hospital in mental health care.

The six forces began to emerge toward the end of World War II and reached their greatest intensity during the period of 1965 to 1975 when slightly over 27,000 fewer persons were resident in state mental hospitals with each subsequent year. One of the leading early forces was the highly evidenced criticism that many of the state mental institutions were little more than warehouses for people with severe mental illnesses who were sometimes abused, deprived of rights others had, and infrequently rehabilitated. Their substantial costs but ineffectiveness led many critics to believe that emerging therapies that could be offered in the community would be less stigmatizing, more effective and less stigmatizing. Of particular importance was the emergence of chlorpromazine and other mind altering drugs in the 1950s that enabled prescribing physicians to control many of symptoms of mental illness allowing people to function in their home communities. The ongoing evolution of drug research has greatly increased the range and effectiveness of these drugs in being targeted toward increasingly specific symptoms with more accurate dosages. President's Kennedy's support of legislation that decentralized the treatment of mental illness from large impersonal state hospitals to a range of local services and the willingness of Congress to begin paying some of the costs of mental health care and research instead of leaving it a total state responsibility were actions that made deinstitutionalization possible. While drugs were important in this movement of people out of state hospitals into a range of local services, the actions of advocacy groups like the National Alliance for the Mentally Ill and the National Mental Health Association have been vital in providing a groundswell of support for peer support groups, lobbying for state and federal legislation to make it happen and providing the leadership and information to change the mental health care system and the stigma associated with using such services. Congress passed legislation in 1972 that enabled the states to greatly reduce their substantial costs of operating state mental hospitals. Before this, states could not use federal matching funds made available through the Medicaid program for persons in the state hospitals if they were between the ages of 21 and 64. The states had to bear 100% of these costs. But the federal government would pay for about one-half the costs of this age group if they were moved out of state institutions into smaller residences in their home communities. This gave the states a huge financial incentive to reduce institutional enrollments at the same time that other rationales were developing that said local, accessible mental health services that would be less uprooting to individuals and their families were better than those in old, distant, state institutions that courts and reports were finding did not rehabilitate.

CHAPTER 5
WAVE II OF
DEINSTITUTIONALIZATION: PERSONS
WITH MENTAL RETARDATION

ISSUES IN THIS CHAPTER.

In the prior chapter we defined institutionalization and deinstitutionalization. These terms apply to persons who were placed in institutions for persons with mental illness, mental retardation, other developmental disabilities and a range of physical disabilities. The names for these institutions have varied historically. They have included such names as insane asylums, mental hospitals, institutions for defective delinquents, schools, training facilities, homes for the mentally handicapped, psychiatric facilities, rehabilitation hospitals, etc. In the last chapter we looked at the processes of institutionalization and deinstitutionalization among those with mental illness and the origins of the social movement that was directed at changing the perceived limitations and cruelties of institutional living. In this chapter the focus is on those with mental retardation—the major subset of those with developmental disabilities. We first look at the meanings of these terms. We then review the pattern of institution building and the decline in the numbers of persons in public residential facilities. After that we review the sources of deinstitutionalization giving particular attention to the role of parents, other advocacy groups and courts in the declining number of residents found in such institutions.

THE MEANING OF MENTAL RETARDATION AND DEVELOPMENTAL DISABILITIES

The American Association of Mental Retardation or its predecessor organization has gone through numerous definitions of mental retardation including relatively recent revisions in 1959, 1961, 1973 and 1992. Each subsequent definition has become more explicit. The AAMR's 1992 definition of mental retardation is used as the benchmark definition adopted by most professionals working in the field. The current definition is: (AAMR, *Mental Retardation*, 1992, 1)

Mental retardation refers to substantial limitations in present functioning. It is characterized by significantly subaverage intellectual functioning, existing concurrently with related limitations in two or more of the following applicable adaptive skill areas: communication, self-care, home living, social skills, community use, self-direction, health and safety, functional academics, leisure, and work. Mental retardation manifests before age 18.

This definition uses three criteria: IQ level under 70, limitations in at least two of ten adaptive skill areas, and age 17 or less. In prior definitions, one of the criteria, IQ level, was used to define four levels of mental retardation: mild = 55-69; moderate = 40-54; severe = 25-39; and profound = >25. However, the 1992 revision dropped this classification scheme and replaced it with a more functional approach delimiting four levels of supports (intermittent, limited, extensive, pervasive) that might be needed in any of the ten adaptive skill areas. The older classification using the four levels of retardation had some utility to it as it enabled teachers, service providers, and researchers to quickly note and communicate the general functioning level of persons with different levels of retardation. Such information was relevant to placement in a variety of programs and enabled researchers to look at prevalence rates of mental retardation at the four levels. In that older classification scheme, of all persons with mental retardation, about two thirds were classified as mild with decreasing proportions occurring in each of the next three descending levels.

Persons with mental retardation are included in the larger and more inclusive definition of "developmental disabilities". The concept of development disabilities is a more recent term. The Administration on Developmental Disabilities uses the following definition of "DD" developed by congress:

The term "developmental disability" means a severe, chronic disability of an individual that—(i) is attributable to a mental or physical impairment or combination of mental and physical impairments; (ii) is manifested before the individual attains age 22; (iii) is likely to continue indefinitely; (iv) results in substantial functional limitations in 3 or more of the following areas of major life activity: (I) self-care. (II) receptive and expressive language. (III) learning. (IV) mobility. (V) self-direction. (VI) capacity for independent living. (VII) economic self-sufficiency; and (V) reflects the individual's need for a combination and sequence of special, interdependent, or generic services, individualized support systems or other forms of assistance that are of lifelong or extended duration and are individually planned or coordinated. ("Developmental Disability", 2001)

This definition of DD will include impairments caused by mental retardation and related conditions like cerebral palsy, epilepsy and other neurological conditions which impair general intellectual functioning or adaptive behaviors. One of the general findings is that mental and physical impairments overlap in many persons. And as the severity of mental retardation increases there is an increasing probability of having physical impairments. Also, persons with mental retardation are about twice as likely to experience mental illness as the population without mental retardation. (Stroman, 1989; Westling, 1986)

PATTERNS OF INSTITUTIONALIZATION AND DEINSTITUTIONALIZATION

The history of institution building for those with mental retardation is interwoven with their perception by the public and the responses of the states where the care of those with mental retardation has been lodged until the federal government began a sharing of that responsibility with the passage of the 1963 Mental Retardation Facilities and Community Mental Health Centers Act. The treatment of one of the nation's most vulnerable populations reflects shifting attitudes over the last 150 years. Wolf Wolfensberger (1976) has conceptualized seven different models of how those with mental retardation have been viewed in that time period. Different groups in society have viewed them differently in the same era of time although there were often dominant motifs existing at any one time that influenced the actions of state legislators, parents and those providing care and education to those with mental retardation. Table 5.1 lists those different models. The developmental model was dominant from about 1850 to 1880 and again starting after World War II. The models of them as subhuman organisms, as objects of pity and as holy

Table 5.1   Wolfensberger's Seven Models of How Those with Mental Retardation Have Been Viewed.

Conceptual Model	Key Ideas
As sick persons	This medical model locates mental retardation in individual biology and likens it to a sickness. Prevention, training in nursing wards in "hospitals" and various forms of medical intervention are seen as the central treatments.
As subhuman organisms	Viewed as subhuman more like vegetables or animals and therefore without rights. Lacking reason, they need to be tamed as are wild animals. As a threat to normal social life they need to be secluded in separate institutions where basic needs can be met.
As a menace	Similar to the above model, this model sees them as a threat to organized society and argues for their incarceration in institutions where their harm as vagrants, criminals and reproducers of their own kind can be controlled.
As objects of pity	Seen as eternal children who never grow up and need paternalistic care in sheltering environments that seclude them from those who would harm or take advantage of them.
As a burden of charity	As users of food, shelter and services provided by others, they are expected to contribute what they can to society without expecting more than the basic necessities of life. This sour humanitarianism sees their separation into institutions as an economical way to meet their basic needs.
As holy innocents	A few see them sent by God as blameless victims who need our loving attention and care.
As capable of development	This developmental model takes an optimistic view of the modifiability of human behavior and argues for the appropriate educational inclusion, progressive integration and humanitarian mainstreaming of persons with mental retardation into all institutional areas of life.

Source: Wolfensberger, 1976.

innocents were minor motifs during the last 150 years. Beginning in about 1880 they were increasingly seen as a burden of charity as the growth in the number and size of institutions accelerated. This stance was particularly prevalent among state legislators who felt a stern duty to care for "less fortunate" citizens. For a period of time they were seen as a menace to society and their containment in remote rural asylums and the development of three policies during the eugenics movement was seen as important to control their growth in numbers by limiting their propagation. These three policies to control their propagation involved segregating the sexes in state mental institutions, prohibiting their marriage among themselves or with "normal" people, and the practice of sterilization of persons with mental retardation residing in institutions. (Scheerenberger, 1983; Stroman, 1989; Trent, 1994; Tyor and Bell, 1984; Baumeister, 1970).

Table 5.2 captures some of the key historical developments in the treatment of those with mental retardation. The treatment of those with mental retardation in a given era reflects its dominant ideological motifs.

TABLE 5.2   MAJOR PERIODS AND DEVELOPMENTS IN THE HISTORY OF THOSE WHO ARE MENTALLY RETARDED

Period	Key Developments
1850-1880	Period of optimistic development of small schools for those with mental retardation and their growth into small institutions.
1880-1900	Growth of size and number of institutions. Growing custodialism as institutions are seen as sheltering inmates from society.
1900-1945	Continued growth of institutions as they become more custodial in nature. During period from 1900-1920 those with retardation are seen as a menace to a society who should best be contained in institutions and not allowed to procreate. Institutional architecture becomes distinctive with large efficient congregate dormitories where understaffing leads to dehumanized treatment, peonage, abuse, and general neglect of inmate welfare.
1945-2000	Developmental theory gains acceptance; deinstitutionalization starts and accelerates; special education evolves into educational inclusion; social mainstreaming and self-determination accelerate as diversified residential programs proliferate; advocacy and civil rights activities for the disabled leads to major legislation that impacts on those with mental retardation and developmental disabilities.

TABLE 5.3   Number of Residents in Public Residential Facilities for
the Mentally Retarded, 1900-1998**

Year	Number	Year	Number	Year	Number
1900*	10,000	1974	166,247	1987	95,637
1910*	20,000	1976	159,058	1988	91,531
1920*	35,000	1977	149,169	1989	88,086
1930*	52,000	1978	142,264	1990	84,818
1940*	102,000	1979	136,737	1991	81,245
1950	128,145	1980	132,515	1992	77,600
1955	143,548	1981	126,354	1993	73,032
1960	163,730	1982	119,229	1994	68,867
1967	194,657	1983	113,907	1995	64,187
1971	189,546	1984	109,619	1996	59,775
1972	181,035	1985	105,380	1997	56,254
1973	173,775	1986	100,511	1998	52,801

*Numbers for these years were estimated from a graph.
**Some sources differed about .5% on their numbers for a given year.
Sources: Lakin et al, 1981;Braddock, 1986; Braddock, 1990; Braddock,
2000; NIMH: *Patients in Public Institutions for the Mentally Retarded,*
1967. This last source points out that between 1950 and 1966, between
54,741 and 37,440 persons with mental retardation were housed in
public mental hospitals where they made up between 26.9% and 19.5%
of all first admissions to such hospitals.

An analysis of the data in Table 5.3 along with other information
shows several conclusions that can be drawn about trends in
institutionalization and deinstitutionalization:
>From the beginning of the development of public facilities for the
mentally retarded they have grown steadily from the last century up
until 1967, the peak year, when 194,657 persons with mental
retardation resided in such facilities.
>In comparison to the deinstitutionalization of those with mental
illness, the deinstitutionalization of those with mental retardation began
a little over a decade later.
>If we look at data in the most recent period regrouped into five
year periods as shown in Table 5.4, we see that the first five years,
1967-72, had the lowest decline in deinstitutionalization in either
numbers or the percentage loss of residents for any five year period
since 1967.

The momentum of deinstitutionalization was highest for the 1972-77 period where the number of residents declined an average of 6,372 per year. The pattern of deinstitutionalization has moved at a fairly steady pace since 1977 and appeared to pick up some new momentum in the 1990s. But since this is a movement controlled by the states, some states have deinstitutionalized at a much faster pace than others. (Braddock, 1990; Braddock, 2000).

>Several others developments were occurring in the deinstitutionalization movement. One of these was that the average number of residents per public institution declined from over 1500 in 1967 to around 500 in 1982. (Lakin, 1982). Also many institutions were closed or in the process of closing as residential facilities for the mentally retarded--sometimes being converted to other uses. In 1967 there were 273 residential facilities. Between then and 1984 there were 24 closures in 12 states and by 1988 there had been a total of 44 closures in 20 states. Braddock (2000) reports that his survey in 2000 showed there were 118 closures already completed or planned to be completed by 2000 and at the rate of closure in the 1990s all institutions should be closed by 2011.

>Over time as many current residents were released and very few new persons admitted to public institutions, the makeup of the residents changed. Those whose adjustment to residential community residential placements was easier were those who were higher functioning and/or were less medically fragile. Over time then the declining populations in many public institutions were increasingly and principally made up of persons with severe or profound levels of retardation, who had behavior problems, who were medically fragile, and those with multiple impairments for whom generic communal services were often inadequate as they needed a greater range of pervasive and specialized supports. (Scheerenberger, 1976; Braddock, 1990).

In reviewing Table 5.3, two central questions stand out: (1) Why did deinstitutionalization occur? (2) If many fewer persons with mental retardation are not living in public residential facilities, where are they living? The next part of this chapter that analyzes "Forces Behind Deinstitutionalization" will review the first question. But first we turn to the second question regarding changing pattern of residential location of those with mental retardation/ developmental disabilities who are not living at home. But it needs to be pointed out that by far the greatest percentage of those with MR/DD are not living in any type

TABLE 5.4   Decline of the number of residents per five year period from 1967-1997 in state public facilities for the mentally retarded.

FIVE YEAR PERIOD	AVERAGE ANNUAL DECLINE PER YEAR	PERCENT DECLINE IN FIVE YEAR PERIOD
1967-1972	2,224	7.0
1972-1977	6,372	17.6
1977-1982	5,988	20.1
1982-1987	4,718	19.8
1987-1992	3,607	18.9
1992-1997	4,269	27.5

of publicly or privately sponsored residential facility. In 1998 of an estimated 3,240,000 persons with DD, only 13% lived in a residential facility, while 13% lived in their own household, 15% with a spouse and 59% (1,922,248 persons) with a family caregiver. (Braddock, 2000).   Out-of-home placement is a choice made by 416,7171 individuals or their families in 1998.   Table 5.5 shows the recent distribution of where MR/DD out-of-home placements lived in 1993 and 1998.   An important classification device has been to call placements in facilities with 16 or more beds an "institution" while those with less than 16 beds are called "community residential placements".   Certainly individual foster home (often called "family living programs") placements are less likely to have "institutional" qualities than a 15-bed ICF/MR—an Intensive Care Facility for the Mentally Retarded.

Table 5.5 shows a continuing trend away from "institutional" placements even though there has been a faster decrease in the number of MR/DD residents in public institutions than in either private institutions or nursing homes.   Some of the depopulation of public institutions has been a transinstitutional transfer to larger private institutions and nursing homes.   This is particularly true for the more severely disabled and the aged MR/DD population.   While the growth of the community residential sector placement has been substantial, it has been most pronounced by the increasing placement of persons in small residential settings of less than 7 persons.   One of the big

Table 5.5 Types of out-of-home MR/DD residential placements in the
United States in 1993 and 1998.

TYPE OF RESIDENTIAL SETTING	1993 Number	1993 Percent of total	1998 Number	1998 Percent of total
INSTITUTIONAL SETTINGS	158,565	44	124,946	30
Public institutions	73,032	20	52,801	13
Private institutions	43,497	12	36,258	9
Nursing homes	41,759	12	35,887	9
COMMUNITY RESIDENTIAL SETTINGS	204,152	56	291,771	70
Group homes for 7-15	28,507	7	29,772	8
ICFs/MR for 7-15	27,064	7	24,203	6
Small settings for 1-6*	148,581	41	237,796	57
Totals	362,717	100	416,717	100

*Small settings in 1998 included 8 categories of living arrangements
with the following percentages of the 237,796 residents in each of the
following 8 types: 28% in group homes of 1-6 residents; 10% in group
homes of 7-15 residents; 7% in ICFs/MR for 1-6 residents; 8% in
ICFs/MR for 7-15 residents; 9% in foster care arrangements for 1-6
residents; 7% in apartments; 28% in supported living arrangements for
1-6 residents; and 3% for 1-6 persons in an assortment of other living
arrangements.
Source: Adapted and modified from Braddock (2000).

projects many states have been pushing is residential placement in
foster care—often called family living programs in some states—both
because they are seen as more homelike or less institutional and
because their costs are lower than most other placements.

FORCES BEHIND DEINSTITUTIONALIZATION AND INTEGRATION.

Many of the forces influencing deinstitutionalization for the
MR/DD population were the same as for mentally ill except there was
no "drug revolution" increasing treatment effectiveness for those with
mental retardation as there was for the mentally ill. Furthermore, the

same weighting of importance for the identifiable change agents was not the same for the MR/DD deinstitutionalization movement. Undoubtedly the combination of public critiques of the warehousing facilities for the mentally retarded and advocacy by parents and others evoked a judicial activism and legislative response that was relatively more far reaching for those with mental retardation.

Six intertwined and mutually reinforcing causes of deinstitutionalization and what was to replace it—a continuum of community services—are here identified. And it is important to note that the social context of the sixties and early seventies was alive with the successes of the civil rights movement for racial and ethnic minorities, protests about the Vietnam war and advocacy thrusts for both those with mental illness and physical disabilities. The six major synergistic forces we identify here are:

>The indictment of the poor quality of life in large public institutions.
>The advocacy movement.
>The spreading of a new treatment philosophy: integration, normalization and inclusion.
>The support of President Kennedy for deinstitutionalization and community care.
>The growing cost of institutional placement and the opportunity for the states to shift costs to the federal government for community care programs.
>The judicial and legislative responses to the first five forces listed in an era of reform, protest and the expansion of civil rights.

The Poor Quality of Life in Large Public Institutions. During the period of institution building that lasted up until the middle 1960s the justification for sizeable facilities for those with developmental disabilities was much like the philosophy of having sizeable hospitals. In one location could be arrayed a range of trained specialists, specialized equipment and facilities, and experienced people to deal with a wide array of mentally and physically disabling conditions. This reservoir of services provided in one location was not only more efficient but more effective in meeting the needs of a diverse population that certainly rural communities and not even many urban communities could provide had been the philosophy for about a hundred years. (Baroff, 1974). However, close on the heels of the criticisms of public mental hospitals reviewed in the last chapter, similar criticisms arouse from parents, some professionals in the field, the mass media and academic investigators who often couched their criticisms in the academic language of research findings.

A variety of criticisms were made by various academic studies of public institutions even though some institutions had more imaginative and individualized programming than other institutions. Some of the points were similar to studies found in mental hospitals—that the very nature of institutional life where decisions are made by a bureaucratically organized staff for the sake of uniformity and efficiency stifle individuality, create dependence, and undermine decision-making skills since all decisions, whether it be meal time, the blocks of time set aside for recreation or the nature of the recreation itself, are all made by the staff. Academic critics found patterns of "block treatment" where all residents did the same thing at the same time—shower time, lunch time, bed-time. Such block treatments robbed persons of their individuality. Residents had little exposure to a variety of people, buildings, different ways of life or other experiences in these total institutions and this dull environment was dulling of experience itself. Residents typically had infrequent contact with family members even when the family was intact. Thus they were deprived of many of the emotional experiences of being part of a family where individual responsibilities and unique identities can be stimulated and grown. Some critics found a pattern of forced idleness that was not developmentally stimulating like a good learning environment should be. Other critics found that institutional placement delayed development, slowed or depressed affectivity, and lowered social connectedness beyond what it was in more stimulating social environments. (Baroff, 1974; Stroman, 1989; Trent, 1994). One of the more strongly worded academic attacks on state asylums came from a California sociologist and his colleagues in the early 1960s when they observed retarded people's living conditions and treatment in Pacific State Hospital. They stated the place constituted a "staggering visual, auditory, and olfactory assault on the presupposedly invariant character of the natural normal world of everyday life." (MacAndred and Edgerton, 1964, 314).

Academic reports had a limited audience compared to some of reports in conditions in state asylums that appeared in mass media magazines or books beginning after World War II and going through the 1970s. One of the most startling exposes was a book primarily made up of grainy photographs taken at five state institutions in four northeastern states that were visited in December of 1995 by Burton Blatt and secret photographer Fred Kaplan. Blatt said in the introduction, "our pictures could not even begin to capture the total and overwhelming horror we saw, smelled, and felt." They showed and described "therapeutic isolation cells" where children were kept in solitary confinement without water, beds, or toilets. They saw children with their hands and legs bound. They saw infants by the hundreds crowded into cribs without toys or any apparent stimulation by ward attendants. They saw attendants hose down the floor covered by excrement in the day rooms where dozens of inmates spent the day doing nothing. After visiting the day rooms Blatt and Kaplan had to have their clothes dry cleaned to remove the stench. *Christmas in Purgatory: A Photographic Essay on Mental Retardation* was published in August in 1966.

In 1965 Senator Robert Kennedy, after visiting Rome and Willowbrook State Schools in New York, told the New York state legislature that inmates in those two institutions were being deprived of education and their civil liberties by living in "schools" easily susceptible to conditions promoting intestinal disease and brutal treatment by staff. One of the persons who exposed conditions in a state school was a physician, William Bronston, who began working at the Willowbrook State School in New York where he found conditions unbelievably bad. He was disciplined by the administration of the school when he tried to organize families and staff to confront it with the terrible conditions at the school. However many parents felt stigmatized about having children with disabilities and for having institutionalized them. They were reluctant to protest conditions there as were most fellow workers who were fearful of losing their jobs. They tried to fire him but he was protected by civil service. When that didn't work, he got the cooperation of a local television reporter, Geraldo Rivera, to report on the conditions at Willowbrook. On January 6, 1972 the film footage aired on national television showing naked residents at both Willowbrook School and Letchworth Village lying in their own excrement, walls smeared with feces, and floors covered with urine. The conditions at these institutions were compared to a Nazi concentration camp. All of the residents contracted hepatitis within six months of moving there. (Pelka, 1997). Rivera later wrote about Letchworth Village:

> Virtually every patient in building Tau was undressed and there was shit everywhere; it looked and smelled like a poorly kept kennel. It was so bad I was afraid that people watching television, emotionally drained from a week at Willowbrook, would either not look at it or not believe it.
>
> The residents of Tau were young girls. Many of them had physical deformities; more were literally smeared with feces—their roommates',

their own. They looked liked children who had been out making mudpies. My stomach still turns just thinking about it.

When we walked into the wards, they came toward us. I wanted to hold them, but it was too frightening. They were like lepers, and I was afraid they would somehow infect me. (Rivera, 1972, 78, 80).

Opened in 1951 and designed for 2,950 residents, by 1955 Willowbrook was overcrowded with 3,600 residents and housed 6000 residents by 1963. After further exposes of staff brutality and the horrible conditions, parents and residents filed a class-action suit with the help of the New York State Association of Retarded Citizens. Dozens of witnesses and hundreds of pages of testimony presented to the courts documented overcrowding, the use of extended seclusion, unhealthy conditions, the lack of meaningful programs all along with staff brutality. For example, one woman had all her teeth extracted because she once bit someone; others were tranquilized in back wards to keep them quiet. In May 1975, Judge John Bartels signed a consent decree that ordered the state of New York to reduce the 5400 residents living there then to 250 by 1981. That number was not reached, but by 1982, 2600 residents had been moved into community living arrangements that cost no more and provided much more human living conditions. (Trent, 1994; Pelka, 1997).

Joseph Shapiro (1993, 295-6), describes conditions at Faribault Regional Center, a state hospital for people with mental retardation in Southeastern Minnesota as reported by a University of Minnesota psychologist, Travis Thompson, who went to work there in 1968, asking to be assigned to work with the "toughest" residents. He was assigned to the Dakota Building where the institution kept what it labeled the "high profounds".

"I was confronted with sights, sounds and smells which I had never before experienced and hoped that I would never witness again," the young psychologist later wrote. "Seated in the middle of a large ward area, shackled to a chair, was a young man in his twenties, all of his skin abraded from his knees and blood running down his shins. Along the seventy-foot wall of the ward were seated approximately fifteen men, huddled in fetal positions, with their heads between their knees." Thompson described finding sixty-seven residents in the crowded room, sitting in urine and feces, rocking or walking aimlessly, or running around the walls of the room. Some were naked or nearly naked. Others gnawed their hands or twiddled their fingers in front of their faces. That night when he got home to his shower, Thompson washed his body for a half hour, trying to get the acrid smell of the ward out of his skin. Thompson worked to train these "high profounds," using behavior modification techniques that would later be imitated at other institutions. . . . Any normal person left in Dakota for six months, Thompson told a reporter at the time, would no longer be normal. "They would fit in with the crowd, rocking and rocking, sitting in their own feces."

The stories of the horrible conditions in state institutions for those with mental retardation could be repeated in many different states and at many points in history. These sickening stories provided the fodder for the advocacy movement to demand improvements in institutional practices and, when significant reforms rarely occurred, for deinstitutionalization. We turn next to the advocacy movement which led to many changes in the treatment of the MR/DD population.

The Advocacy Movement for those with Mental Retardation. The advocacy movement for those with mental retardation has been led mainly by parents but also with the help of concerned professionals working in the field. The goals have generally progressed over time from first getting better treatment in state institutions, more and better services in the community, then deinstitutionalization, and finally mainstreamed public education. But all of these overlap and are ongoing concerns of a variety of disability rights groups.

The premier parent's advocacy group was formally founded in 1950 when representatives from about 80 local and state groups of families with children with cognitive disabilities met to form the National Association for Retarded Children. Since its founding it has advocated for self-determination for persons with mental retardation along with prevention programs, research, education, and support services for persons with mental retardation and their families. The organization changed its name in 1974 to Association for Retarded Citizens to reflect the fact that persons with mental retardation include many adults who are not perpetual children as depicted in some stereotypes. After People First, a self-advocacy group of persons with cognitive disabilities was formed in 1974, there was a growing discussion of changing the organization's name again because the label "retarded" made many persons with mental retardation, their parents and professionals working in the field feel uncomfortable with its too frequent and stigmatizing use. In 1991 the organization changed its name to simply "The Arc" with that title no longer an acronym. (Pelka, 1997). The Arc's web site tag line now describes it as "The national organization of and for people with mental retardation and related developmental disabilities and their families." ("About The Arc",

2001).   Its state chapters have provided services to member families, lobbied for changes in state legislation and services impacting on the MR/DD population, and filed class action suits on behalf of its constituents.   The national organization with a membership over 150,000 and with over 1,200 state and local chapters supports research, information sharing, improved services and a variety of lobbying and other efforts.   It has national offices in Silver Spring, MD, Washington, D.C., and Bedford, TX.

The Arc's predecessor local chapters in the 1950s and 1960s "focused on education.   Parents, seeing their children rejected by the public schools, formed their own schools in church basements and private   homes,   and   they   worked   to   pressure   their   elected representatives to make changes in state laws and funding." (Pelka, 1997, 23).   Perhaps one of the most significant actions by a state chapter was the filing of a class action lawsuit by the Pennsylvania Association of Retarded Citizens against the Commonwealth of Pennsylvania in 1969 because of the exclusion of children with retardation from local schools and the appalling lack of education at state institutions for the mentally retarded.   These and a number of subsequent law suits established litigation, including appeals to federal courts regarding equal treatment and due process rights, as a powerful tool in the struggle for disability rights.   Three lawsuits in particular, *PARC v. Pennsylvania* (1972), *Wyatt v. Stickney* (1974), and *Mills v. Board of Education* (1972) opened up the floodgates for two developments: deinstitutionalization out of state training schools (often called   "developmental   centers"   starting   in   the   1990s)   and mainstreaming of children in public educational facilities due to the injustices of institutional practices and the exclusion of students with disabilities from regular public education.

Another   strand   of   the   advocacy   movement   for   educational inclusion came in 1973 when Marian Wright Edelman, a civil rights activist who had worked to force Mississippi to fund head start for Black Children, found in a survey that 750,000 kids were being excluded from schools because of a disability.   She was amazed at the depth and rationales provided for this exclusion by schools.   These disabilities included not only mental retardation, but also autism and physical disabilities that did not diminish learning capacities.   Edelman launched the Children's Defense Fund to help establish the right of all students to a public education.   The efforts of many advocacy groups helped significantly to get the Education for All Handicapped Children Act passed in 1975 to promote educational integration of those with a variety of mental and physical disabilities. (Shapiro, 1994; Fleischer & Zames, 2001)

A new part of the advocacy movement was the self-advocacy movement begun by people with developmental disabilities first in British Columbia and then later in the United States in 1974 with the title, "People First". Since then it has developed more than 500 worldwide chapters—in many states and 43 in other countries with over 17,000 members worldwide. Its 4th international conference in Anchorage, Alaska in April, 2001 was attended by about 1000 people. The members of People First report that they live in a variety of places: state schools, foster homes, their parent's homes, group homes, and their own homes and apartments. (Stroman, 1989; "Self Advocacy has reached the Last Frontier", 2001). Members of People First report:

> We go to school, we work in sheltered workshops and many of us work in community businesses.
> We serve on state and local ARC boards. We sit on the Governor's Commission for the Handicapped and State DD Councils. We have served on the President's Commission on Mental Retardation. We serve on local advisory committees and employment councils. ("Who are People First Members?" 2001, 1)

The People First chapter of Salem, Oregon has a web presence as do many of the People First chapters. As part of People First International, they say that "People First is developmentally disabled people joining together to learn how to speak for ourselves. We want others to know that we are PEOPLE FIRST, and that our disabilities come second." In describing their goals, they list a number of things they wanted: (1) "to speak for themselves", (2) "to be treated with dignity and respect. We want to be in control of any plans that have to do with us. We want the right to make our own decisions. We want to be recognized as a primary advocacy group for people with developmental disabilities," (3) "to live in a safe. . .accessible environment" of our choosing that is affordable and offers privacy, (4) to not live in poverty and to "be paid a fair wage when we work," (5) "transportation to get where we want to go", and (6) "full medical and health benefits." ("What Are People First Goals? 2001, 3). A complete history of the disability rights movement would have to include stories of this grass-roots groups at both the local and state levels. One of the state chapters—California People First—did an extensive investigation of the service system in their state for persons with developmental disabilities. Their report, *Surviving the System: Mental Retardation* *and the Retarding Environment*_(1984) "was a devastating portrayal of the way a paternalistic social service system harms the people it is intended to serve." (Pelka, 1997, 244).

The umbrella organization for all local and state People First organizations was formally organized in 1991 at the second North American People First Conference which met in Nashville.   Their acronym is S.A.B.E.—Self Advocates Becoming Empowered. S.A.B.E has developed a rich web site that enables users to connect to many other web sites, and understand the organization's history, goals, strategies and services.   This international organization, principally serving members in the United States and Canada, lists its three goals as follow: ("Our goals", 2001,1).

>Make self-advocacy available in every state including institutions, high schools, rural areas and people living with families with local support and advisors to help.

>Work with the criminal justice system and people with disabilities about their rights within the criminal justice system.

>Close institutions for people with developmental disabilities labels nationwide, and build community support.

In 1999 S.A.B.E participated in the National Leadership Summit on Self-Determination and Consumer-Direction and Control where it shared with the 120 "leaders" invited to the conference its own "Declaration of Self Determination' that it adopted in 1997. (Ward, 2001).

Another advocacy organization whose purpose and constituency have evolved over time is TASH.   In fact four name changes or patterns of usage of its 1983 Acronym reveal the changing nature of the advocacy movement.   In 1974 the American Association for the Education of the Severely Handicapped (AAESPH) was formed to focus on educational advocacy for those with severe and profound disabilities by special education and rehabilitation specialists.   In 1980 it changed its name to reflect a broader mission and constituency to TASH—The Association for the Severely Handicapped.   In 1983 it changed its name slightly to The Association for Persons with Severe Handicaps but continued to use the acronym TASH because it was widely known.   In 1995 the Board decided to keep only the acronym but drop the full name of the organization to better reflect the directions and current values of this international organization with its largest membership in the United States.   Representing over 8,000 members worldwide with 32 chapters in the United States and Canada, the Board of this advocacy group had developed 21 resolutions or position statements by 2001 on such topics as "deinstitutionalization policy" and "resolution on inclusive education". It is an inclusive organization whose members include persons with disabilities, family members, professionals, advocates, researchers and students. It publishes the TASH *Newsletter* and the *Journal of the Association for Persons with Severe Handicaps (JASH)*.("TASH" 2001). TASH has advocated for amendments to the 1973 Rehabilitation Act to enable it to provide more services to the disability community, played a leading role in advocating for the 1986 Handicapped Children's Protection Act, supported the passage of the ADA in 1990, and was the "first national organization to call for the complete end to institutions for persons with disabilities." (Pelka, 1997, 30).

In summary, the advocacy movement for those with developmental disabilities was not only instrumental in getting the deinstitutionalization movement started. It has been critical in widening the concern from inclusive residential settings for those with developmental disabilities to inclusive education, better employment and training programs, inclusive employment opportunities and the inclusion of such persons in all aspects of community life. The advocacy movement began with small local groups of parents fighting for the needs of their children. It has expanded to national and then international stages.

The Spread of a New Treatment Philosophy: Normalization and Integration. Concurrent with the growing criticism of state asylums and the desire of advocates first to reform and/or then shut them down was the growth of a new perspective and treatment philosophy. The new philosophy was a developmental philosophy that persons with cognitive disorders could learn or be trained even though the pace of learning might be different than for those without cognitive disorders. It particularly emphasized a social model of disability that emphasized both the environmental origins and the social/educational origins of developmental disabilities. The expanding developmental philosophy has supported early interventions to minimize both the hereditary and social origins of disability. Baroff (1974) saw three developments that were coalescing in the late 1960s and early 70s to help frame this new treatment perspective. The first of these was the idea and growing international support for the "rights" of persons with mental retardation to be served well and fairly who up to that point had been isolated, excluded, ignored or at best "grudgingly served." This was seen in the proclamation in 1968 of the "Declaration of General and Special Rights of the Mentally Retarded" by the International League of Societies for the Mentally Handicapped. It was secondly seen in the principle of "normalization" first developed in Europe and then diffused and adopted as a service ideal among many advocates in America. And thirdly it was accompanied by proposals and then programs to provide a continuum of services to those with mental retardation that were designed to prevent mental retardation and maximize the development of affected persons. These programs were to provide an array of services from prenatal care to old age and to cover various "institutional" areas of life such as health care, education, family care, vocational programs, recreational programs, varieties of residential opportunities, transportation, spiritual opportunities and the like. Simply to reform or flee from what seemed to be almost incorrigible institutions was not enough. There needed to be humane programs to which to flee and a variety of community-based programs that were first conceptualized in the 1960s and 1970s and which evolved to fill those needs in the succeeding decades. (Baroff, 1974; Dybwad, 1990)

Thinking about the "rights" of the disabled as another minority group was emerging about a decade after the civil rights movement exploded on the American landscape in the 1950s. In the sociological minority group theory, minority groups are disenfranchised groups who are stigmatized and treated in discriminatory ways without full recognition of their basic sameness with other humans. There are many forms that discrimination may take--ranging from residential segregation, educational and employment discrimination to maltreatment in the various institutional sectors of life like religion, family, health care, recreation, and work. (Stroman, 1982). Table 5.6 provides the author's condensation of the 1968 Declaration of the General and Special Rights of the Mentally Retarded that came out of the advocacy work of the International League of Societies for the Mentally Handicapped. The social constructionist model of rights would argue that "rights" do not adhere in the very nature of social life but emerge as normative statements reflecting the dynamic forces at work at a particular time in history.

The normalization principle was first developed in several Scandinavian countries in the 1950s and popularized by Bengt Nirje, Bank-Mikkelsen and Wolf Wolfensberger in this country starting in 1969. Some were skeptical of the philosophy because of the radical changes it involved, but over time it became widely accepted. The basic idea was that persons with disabilities should be offered the same experiences as nondisabled persons. Instead of being segregated in special asylums, training schools, special education classes, or hospitals

TABLE 5.6   Abbreviated summary of the "Declaration of General and Special Rights of the Mentally Retarded" proclaimed in 1968 by the International League of Societies for the Mentally Handicapped.

I	Has same basic rights as other citizens of their same country and age.
II	Every mentally retarded person has right to medical care, rehabilitation, education, training and guidance to develop their potential to the fullest possible extent irrespective of the severity of the disability or its cost.
III	Has right to economic security, decent standard of living and a meaningful occupation.
IV	Has right to own family life and to participate in all aspects of community life as normally as possible.
V	Has right to a guardian if needed but guardian should never be a direct service provider.
VI	Has a right to a fair trial that recognizes his degree of responsibility and a right to protection from abuse, exploitation or degrading treatment.
VII	Any modifications of their rights due to the severity of their handicap should be protected by legal safeguards, based on expert evidence and subject to periodic review and the right to appeal to higher authorities.

Source: Abstracted from original found in Baroff, 1974, 120-121.

they should be integrated into all aspects of community life: regular type residences, schools that others attend, the same hospitals, stores, places of work, churches, and recreational facilities that others in their same communities use. It meant that persons with cognitive disabilities should not be totally protected from risk but that limited risk relative to a person's ability to determine life-threatening risks and take appropriate action should be provided to them. In part the philosophy of normalization was a reaction to the over control of behavior that had occurred in many institutional settings. Normalization was a management principle to allow persons to experience and grow in response to a varied and changing environment rather than secluding them in a non-stimulating environment like the confines of one or two buildings in an institution for those with mental retardation. Wolfensberger enlarged Bank-Mikkelsen's idea beyond simply integrating persons with mental retardation in new social and educational physical environments but also stimulating them with a variety of social interactions in those environments. (Stroman, 1989;

Baroff, 1974; Wolfensberger, 1972; Pelka, 1997; Tyor and Bell, 1984) Thus, at first, normalization meant primarily physical integration but over time it has also come to mean social inclusion in interpersonal ways.

One of the criticisms of the normalization movement was the very term itself and the implication that persons with MR/DD should become as normal as possible by living in "normal" places and following "normal" daily, monthly and yearly rhythms of life as others do. But self-advocates have argued that this emphasis denies them the opportunity to develop a self-concept based on their disability as well as the right to associate with other people with disabilities.   By emphasizing normality there is still an underlying stigma that they need to become more like others rather than maintaining their distinctiveness.   Despite this criticism, the normalization philosophy was the predominant philosophy justifying deinstitutionalization and its integrating counterparts—educational mainstreaming and community inclusion found in the Section 504 of the 1973 Rehabilitation Act and the 1975 Education for all Handicapped Children Act. (Pelka, 1997)

If there had been serious problems in developing community care programs and the persons who had been relocated into community residential programs didn't like them, the deinstitutionalization movement might have petered out. But such was not the case. While the states faced challenges in developing community residential programs, the outcomes were generally seen as good—by persons with mental retardation living in the communities, by their parents or other relatives, and by professionals. For example, a variety of studies found that residents who had formerly lived in large state institutions: (1) preferred living in the community; (2) were able to form new friendships both inside and outside their new residence; (3) were often involved in educational or vocational programs in their communities; (4) were satisfied with the food they were getting; (5) had greater freedom than formerly in decorating their rooms, going outside their home, selecting clothing, going to new places they had never seen before, having spending money for things of their own choice; (6) had opportunities to make money; and (7) were able to develop boyfriend/girlfriend relationships through which they could express affection. While parents and professionals often had misgivings about the gains from living in the community before the move was made, most changed their mind positively after the change. (Bercovici, 1983; Stroman, 1989; Halpern, Close and Nelson, 1986; Westling, 1986).

The Support of President Kennedy for Deinstitutionalization and Community Care.   As indicated in the prior chapter, the role of a popular president in suggesting and strongly supporting new legislation needs to be emphasized. The president was supportive of the various committees and commissions that had suggested depopulating state institutions for both the mentally ill and mentally retarded and replacing them with care in the local community. This proposal came on the heels of many civil rights activities on behalf of blacks and the poor in American society. It followed rather closely the rising call to restore the rights of those who had been incarcerated in state mental hospitals. The president's support for releasing institutional inmates to their home communities for care resonated well with the images presented by advocates which depicted those confined in deadening institutions as another minority who needed to have their rights recognized and to be freed to live in integrated communities. (See Pelka, 1997; Kent, 1994)

The Growing Cost of Institutionalization and the Opportunity for the States to Shift Costs to the Federal Government for Community Care Programs.   A concern for both state governments and the federal government has been the growing cost of care in large public institutions (operationally defined as PRFs—Public Residential Facilities with 16 or more beds). The cost of operating such facilities remained relatively stable over many decades when increases in operating costs were below or in line with increases in the cost of living until about the early 1970s when operating costs began to rise as substantial architectural and program improvements were being made at aging state training schools. Table 5.7 shows the rising costs of care. The data in this table also points to another important fact—state variation in the costs of operating such institutions is very large.

A complex set of interwoven variables help explain in a general sense why the costs of operating such large public facilities has increased at a faster rate than inflation in the last several decades. Many of the same variables help explain the large variation in annual costs per resident among the states. The factors that explain these rising costs include at least the following variables: (1) staff to patient ratios increased substantially over time and staffing costs are the greatest proportion of all costs; (2) improvements in programming were made progressively in many institutions that required capital repairs or improvements and more intensive staffing; (3) a decreasing number of residents were often using the same facilities which meant that the costs of operating the facility were being spread over fewer residents; (4) the release of

Table 5.7   Average per diem and average annual costs of operating public residential institutions for the mentally retarded 1970-1998.

Year	Average per diem cost	Average annual cost per person	Range of per diem costs among states
1970-71	$10.86	$3,964.	
1974-75	36.10	13,177.	
1980-81	77.99	28,466.	$25.60 to $213.00
1984	106.97	39,044.	
1988	153.54	56,042.	$85.99 to $302.82
1993	219.86	80,249.	$120.86 to $472.29
1998	290.51	106,215.	$185.53 to $1,037.83

Sources: Westling, 1986; Braddock, 1990; Braddock, 2000.

higher functioning residents so that the remaining residents required more intensive care inasmuch as there was a proportional increase in medically fragile, lower functioning residents who often exhibited multiple disorders and behavior problems requiring more intensive staffing; and (5) the growing unionization of state employees in public residential facilities along with planned improvements in wages and salaries at such institutions. (Stroman, 1989; Westling, 1986, Braddock, 1990).

States had a double economic motive to decrease institutionalization as well as finding it desirable to clothe it in the rhetoric of humanitarian normalization principles. The two economic motives were that other kinds of "residential programs" for those with MR/DD were less expensive and with new and ever evolving federal legislation starting in the early 1970s, the federal government would pick up an increasing proportion of total state expenditures for MR/DD programs. Table 5.8 shows the relative costs in 1998 of five different kinds of placement other than large public institutions reported on in Table 5.7. In the last three decades the federal government has picked up a growing percentage of the funding of MR/DD programs. Braddock's analyses in 1990 and 2000 distinguish between two types of spending for services for the MR/DD population: (1) services provided in large/congregate institutions of 16 or more beds, and (2) "community" services including smaller residential services, early intervention programs, workshops, and day treatment programs. In 1977, the federal government's outlay for congregate services far exceeded its outlay for "community" services. But by

Table 5.8   Average annual costs of care per resident and range of costs among the states of five types of residential placement, 1998

Type of Residential Placement	Average annual cost of placement	Range of annual costs among the states
Public ICF/MR, 1-15 residents	$76, 115	$127,615--$32,357
Private ICF/MR, 1-15 residents	$59,055	$152,025--$33,962
7-15 person settings	$33,776	$180,216--$14,585
1-6 person settings	$40,809	$131,607--7,861
Supported living	$14,396	$72,230--$1,303

Source: Braddock, 2000.

1998, the federal contribution had grown much more rapidly for community services while federal dollars for institutional care had remained fairly stable due to the increasing costs per person even while censuses of large institutions were declining steadily over that period. By 1988, federal payments had reached 26.4% of $5.637 billion spent on community services that year. But 10 years later, the federal share had increased from 26.4% in 1988 to 46% of $17.442 billion in 1998. By 1998, 72% of all funding from all sources was going into community services. The states were happy to see this shift—the local/county share of MR/DD community services dropped from 5.8% to 4% of all outlays while the states' share declined from 63.2% in 1977 to 50% in 1998. (Braddock 1990; Braddock, 2000). The biggest component in 1998 of "community services" was for the HCBS Waiver program which accounted for 47% of all services. First authorized in 1981 by Congress, the Home and Community Based Services Waiver program has grown from $1.2 million in 1982 to $1.1 billion in 1993 to $4.0 billion in 1998. This is huge! While no state offers all the possible programs available in this program, this funding stream provides for the following array of community based services to the MR/DD population: case management, home health aides, personal care, homemaker assistance, day habilitation, respite care, residential habilitation, adapted equipment, home modification, supported employment, and occupational, speech, behavioral and speech therapies. (Braddock, 2000).

Braddock (2000, 31) comments on the huge significance of this shift to federal funding for MR/DD services:

It is clear that Medicaid is the essential financial underpinning for MR/DD services in the U.S. Combined federal and state Medicaid spending in 1998 constituted 72% of all MR/DD spending of $25.6 billion, advancing from 68% in 1993. States rely on Medicaid's stability, especially when undergoing major service system reform efforts including institutional downsizing and closure.

Medicaid funding is attractive to states, because state spending is matched by federal reimbursement of between 50 - 78%, depending on state wealth. Medicaid therefore represents an *unsurpassed opportunity* (emphasis added by author) for states to expand their services beyond what the allocation of their own resources would otherwise allow. The proportion of states' community services budgets that are used to match federal Medicaid funds has increased substantially in recent years, from 43% in 1990 to 81% in 1998. Much of this expansion, of course, can be attributed to growth of the HCBS Waiver program.

Braddock (2000) has developed a measure of how much the nation and each state financially contributes to services to those with disabilities in the MR/DD area. He calls this variable the "Fiscal Effort for Developmental Disabilities" which measures the dollar amount of each $1,000 of personal income that goes to funding developmental disabilities services. Furthermore, to show trends in the growth and/or decline of institutional versus community services, the portion of the fiscal effort that goes to each of these is broken out. Table 5.9 shows that total fiscal effort (combining state and federal efforts) has grown 63% between 1977 and 1998 and how the proportion going for institutional services (residential placements in institutions holding 15 or more persons) has declined 39% while the proportion going for community services has increased from 25% of total expenditures in 1997 to 72% in 1998. For persons with disabilities, their families and the professionals working in that field, this table reveals two good pieces of news. In 21 years the country has made a substantial increase in spending on MR/DD services and more of that spending is going for community based services rather than "institutional services".

However, there were very substantial differences among the states. In 1998, Nevada lagged behind all other states by spending just $1.05 on MR/DD for each $1,000 of earned income while Rhode Island was the leader at $7.22. By 1998, two states, Rhode Island and Vermont plus the District of Columbia, were no longer using large institutions. However, two states lagged way behind in deinstitutionalization— Mississippi and Arkansas which in 1998 were still spending 73% and 52% respectively of their MR/DD money on large institutional placements. (Braddock, 2001).

TABLE 5.9. Fiscal Effort for Developmental Disabilities in the United States, 1977-1998.

Spending per $1,000 personal income for:	1977	1993	1996	1998	Percent Change 1977 to 1998
Institutions	$1.69	$1.37	$1.16	$1.03	-39%
Percent of Total	75	40	32	28	
Community Services	$.57	$2.06	$2.50	$2.66	+367%
Percent of Total	25	60	68	72	
Total	$2.26	$3.44	$3.66	$3.69	+63%
Total Percent	100	100	100	100	

Source: Modified and adapted from Braddock, 2000, p. 33.

Braddock did a further analysis of this data to determine which were the best predictors of how much states increased their spending on MR/DD services between 1977 and 1998. His answer throws some light on the relative importance of litigation, advocacy, and state leadership in trying to draw more federal money into the state to provide community based services. He found that neither the size of the state's population nor its relative wealth compared to other states had any apparent influence on how much a state had increased its MR/DD fiscal effort over the 21 year period. However, three other variables did reveal a powerful explanation of such increases. These were (1) the degree of civil rights activity in the state measured by the rapidity of adoption of three civil rights laws between 1937 and 1966; (2) interest group activity as measured by per capita membership in state Arc organizations since 1966, and (3) per capita growth in the state's matching funds for HCBS Waiver since 1982. He found these three variables explained about 70% of the variation among the states in the growth of their MR/DD funding. Of special significance is the role of civil rights activity in a given state in prompting it to develop alternatives to institutional care. Braddock (2000, 37) comments, "There have been more than 70 pending and completed class action right-to-habilitation suits in 38 states between 1970 and 1996." He goes on to conclude,

Significantly, most of the cases filed or reformulated after 1974 resulted in court orders or consent agreements requiring the states to develop community-based alternatives to institutions. . . . This stimulated many defendant state governments to request substantial additional funds from their legislatures to implement new community services initiatives. (Braddock, 2000, 37).

In addition to this information, Braddock points out the most rapid growth of community services has been in those states where there was the presence of class action suits. In many states state protection and advocacy agencies have played a significant role in initiating these suits. "Nationwide, Protection and Advocacy agencies are currently involved in more than 30 cases related to community integration, rights violations in facilities, and access to housing in the community for persons with developmental disabilities." (Braddock, 2000, 38).

In conclusion, one of the powerful forces that has pushed and is still pushing deinstitutionalization of the MR/DD population is an economic one. By deinstitutionalizing this population group, states have not only be able to fund a greater variety of community institutional services that are both more viable and culturally acceptable, but additionally draw down more federal money to come up with anywhere from a 50% to 22% match of their own funds. By spending more state dollars they earn more federal dollars. While such matching funds were not a powerful factor in deinstitutionalization when that movement began, over the decades it has become a powerful driving force that appears to be growing in significance. But it is also important to note that many state governments have had to be pushed to draw down this federal money by class action suits by advocacy groups acting on behalf of the disabled.

JUDICIAL AND LEGISLATIVE RESPONSES TO THE DISABILITY RIGHTS MOVEMENT.

While many would like to think that our state and federal legislative bodies lead the way in formulating legislation to provide for greater equality of opportunity and the enforcement of basic civil rights, many see them as following popular movements to which they react. One can make a case with good evidence to support either side of this argument. Without clearly saying that one set of forces was dominant, it is certainly fair to say that federal and state legislatures as well as a variety of advocates and advocacy groups were involved in complex and interactive ways in what is called the disability rights movement. Furthermore, advocacy for persons with psychiatric disabilities seemed to generally precede those with cognitive disabilities yet there were systemic feedback loops between these two types of groups as well as those advocating for persons with physical disabilities. Furthermore, we must remember that advocacy groups were not necessarily advocating for the same things—some wanted improved institutions, some wanted to move persons with disabilities out of public institutions back to the community while others wanted particular types of services in the community such as teachers able to deal with students with learning disabilities or behavioral problems or school to work transition programs or sheltered workshops or new types of residential placements. The "needs" of those with disabilities are constantly being redefined and upgraded to provide more, better, or refurbished services to improve them.

Two of the key ways advocacy movements work are through either the judicial system where current practices are pleaded to be inadequate or unfair in some way or through legislative systems where new or modified programs or practices are defined and funded to replace those defined as inadequate in some way. Probably the five judicial cases that stimulated deinstitutionalization the most in the 1970s were:

(1) *PARC v. Commonwealth of Pa., 1970* which established the right of persons with mental retardation to receive a free public education.

(2) *Mills v. Bd. of Ed. of the District of Columbia, 1972* which established the right of persons with physical disabilities to receive a free public education.

(3) *Wyatt v. Stickney, 1972* in Alabama which established the right to habilitation rather than just custodial confinement in state mental hospitals.

(4) *New York State Association for Retarded Inc. v Rockefeller, 1974* which established the right to habilitation rather than just custodial confinement in state institutions for those with mentally retardation.

(5) *Pennhurst State School and Hospital v Halderman,* in 1977 where the court found that habilitation should occur in the least restrictive environment. Collectively these significant court cases meant that custodial institutions should be reformed to provide habilitation and that habilitation should occur in the least restrictive environment which was interpreted to mean outside of large institutions and in a person's home community.

The three pieces of legislation that were most instrumental in deinstitutionalization in the 1970s were:

(1) The Rehabilitation Act of 1973 which had many components the most important of which provided money to the states and agencies to provide the disabled with a variety of rehabilitative services to prepare them for work or greater independence, created a new definition of disability that was both social and medical, and, perhaps, most importantly under Section 504 of this act, forbade discrimination against those with disabilities under any program or activity receiving federal aid.   (This meant such agencies as schools, universities, hospitals, courts, nursing homes, airports, contractors receiving federal funds, museums and the like could not discriminate against people with disabilities).

(2) The Education for All Handicapped Children Act of 1975 which required a public school education for all disabled children in the least restrictive environment that was to be tailored to the needs of the child as developed by a family/interdisciplinary team who created an "Individual Education Plan" which in turn was to be reviewed and updated at least annually.

(3) The Developmentally Disabled Assistance and Bill of Rights Act of 1975 which required (i) the withholding of money from state institutions for the developmentally disabled if they didn't provide appropriate treatment, medical care, diet, and limited physical restraints to those absolutely necessary; (ii) the establishment of a network of "Protection and Advocacy" agencies to inspect violations of and to promote the rights of those with disabilities.

These three pieces of legislation were significant in expanding the role of the federal government in not only defining the rights of the disabled but in funding programs which had principally or exclusively been the province of state governments up to that time.   The various strands of the disability rights movement had moved the nation forward in recognizing that those with disabilities had the same rights as others.

SUMMARY

This chapter reveals that the term of mental retardation is used to define persons who have substantial limitations in intellectual functioning that exists concurrently with limitations in two or more of ten adaptive skill areas such as self-care, communication, home living, functional academics or work occurring before age 18. It is an older term that encompasses over half of those with developmental disabilities who have chronic mental or physical limitations occurring before age 22. A brief review of the history of this category of persons found that many of them were placed in training schools or asylums starting in about 1850. The numbers of such segregating institutions and their resident populations grew in number up to 1967 when their numbers peeked at 194,657 residents. During the last 150 years, various images of such developmentally disabled persons existed that substantially influenced their treatment. They have been depicted is sick, sub-human, a menace to society, as objects of pity, as burdens of charity, as holy innocents and finally as capable of growth under the developmental model which reemerged in the 1960s. However, even under different images of them, the more severely disabled were usually sent to public institutions that started out as schools but largely became custodial warehouses that separated them from their families and communities.

But a series of synergistic forces began emerging in the 1960s which led to a deinstitutionalization movement that relocated many former residents back to a variety of housing options in their home communities. These forces included exposes on the terrible living situations in some of the large public residential facilities and the inhumanity of all of them to some degree. The exposes were often led by parental and professional advocates who filed court cases and pleaded with legislators to rectify these conditions and/or close depressing asylums. Simultaneously, new treatment philosophies of normalization and inclusion emerged which proposed the movement of institutional residents back to the schools and communities from where they came. President Kennedy, the courts and federal and state legislative bodies along with many new service providers responded to the exposes, advocacy movement and new treatment philosophies with programs to depopulate unpopular institutions with better and more diverse localized educational, residential, and work programs that used local generic services whenever possible. The federal legislation progressively provided states more money if they replaced institutional residential services with community services. This funding carrot has led to extensive depopulation of state schools for those with cognitive disabilities. A review of the evidence suggests that community residential placements have largely replaced public residential facilities as the homes of the developmentally disabled and that the federal government is paying an increasingly larger portion of the total care costs of those with developmental disabilities. While the wave of deinstitutionalization that began in the late 1960s is not over yet, much of its work has been done even though waiting lists to get community services still plagues many states. The wave is receding while a new reform movement called self-determination has been growing in the 1990s and touching all aspects of the lives of the disabled, their families and supporters, legislators, and providers. That spreading wave portends immense new system changes. We will review this cresting wave in chapter 7.

CHAPTER 6
MULTIPLE WAVES OF CHANGES FOR PERSONS WITH PHYSICAL DISABILITIES

ISSUES IN THIS CHAPTER

In this chapter we will look at a number of issues that pertain to those with physical disabilities. First we will note that in comparison to those with cognitive disabilities or psychiatric disabilities, there is a greater diversity within this category of people. While each of the disability groupings described in the prior two chapters are quite diverse, the range of disabilities captured under this rubric is very diverse which, when coupled with age, sex, ethnic and socioeconomic differences produces awesome variations in types, severities and responses to disabilities.

The second pattern to be noted and discussed is that there have been multiple waves of change that have impacted on those with physical disabilities. While distinctive reform movements have been noted for those with developmental disabilities and mental illness, the first reform movements for those with physical disabilities were stimulated by industrial or job-related accidents soon after 1900 while the second and largest reform movement resulted from the injuries of war. The first wave of change started before World War I when states began developing workmen's compensation insurance in response to the toll of injuries from work. The second and third waves of reform came after World War I and II respectively when a grateful nation felt a special obligation to those who had put their lives both on hold and in jeopardy and now were injured. These post war waves put a large emphasis on *vocational* rehabilitation mainly for war veterans but to a lesser extent for those injured at civilian work. Under an emerging welfare state, the goal was not only a humanitarian one of care-giving to the veteran but an economic one to restore economic functioning to minimize long term subsidy by the state to those unable to work. The fourth wave also occurred mainly after a war, the Vietnam War, but in this case involved more than rehabilitation for work. It increasingly focused on other issues such as where the rehabilitation took place and a growing demand for inclusion and accessibility in all areas of life. Rehabilitation was no longer simply to be given by the welfare state but demanded by activists who saw it not as a charitable gift but as a human right.

The third difference to discuss is the greater degree of self-advocacy by those with physical disabilities in comparison to those with cognitive or psychiatric disabilities. While often stigmatized like the mentally retarded or psychiatrically disabled, but perhaps to a lesser degree, those with physical disabilities were often seen as more competent to manage their own affairs and demand equal opportunities.

A fourth issue we want to look at is the evolving nature of rehabilitation. The disability rights movement here has focused not only on deinstitutionalization and its community counterpart— "independent living" outside of institutions but also changing patterns of institutionalization. In this section of the chapter we will look at the operation of a rehabilitation hospital in the 1960s and look at the growth and change in the rehabilitation business today.

THE DIVERSITY OF PHYSICAL DISABILITY AND RESPONSES TO IT

The range of medical conditions, injuries and the social responses that often magnify or exaggerate the subsequent limitations in functioning are indeed vast, complex and variably interconnected in individualistic ways. One of the historic ways to get at the various sources and types of disability is that undertaken in the National Health Interview Survey where a sample of U.S. citizens is asked if they have some "Activity Limitation" from a variety of conditions and then to ask them which is the main cause of their activity limitation. Naturally there may be only one "main cause" even though other conditions may be present. Table 6.1 shows the responses to these questions during the 1983-85 period when the interviews were carried out. It is instructive to note that 39.8% of the main causes of activity limitation are due to three causes: orthopedic impairments, arthritis and heart disease while only 6.9% are due to sensory impairments—visual or hearing impairments. Types of limitations can be regrouped in these five categories: mobility limitations—38%; chronic diseases—32%; sensory limitations—7%; intellectual limitations, including mental retardation—7% and other—16%. With each succeeding older age cohort, mobility limitations, chronic diseases and sensory limitations grow as primary causes while intellectual limitations are highest among those under 18 (during the period of schooling) and over 85.

As noted elsewhere, a growing proportion of the population is admitting or reporting a disability. This is due to a variety of factors including an aging population, advances in medicine and quick response emergency medical programs that enable more of those injured, diseased, born prematurely or with potentially disabling conditions to be saved from death for a longer life span, and perhaps, a growing ability to recognize and/or admit the presence of disabilities.

David Thomas (1982, 3-4) concludes that "the most significant feature of disablement is its diversity". He goes on to illustrate:

Not only do we have difference of causation, type of impairment, severity and prognosis, the conditions span the entire age-range and is no respecter of race, sex or social class; there are also important differences between acquired and life-long disabilities. Equally varied are the responses to disability which produce not a unitary but a variegated picture. Within the world of disabilities we can find contradictory images of success and failure, optimism and pessimism, tragedy and humor, 'matter of fact' reactions and pathological responses, acceptance and stigma, recognition of individual differences and stereotyping, superb support services and inadequate ones, sensible and silly legislation, community support and social isolation, resignation and rebellion, successful careers and appalling job prospects, deeply satisfying personal relationships and loneliness, acceptance and rejection.

As varied as the individual disabled person's condition and reaction are public responses, from 'they're just like everyone else', imaginative concern, mawkish sentimentality, indifference, rejection and hostility.

Thomas goes on to point out several other variations in response and how these have varied over time. In the 1800s humanitarian charity was primarily only available to children who were blind, deaf or crippled. After World War I aid was extended to those crippled by war or industry. Following this came a widening of the definition of disability and a growing range of services for those with disabling conditions starting in the 1950s. And another increasing varied set of

TABLE 6.1   Percentage of Persons with Activity Limitation Reporting Specified Causes Of Limitation, All Ages: United States, 1983-85.

MAIN CAUSE	%	ALL CAUSES	%
Orthopedic impairments	16.0	Orthopedic impairments	21.5
Arthritis	12.3	Arthritis	18.8
Heart disease	11.5	Heart disease	17.1
Visual impairments	4.4	Hypertension	10.8
Intervertebral disk disorder		Visual impairments	8.9
Asthma	4.3	Diabetes	6.5
Nervous disorders*	4.0	Mental disorders	5.6
Mental disorders	3.9	Asthma	5.5
Hypertension	3.8	Intervertebral disk disorders	5.2
Mental retardation	2.9	Nervous disorders*	4.9
Diabetes	2.7	Hearing impairments	4.3
Hearing impairments	2.5	Mental retardation	3.2
Emphysema	2.0	Emphysema	3.1
Cerebrovascular disease	1.9	Cerebrovascular disease	2.9
Osteomyelitis/bone disorders	1.1	Abdominal hernia	1.8

*Note: nervous disorders include epilepsy, multiple sclerosis, Parkinson's disease, and other selected nervous disorders. Mental disorders include severe mental diseases, neuroses, senility, alcohol and drug dependence, and special learning disorders.
Source: Pope & Tarlov. 1991. *Disability in America*. 57.

responses to disabilities are the different perspectives that professional groups bring: physiatrists, orthopedic physicians, physical therapists, occupational therapists, social workers, psychologists, vocational counselors, art therapists, sociologists, employers, disability advocates, communication specialists, insurance companies, and a wide range of other health care providers.

WIDENING WAVES OF REHABILITATION SERVICES

The welfare state in western societies has generally expanded as democratic principles are increasingly refined and the scope of human needs is widened to include new areas where the state may or should intervene if capitalism is unable to meet some human needs. Many such needs were met at the communal level stimulated by religious and other humanitarian motives in earlier times. But as communities grew and societies became more complex, the umbrella of humanitarianism was often not wide enough to cover all the need and governments slowly defined their wider responsibilities.

Early Vocational Rehabilitation. The first Workmen's Compensation Act was passed in 1910 in New York state; 42 states had passed such laws by 1921; Mississippi was the last state to pass such a law in 1948. Before such laws were passed, becoming disabled and thereby being unable to work was a sure ticket to poverty. The demand for such reforms to make industry responsible for the risks of injury stemming from hazardous work were slow to take place in the progressive era. While these laws are state laws, which means there are substantial variations in their provisions among the states, and have been amended and often expanded over time, they typically provide several types of benefit for those killed or injured while working. Usually there are payments to the survivor's dependents if there is loss of life. Variable payments to survivors and rehabilitation agencies are made that reflect whether the job-related disease or disability is seen as partial or total, the loss of income from time lost from work, the cost of medical care provided and the costs of rehabilitation services if undertaken. While Workmen's Compensation was not directly designed to pay for vocational rehabilitation costs, these services may be paid for if they avert paying for life-time benefits were the impaired person not to receive vocationally related rehabilitation services. These state laws were passed as part of the reforms of the progressive era. (Rubin & Roessler, 1983; DiNitto, 2000)

A second act that set a precedent was The Soldier's Rehabilitation Act of 1918. In earlier wars, disabled veterans were given only a pension. But this was breakthrough legislation because it offered vocational rehabilitation services to those who had a disability stemming from military service that presented a limitation in returning to work. Some 236,000 World War I veterans received services. Many persons in the field saw the need to provide the same rehabilitation service to an even larger number of civilians who were disabled. Such legislation failed in 1918, partly because there was inadequate staff to run such a program. But in 1920 the Smith-Fess Act formally titled The Federal Civilian Vocational Rehabilitation Act passed which provided a limited amount of money for physically disabled persons if the states matched the federal money dollar for dollar. The legislation was renewed for another six year in 1924 even though 12 states had not yet participated in the vocational rehabilitation program for persons with partial or total disabilities that inhibited them from working. Furthermore, the federal act was so underfunded that only about 5% of eligible persons received services. During the 1920 and 1930s, it was commonly believed that the visually handicapped had few good prospects of competitive employment and were usually employed in home vocations or sheltered workshops. But in 1936 the Randolph-Sheppard Act allowed them to operate vending stands on federal property. (Rubin & Roessler, 1983).

Vocational Rehabilitation during the 1940s and 1950s. During World War II, with 12 million persons in the military, and a shortage of workers, many women and disabled people who had not been in the labor went to work. This was helpful for both groups for it showed they were as capable of doing good work as nondisabled men. In 1943 the vocational rehabilitation act passed in 1920 and extended in 1924 was extended again with the provision that it could also include those with mental illness, mental retardation and the blind. While vocational rehabilitation services were available for all, medical restoration services could only be provided to the poor because of legislator's fear that providing such restorative services would set a precedent that might be interpreted as leaning toward socialized medicine. Advances in antibiotics and the recognition of the medical specialty, physiatry or physical medicine, and the opening up of 21new rehabilitation centers in preparation for many war casualties were major gains during the war years and immediately thereafter. The period after World War II was the golden age of Veterans Administration hospitals and rehabilitation programs as their services were expanded to serve many veterans with disabilities. (Gritzer and Arluke, 1985). In 1954 under President Eisenhower's strong support for vocational rehabilitation, amendments were made to the original act which increased federal funding from $3.5 million in 1940 to $65 million in 1958, put more of a carrot in front of the states to promote rehabilitation by increasing the federal share from 50% to 60%, and extended more services to those with mental retardation and mental illness.

One important amendment to the social security act occurring in 1956 was the extension of an income maintenance program for those who became disabled while covered under social security. This program, Social Security Disability Insurance (SSDI) was a major expansion of social security by providing lifetime income to those who became permanently and totally disabled. In 1972 the Social Security Act was again amended to provide Medicare—federal health insurance—for those on SSDI. The 1956 amendments also provided money for vocational rehabilitation for those who became disabled. (Rubin & Roessler, 1983).

  The First Magna Carta of Disability Legislation: The Rehabilitation Act of 1973. This major piece of legislation was a billion dollar program because it provided enough money each year based on 80% federal 20% state match to provide a billion dollars a year for a range of rehabilitation related services. As amended over the next several years, the major mandates that came out of 1970s and reflected the spirit of the times in the field of rehabilitation were these five mandates: (1) give priority treatment to the severely handicapped instead of "creaming"—serving those most easily rehabilitated, (2) develop program evaluation to determine if programs are effective and efficient, (3) protect and advance the civil rights of those with disabilities, (4) promote consumer involvement, and (5) provide support for research. (Rubin and Roessler, 1983). However, one of the most important parts of this act did not come until 1977 when the final regulations were issued, after multiple demonstrations by disability advocacy groups, that prohibited discrimination against the disabled by firms or agencies receiving federal funding. This opened up a whole new avenue to press for gains because now the social sources and implications of disability were recognized in federal law. This legislation enabled lawsuits to be leveled against employers having federal contracts by persons who believed they had been discriminated against because they had a disability, were regarded as having a disability or formerly had a disability.

  As outlined in Table 2.3, much additional legislation was passed in the 1970s and 1980s to open up opportunities for (1) deinstitutionalization, (2) reduction of physical and cultural barriers to integration, and (3) provide services to enhance opportunities for independent living in the community. One of the most important pieces of legislation was the Americans with Disabilities Act of 1990 which provided an expanded legal basis for protecting the employment and access rights of those with disabilities. Much of this legislation came at a time when self-advocacy by the disabled themselves rather than advocacy by parents and professionals created a strong push for change for those with disabilities. We turn next to an analysis of self-advocacy.

THE GROWTH OF SELF-ADVOCACY AND CROSS-DISABILITY ORGANIZATIONS

An analysis of the private organizations (those not listed as government, university-related or for trade purposes) listed in Table 2.2 indicates that nearly an equal number were started in the entire period up to 1970 as in the 1970s alone—about 20 in each time period. The number declined to about 9 in the 1980s and 7 in the 1990s. This somewhat inexact quantitative approach suggests that the 1970s was the most active period of the emergence of self-advocacy organizations. About 13 of the private organizations founded in the 1970s listed in Table 2.2 were cross-disability organizations whereas only seven were organizations representing just one category of disability. The decade of the 1970s was a period of the emergence of cross-disability organizations. This enabled such groups to say they represented larger constituencies and draw upon the resources of a larger number of members. It gave them a more powerful voice. But it was also a time that persons with somewhat distinct stigmas associated with particular types of disabilities recognized that all persons with disabilities were in the same stigma pool. They grew toward sharing a common identity because they were stigmatized not because they had similar types of disabilities but because they had any kind of disability.

Barnartt, Schriner and Scotch, (2001) did an analysis of "protest activities" by culling reports on them from four national newspapers, over 100 regional newspapers, and other sources for the 30 year period of 1970 to 1999. Their findings differed from the perceptions of journalists who perceived that protest activity in the 1970s was greater than in the two succeeding decades. But Table 6.2 provides data that the number of protests in the 1990s exceeded the number in the 1980s which in turn exceeded the number in the 1970s. However, such a quantitative analysis does not indicate their relative qualitative impact on the public, the mass media or elected representatives. In fact, some of the protests in the 1970s were quite demonstrative and gained national attention from the media. Tarrow (1996) argues that "contentious politics" sets itself apart from politics as usual because the participants engage in risky behaviors by adopting tactics and strategies that are outside the normal activities of political institutions. While social movements may use lawsuits, letter-writing campaigns, voter registration drives, newspaper ads, media blitzes and the like, the use of disruptive tactics often gains a level of attention, attention that less disruptive tactics won't achieve. Barnart, Schriner and Scotch (2001, 438) point out, "Actors who participate in contentious politics tend to be angry, emotional and demanding. They are protesting issues about

Table 6.2   DISABILITY PROTESTS IN THE U.S. BY YEAR, 1970-1999.

YEAR	N	YEAR	N	YEAR	N
1970	0	1980	8	1990	35
1971	0	1981	14	1991	55
1972	9	1982	5	1992	57
1973	6	1983	13	1993	49
1974	5	1984	9	1994	18
1975	0	1985	17	1995	29
1976	7	1986	13	1996	40
1977	18	1987	10	1997	80
1978	4	1988	41	1998	26
1979	10	1989	39	1999*	30
1970s	59	1980s	169	1990s	419

*Through 7-26-99.
Source: Adapted and modified from Barnartt, Schriner & Scotch, 2001.

which they feel so strongly that they are willing to engage in risky behavior and angry rhetoric, even if they sometimes alienate potential supporters. Disability protestors have been willing to confront public officials, block traffic, occupy public places and government offices, or be arrested for their causes." Historians for the disability rights movements cite these examples as illustrative of disruptive protest behaviors (Shapiro, 1993; Pelka, 1997):
>In 1972 Disabled in Action blocked traffic in New York's financial district to protest lack of access to public transit by wheelchair users.
>In 1977 disabled protestors from around the country occupied federal offices in 10 cities in order to push for a speedy release of Section 504 regulations on employment discrimination language.
>In 1988 students at Gallaudet University closed the campus for a week as they successfully struck for a deaf president.
>Over the years, ADAPT—first called American Disabled for Accessible Public Transit, carried out dozens of protests over the lack

of public buses with wheelchair access. Hundreds of protesters have been arrested in seeking to change public policies in this area. Are such disruptive tactics successful? Barnartt, Schriner and Scotch (2001, 438-9) conclude:

> While mainstream research in politics has traditionally tended to view protests and other nonelectoral political activities as ineffective, social movement research suggests that protest activity, particularly when it is disruptive, may be successful in influencing public policy. . . . Disability movements appear to be influential in securing short-term policy goals and in changing the terms of the larger debate over how government and society at large ought to address the role of people with disabilities.

There are a number of dimensions of the role of self-advocacy in making more Americans aware of the stigma and treatment of those with disabilities and changing the political climate regarding Americans with disabilities. Several of these need to be pinpointed as significant.

>There has been a growth in protests by the disabled. This is seen in the increase each decade in the number of protests since the 1970s as shown in Table 6.2. One interpretation of this that is supported by evidence is that over time a greater proportion of these protests have involved an organization. In the 1970s, about 56% of known disability protests had an organizational base. But this increased to about 69% in the 1980s and 64% in the 90s. (Barnartt, Schriner and Scotch, 2001). Such organizations can provide the know-how, resources and a national network to organize effective protest action.

>The political climate changed around 1988 after the successful Gallaudet strike, the introduction of the Bush administration that included more officials with some sympathy for the disability rights movement, and the protests over the issues found in the first but unsuccessful draft of the ADA submitted in 1988. Perhaps as a results of these developments, there appeared to be "more sympathy and empathy for disability issues in Congress than had heretofore been seen."(Barnart, Schriner, and Scotch, 2001, 441).

>There had been a growth in lobbying by many disability advocacy groups on issues of concern to them. Not only are there more disability self-advocacy groups than ever before, more of them have lobbies in the nation's capital while many of them have offices in the state capitals. And these groups have become more sophisticated in making radio and TV stations and other mass media aware of their agendas. (Fleischer & Zames, 2001). According to Shapiro (1993), 180

national organizations endorsed the ADA and helped to get this monumental piece of legislation passed. One of the outcomes of this lobbying and the changing political climate has been that people with disabilities are increasingly being involved in framing the legislation that impacts on them. "Most American disability policies since the mid-1970s, including the landmark Americans with Disabilities Act, were drafted with the active participation of representatives of organizations of disabled people." (Barnartt, Schriner, Scotch, 2001, 437).

>One area where disability rights groups have been successful has been to end the fund-raising campaigns that were framed in the medical language of people "suffering" from a disability as if it were a disease. While the use of "pity" for "unfortunate" people who had undergone personal "tragedies" was often successful in raising money in Jerry Lewis telethons, people with disabilities hated them because of the way they presented those with disabilities as sick, abnormal, "stuck in a wheelchair", or as one of society's charity cases unable to cope on their own. The smiling poster children or the crippled children shown on TV fund raising programs from the 1930s to the early 1990s were usually aimed at finding a "cure" for the debilitating diseases of muscular dystrophy, polio or cerebral palsy. But with the exception of Polio, cures for disabilities are not usually available and the depiction of the disabled as needing cures for their condition did little or nothing for ending the stereotypes about them. In fact, they often exacerbated the stigma associated with having an impairment.

>One important consequence of the growing voice of self-advocacy groups has been the inclusion of those with disabilities into government agencies responsible for framing legislation and implementing policies for the constituencies from which they were drawn. While there are many examples of the growing inclusion of persons with disabilities in government, several examples will help show the inclusion of those with disabilities. Max Cleland, a Vietnam veteran was badly wounded in 1968 when he lost his right leg and right arm and received a severed windpipe from a grenade explosion. He later had to have his left leg amputated due to that wartime injury. After a year recuperating in VA hospitals, he returned to Georgia, ran for and won a seat in the Georgia State Senate at the same time Jimmy Carter was running for governor of that state. He was reelected in 1972 to the same seat. In 1975 he moved to Washington where he became an aide to Senator Alan Cranston specializing in veterans' affairs. In 1976, newly elected President Carter made Cleland his first appointee who began serving as the youngest person to ever be the Director of the Veterans Administration. He served in that position to 1981 when he

returned to Georgia to be elected as its Secretary of State. In 1996 he was elected to the U.S. Senate from Georgia. Another example is Frank Bowe, who lost his hearing at an early age but earned multiple graduate degrees, has been a prolific writer of more than a half dozen books and from 1978 to 1983 was a consultant to the U.S. Congressional Office of Technology Assessment and from 1987 to 1989 on the Task Force on the Rights and Empowerment of the Americans with Disabilities. He has been a consultant to many public agencies as well as a college teacher. (Pelka, 1997).

From a sociological viewpoint of determining how social change occurs in a society it is clear that one important engine of social change comes from persons who organize to protest and try to change stigmatizing attitudes and discriminatory behavior toward their particular group. Persons with physical disabilities, alone and in cooperation with allies from other disabilities groups, have organized for multiple purposes and often use a rich array of tactics to effect social change. These purposes include reducing stigma in its many forms and channels, getting legislation to make discrimination against them illegal, providing for a variety of services either through government agencies or through their own auspices and engendering members to help shape the environment that daily impacts on them. The tactics may include organizing, lobbying, educating members through a website or publications, offering services, raising money, and networking with other groups and agencies whose mutual support will empower all.

ANOTHER WAVE OF DEINSITUTIONALIZATION— THE PHYSICALLY DISABLED.

While one might consider those with significant visual and hearing impairments to have physical or organic ones, persons with these two disabilities were among the first institutionalized and then deinstitutionalized—most of it occurring in the period of 1850 to 1975. This section of the chapter principally focuses on those with other forms of physical disability—orthopedic impairments, muscular dystrophy, traumatic brain injuries, arthritis, heart problems and the like as listed in Table 6.1. Those persons with significant disabilities and often unable to work were often confined to asylums, poorhouses, jails, almshouses, training schools, and hospitals in the mid to late 1800s and up to the civil rights era. But starting after World War I we see the growth of vocational rehabilitation programs, most of them located in hospitals. Most of these rehabilitation hospitals operated long-term residential programs where patients often stayed for very substantial periods of time.

The Ingredients, Processes, and Goals of Rehabilitation. After the World War II, many veterans with injuries that interfered with work were sent to rehabilitation hospitals and sometimes outpatient vocational rehabilitation facilities. At this point it is necessary to make a distinction between rehabilitation, habilitation and vocational rehabilitation. Rehabilitation means to restore something that was lost. The loss often comes from an injury but may come from a disease or is a product of general degeneration associated with aging. Habilitation means adding a capacity or skill—but one that has not been lost. Thus a person born deaf would not be rehabilitated to use sign language but habilitated to use it to communicate. "To be vocationally disabled means to have lost a part of all of an ability to carry on a gainful activity. Vocational rehabilitation is the means of restoring part or all of this ability." (Conley, 1965, 36). "Rehabilitation comprises any process, procedure, or program designed to enable the affected individual to function at a more adequate and personally satisfying level. In its fully developed form this functioning includes all aspects of the individual's life—physical, psychological, social, vocational . . . ." (Goldenson, 1978. xvii). Very often rehabilitation, whether directed principally toward improving functioning for a job or for other purposes of enlarging independence, includes the processes defined as habilitation.

Rehabilitation in the most general sense usually includes four forms. (1) One is physical restoration—which is designed to eliminate some disability—e.g., a carpel tunnel syndrome operation to reduce pain and restore flexion from long term repetitive motion or wasted muscles restored by extensive physical therapy (2) A second is the use of orthoses (braces) or prostheses (artificial limbs or joints or false teeth or hearing aids) to support or replace improperly functioning or lost body parts. (3) A third form of rehabilitation is to train a person to use compensatory skills to replace those lost or to place a person in new tasks where the former abilities they once needed are no longer needed. A night watchman may be able to do his job with one arm and a physician who did stand-up surgery may turn to pediatrics or radiology if he or she becomes paraplegic. (4) Or jobs and the access to the job may be altered by lowering work tables, widening doorways, installing curb cuts and ramps, replacing hand levers with foot levers, and using a variety of other assistive technologies. All of these basic forms of rehabilitation need to be accompanied by careful assessment of the capabilities and interests of the person as well as dealing with the psychological and social needs of the person and their family who is experiencing the disability. The framework of rehabilitation counseling and programs historically has been heavily centered in a medical model where the limitation was located in the individual rather than in the environment or the disabled individual in interaction with his/her environment. (Conley, 1965; Rubin and Roessler, 1983; Schriner, 2001). The variety of specialists engaged in rehabilitation work have typically been trained in a medical model of disability and focus most on the individual person.   These rehabilitation specialists include physiatrists (physical medicine doctors), physical therapists, occupational therapists, speech therapists, specialists in orthotics and prosthetics, therapeutic recreation specialists, art therapists, psychologists, vocational counselors, social workers and others.   And on average, persons with disabilities are more prone to sickness and therefore may need the same range of health care providers as do other persons but they may need to use them more intensively.

A Rehabilitation Hospital in the 1960s.   To understand the social context of deinstitutionalization of those with physical disabilities, a review of some of the key findings by two sociologists in one rehabilitation hospital fictitiously named Farewell Hospital will be undertaken.   The authors of *Rehabilitation for the Unwanted*, Julius A. Roth and Elizabeth M. Eddy, (1967) believe that the hospital they studied was probably like many other rehabilitation hospitals then in operation.   Some descriptions of the hospital were not specific to help maintain the secret identity of the hospital.   The hospital, staff and patients the authors and four graduate students studied had nearly 2,000 beds.   The turnover in the hospital each year ran at about 800 new admissions and 800 discharges.   But because 80% of the patients were over 60 and often had multiple disabilities, many of them beyond successful rehabilitation, nearly two-thirds of those discharged each year were discharged dead.   The hospital had multiple wards organized under four general "services"—nursing, psychiatric, self-care unit, and nursing rehab unit.   Even though Farewell Hospital was called a rehabilitation hospital, only about 100 patients at any one time were in the nursing rehab unit.   Most of the units were custodial units from which few would ever return to a family—sometimes because they had no family and sometimes because the elements of a family they still had did not want them or felt they could not cope with them with their level of disability in their particular residential setting.   Some of the key findings of the authors about the inhabitants sometimes called patients and sometimes inmates were:

>To be selected for admission to the rehab unit, which had the highest staff to patient ratio in the hospital, it was better to be younger (half were under 60 compared to only 20% under 60 in the hospital as a whole) and had the "right" disability. The right disability included stroke victims, amputees, those with spinal cord injuries, multiple sclerosis, arthritis, muscular dystrophy or improperly healing fractures. Persons with a history of alcoholism, mental illness, or extremely poor communication skills were likely to be seen as poor candidates for rehabilitation.

>The selection process of who got to go to the rehab unit was largely made by doctors based on quick reviews of a patient's history at what was called the "selection clinic". Occasionally if a potential client for the rehab unit vociferously pursued entry there they might get it. "In most cases, patients have no part in the selection decisions." Usually they "do not know why they are there, and when questioned a short time afterward, most are not aware that important decisions have been made about them." Being uninformed about the decision of whether they do or do not get into the rehab unit is not related very much to their personal, social or disability characteristics but "rather related to their subordinate status and the fact that they are not defined as those who must or should be fully informed about what is happening to them." (Roth and Eddy, 1967, 14-15).

>In describing the daily and weekly routines of patients on the rehab unit, in Chapter 9, "Life in slow motion—the therapeutic pace" Roth and Eddy (1967) point out that only a small amount of time, usually less than an hour a day, was spent in a rehab activity. And some of that time was waiting to see a physical or occupational therapist or some other staff person with only about 15 minutes involving direct attention from a staff person. It typically took the staff three weeks to evaluate a person and formulate a therapy plan. Once prosthetic legs for recent amputees were ordered, patients had to wait between 3 and 8 months before they were delivered and final adjustments made in their fit before patients could be trained in their use. It often took the rehab staff several months to determine if a particular patient needed a wheelchair. And since nearly all the persons needing a wheelchair were poor and on welfare, they needed a welfare department approval to order a wheelchair for them. The median time for the delivery of a wheelchair from the time it was ordered was 5 months. Team meetings were often held on determining a plan of care for a given patient, its intensity and then a transfer to another unit, to another hospital or nursing home, or to the community. These meetings were sometimes delayed if one of the team members could

not make it. "The chronic custodial treatment institution, in comparison with a short-term treatment institution, seems like a study in slow motion." Even staff find that next week's decision, often becomes next month's decision because of bureaucratic delays in processing information. How do patients feel about this? "It is something the patients become accustomed to also, but often with much bitterness." (Roth and Eddy, 1967, 99).

>Patients often adapted to the slow life of a custodial institution and the more self-aware and higher functioning ones usually developed social circles that reflected differences in age, gender, socioeconomic background, and sometimes types of disability. Like at other "total institutions" where daily life is regulated, Farewell Hospital is no different. First, patients are processed by codifying and categorizing them in such a way that their unique characteristics and their desires "tend to be treated as inconsequential or even disturbing to the total program." Roth and Eddy, (1967, 102) go on to comment:

> The round of life is one that tends to make the inmates' time and effort seem worthless. On rehab, for example, the slow pace of the therapeutic program (a little each day), the long delays in getting equipment and appliances, the long wait for community placement in case of discharges, the weeks and months spent on another ward waiting to be returned to rehab after receiving some specialized medical treatment, and many other instances of frittering away the inmates' time might be cited.

In such a total institution, a patient finds that all the information that is known about him and collected from him and from other institutions like hospitals and the welfare department may be used to chart his course in the hospital. With all this knowledge available and usually shared by various staff members, there is a sense that one's privacy has been invaded and often used to manipulate what happens to a person. "The patient finds that his needs for service are defined by the employees, not by himself." (104)

Modifying the original analysis of Goffman in *Asylums* (1961) by changing the terminology for the four types of inmate response to asylums, Roth and Eddy (1967) find patients predominantly choose the third type of the following four responses. (1)"Escape" was the first type of response that ranged from social withdrawal to their own "cubicles" and away from shared social spaces, to not showing up for rehab sessions to suicide. About 15% adopted this response mode. (2) "Attack" occurs infrequently in the career of a patient. It involves attacking one's assumed helpers by criticizing them or engaging in a flagrant refusal to cooperate with them. This tactic was very rare among older people and was occasionally used by a younger person who wanted to get on with their life and was dissatisfied with the pace of treatment or the bureaucratic delays in making decisions about treatment and release. (3) Turning the institution into their "home" or colonizing it by carving out a lifestyle and a circle of friends or activities within it was the most common response adopted by about two-thirds of the rehab clients. Roth and Eddy (1967, 109) explain the bases for this most common choice:

> If you don't have much choice—and those who are seriously disabled and have no funds or interested family or friends outside the hospital have little choice—you may well be inclined, not only to make the best of what you have, but to insist that it isn't so bad a life after all.

The majority of patients who go through rehab will stay in Farewell Hospital once they leave the rehab unit. (4) The "party line" response involves converting to the staff's ideal of a perfect patient is a minority response of less than a quarter of all patients. However this takes one of two forms. The "custodial" party line is mainly adopting the aides and nursing staff's views inasmuch as they are the ones who see the patients the most. The custodial view is that a good patient is one who is able to take care of his own needs and make few demands on the custodial staff. In contrast the therapeutic staff made up of physicians, physical therapists, occupational therapists and counselors define a good patient not by their activity and attitudes on the wards but on the rare occasions when they see them during therapy. They define a good patient as one who is motivated to improve or maintain his functioning level, who doesn't challenge their decisions and who makes progress in rehabilitation according to the basic philosophy of rehabilitation.

>When patients are discharged from the rehab unit, they are usually discharged to other wards in the hospital—nursing, nursing rehab, psychiatric ward, and nursing self-care. A few are released to other hospitals or nursing homes. And a few are released to the community but their lives may still be under the following types of custodial care that retain some degree of supervision over their lives: foster care, boarding homes, hotel or rooming houses and the one with the least supervision—the family.

>When patients are discharged to other wards they are not usually involved in the decision and told about it beforehand. Transfers often come abruptly and give them little time to prepare for them. Patients

usually know that plans may be under way to transfer them to the community; but the timing of it and the exact type of residence where they will be located are often unknown to them until immediately before it happens with the decisions made by others in the welfare department of the state in which they reside.

>The ideal patient at Farewell is a young person in relatively good health with normal physical functioning but with a serious disability, who, after a period of rehabilitation, can be returned to a stable family.   Such an ideal patient is rare since most of their patients were poor, without a stable family, old, and often beyond extensive rehabilitation. But persons with money or good health insurance go to private rehabilitation hospitals with rare exceptions. "Farewell Hospital is a home for the unwanted."   It was called "Farewell" because few will ever leave it. (Roth and Eddy, 1967, 197).

Rehabilitation hospitals or rehabilitation departments in general hospitals operate much differently today than earlier ones although there is much variation in the demographic composition of patients in various hospitals. But with the greater subsidy of rehabilitation costs by the federal government, workmen's compensation insurance companies, private insurance and the emphases in managed care on efficiency, outcomes analysis and cost cutting, there is a greater emphasis on restoration of function in the minimum amount of time and less opportunity for custodialism except for the very aged and/or those judged beyond rehabilitation.

Today a wide variety of rehabilitation programs exist. They can be found in a variety of both public and private rehabilitation hospitals that may serve a wide range of patients or serve just a particular age group or a particular cluster of disabilities.   While such hospitals have inpatient beds they may also serve outpatients as well. Many general hospitals have a rehabilitation department that serves both inpatients and outpatients. For example, Wake Forest University Baptist Medical Center has three related rehabilitation units.   One is called the "Acquired Brain Injury Unit" that provides care for persons with both traumatic and non-traumatic brain injuries. The typical patient stays in this unit three weeks and 90% of them are released to the community. The second unit is a 27-bed "Comprehensive Inpatient Rehabilitation Unit" that provides short-term skilled nursing or rehabilitative care. The third unit is a 49-bed Medicare-certified and CARF-accredited "Transitional Care Unit" that serves a wide age-range of patients but who average 74 years of age. This subacute unit provides rehabilitative services to medically stable persons who need to restore or improve their skills of daily living. This unit provides transition services from the hospital to a nursing home or to other community programs. ("Rehabilitation Services," 2001). A variety of specialized service and research programs are organized around specific disabilities. For example, in 1987 two federal agencies collaborated to start the "Traumatic Brain Injury Model Systems" to develop model programs that stressed continuity and comprehensiveness of care at 17 rehabilitation hospitals or departments geographically distributed around the country. These 17 facilities receive funding from the U.S. Department of Education and the National Institute of Disability and Rehabilitation Research to not only provide services but to maintain a standardized national database for analyses of traumatic brain injury treatments and outcomes. ("Traumatic Brain Injury Model Systems", 2001).

There are also **sheltered workshops** where persons with a variety of disabilities received diagnostic workups for vocational rehabilitation, receive training and may be temporarily or permanently employed. Those seen as potentially capable of competitive employment may be able to move out of the sheltered workshop to jobs in the outside world. Some of them transitioning to competitive community employment may get one-on-one help from a job coach in what is known as "**supported-employment**" programs. Some people who go into supported employment programs may get there directly from their homes by means of state or private vocational rehabilitation programs, or are transitioned from high school vocational programs to supported employment programs where job coaches help new employees with disabilities adjust to a job and then phase out that support as is feasible. Other vocationally-related programs exist such as day-activity programs or partial hospitalization programs for persons with relatively severe disabilities who are engaged in a variety of activities that may prepare them for sheltered workshops or which occupy their time in ways seen as more therapeutic than watching television all day.

Overall, the Vocational Rehabilitation program funded by the federal government (at 80%) and the states (at 20%) provides a range of rehabilitation services to the public. In 1999 the Rehabilitation Services Administration reported that in that year it provided services to 1,204,233 and 231,714 were counted as rehabilitated. ("Research and Statistics", 2001) But over time, the rehabilitation model that follows the medical model of locating disabilities in the individual and solutions with the professionals have had to yield to the independent living paradigm where the locus of the problem is often in the environment and the solutions need to be directed by the consumer. (DeJong, 1984)

GROWING CRITICISMS OF REHABILITATION AND EMERGENCE OF THE INDEPENDENT LIVING MOVEMENT.

Starting in the late 1960s and going into the 1990s there was a crescendo of criticisms aimed at how and where rehabilitation was being carried out and the lack of it for some groups or categories of people. These criticisms were also accompanied by potential answers in how to better meet the needs of many of those with disabilities that coalesced into the Independent Living Movement (ILM). Some of these criticisms came from academics, some from parents, some from providers, some from professional advocates, but perhaps for the first time those with the disabilities themselves were the most vociferous about what was wrong with the system. The following list of criticisms is not exhaustive but it does provide a range of the concerns being voiced by a growing chorus of stakeholders with some kind of involvement in the burgeoning disability business: (Thomas, 1982; Shapiro, 1993; Pelka, 1997; Pope and Tarlov, 1991; Seelman, 2001; Braddock and Parish, 2001; Drake, 2001; Barnartt et al, 2001; Basnett, 2001; Davis, 2001; Shaw (Ed.), 1994).

>Too much of the rehabilitation was seen taking place in large institutions—very often some distance from the consumer's home. This reduced contact with family and friends and secluded them from normal activities in their home community.

>Much of the rehabilitation was seen occurring at a slow pace—at the pace the provider sets rather than at the pace that would be most beneficial in the view of the consumer. To some, the slow pace was undemanding, stifling and did not function to get more people back to work or living on their own in the community in a timely manner.

>Only a small percentage of those who could benefit from a variety of forms of rehabilitation were getting it. For example during the 1950s, only about 60,000 persons a year were getting vocational services out of a population of over 2 million disabled workers. Those not seeking vocational rehabilitation were even less likely to get rehabilitation unless they had money to pay for it. Some of this was due to the stigma of disability but some of it may be attributable to the gross underfunding of disability services, the pace and methods of rehabilitation, and the focus on vocational rehabilitation.

>Too many young people with disabilities were in nursing homes that typically were oriented to custodial care rather than rehabilitative care. There lives were permanently put on hold.

>There were inadequate forms of rehabilitation in the local community where people live. There was beginning to emerge the idea of a full continuum of care ranging from custodial care for the aged and medically fragile to intense comprehensive inpatient rehabilitation centers, to a variety of community out-patient programs and support services for children, adults and older persons who had disabilities.

>Most rehabilitation and care had followed the medical model where a range of providers made the **diagnosis** of what disabilities a patient had, what **treatment interventions** were needed and **where** and **when** those were to occur rather than involving the patient in meaningful ways in those diagnoses and interventions. As the social model emerged, greater attention was given to how the patient saw their disability, the kinds of interests they had in different vocations, and the timing and location of services they wanted, and their desire to live in their own homes. Most of all, the emergent social model put them at the center of decision making rather than at the periphery.

>Once in the community there were often architectural barriers and related social barriers that limited access to many places that persons with mobility limitations want to go from jobs, theaters, and post offices, to hospitals, educational institutions, and the forests for hunting. There were architectural barriers in many homes that needed to be changed if persons with a variety of impairments were not to be further limited in what they could do.

>Once in the community there were often attitudinal and behavioral barriers to being included in the basic institutions of education, health care, work, recreation, and religion.

>Once in the community there was often inaccessible public transportation to enable people to go where they want to go. Disabled people who wanted to live in the community often could not get the personal assistance they needed on a schedule that best fits their daily schedules rather than the pattern of providing personal assistants that fit the schedule of the organization providing the assistants. Shapiro (1993, 250-51) writes,

> Most disabled people know that there is a thin line of luck between independence and institutionalization. Often it hinges on something as simple as having someone around to roll on your deodorant, get you out of bed, or help you eat. Evan Kemp, who left the Equal Employment

Opportunity Commission in 1993, depends on personal assistants three hours a day, every day, to help him get out of bed, use the bathroom, wash, dress, cook breakfast, and get into a wheelchair so he can go off to work. Kemp has the money to afford assistance whenever he needs it. But he has "met disabled people in nursing homes who are more capable, brighter, better advocates than I will ever be. There is a fine line between me as chairman of the EEOC and a patient in a nursing home."

As we shall see in Chapter 7 on the self-determination movement, this issue of having the central say in how and when to use such services and the power to change them when they are unsatisfactory is one of the central issues in that movement.

There were a number of advocacy responses to the growing awareness that people with disabilities were facing exclusion, barriers and a lack of responsive services to their needs. While there was lobbying, protests and public demonstrations to create better legislation to answer their needs, one of the first responses was the emergence of a self-advocacy group that evolved into the Centers for Independent Living Movement. A 1953 survey conducted by Los Angeles County revealed that respiratory quadriplegics (most often polio survivors) could get comparable or better personal care in the community for less than a third of the money it cost to keep them in hospitals or nursing homes. Until 1959, when the program was discontinued, the National March of Dimes provided monthly stipends of $300 to polio survivors to enable them to live at home. A program at the University of Illinois at Urbana-Champaign, established in 1948 to accommodate disabled students, offered many of the features of independent living, though its services were limited to university students. The National Rehabilitation Association passed a resolution supporting the independent living concept in 1956, while early independent living legislations was introduced in Congress in 1957 and 1961, with neither bill generating much support. (Pelka, 1997, 166). In Virginia Laurie's landmark book, *Housing and Home Services for the Disabled: Guidelines and Experiences in Independent Living* (1977), she reported that "four severely disabled individuals can live at home for the cost of maintaining one in a nursing home. For both economic and humane reasons, the rules of government must be amended to make independent living as feasible as nursing home subsistence." (Quoted in Pelka, 1997, 190).

These were some of the early seeds of the independent living concept which simply means that disabled people live their day-to-day life in the community and not in institutions or hospitals and enjoy self-determination—making the decisions that impact on their lives rather than others making them. The actual start of the "movement" began in the fall of 1962 when a student in an iron lung, Edward V. Roberts, was admitted to the University of California at Berkeley. The dormitories there were both inaccessible and unable to accommodate his iron lung. Consequently he lived at Colwell Hospital on the campus and there his older brother and fellow student helped with his daily personal needs. His enrollment brought other students with disabilities to the campus. Roberts and John Hessler and Hale Zukas formed the "Rolling Quads"-- a group oriented to political advocacy. They also helped initiate the Physically Disabled Students' Program. In 1972 they founded the Center for Independent Living and Roberts became the center's first executive director. Because of his creativity and leadership he was later appointed as the Director of the California State Department of Rehabilitation. The idea of "Centers for Independent Living" evolved over time so that as the number of centers grew so did the number of services they offered. Other similar centers were established by Roberts in California showing that they worked well in meeting the fundamental needs of people who wanted to live outside of institutions in places that felt like a home. In 1978 the 1973 Rehabilitation Act was amended to allow federal funding for Centers for Independent Living (*CILs*). This funding promoted their fast spread across the country and around the world. In 1985 there were 298 CILs, by 1995 more than 400 worldwide as the American development of this program rather quickly diffused around the world. Centers for Independent Living have spread around the globe and as of 2000 there were 336 centers for independent living in the United States with an additional 253 subordinate sites in the U.S. In order to represent the interests of CILs to Congress and to share information and training programs among the CILs, the National Council on Independent Living (NCIL) was created in 1982. By 2001, NCIL represented over 700 organizations and individuals including CILs, Statewide Independent Living Councils (SILCs), individuals with disabilities and other disability advocacy organizations. (Pelka, 1997; Braddock, 2001; "About NCIL", 2001).

Functions of Centers for Independent Living. Centers for Independent Living serve somewhere over 200,000 people annually in the United States. Three tiers of organization exist—local centers, Statewide Independent Living Councils, and the national level represented by NCIL—the National Council on Independent Living.

NCIL's mission statement says "The National Council on Independent Living is a membership organization that advances the independent living philosophy and advocates for the human rights of, and services for, people with disabilities to further their full integration and participation in society." ("NCIL's Mission Statement", 2001). NCIL points out that it is the "oldest cross disability, grassroots organization run by and for people with disabilities." ("About NCIL", 2001, 1.) Its primary goal is to represent its member's interests to the administration and Congress. As part of the philosophy of the independent living movement, it emphasizes at all three levels of its governance structure that people with disabilities must make up a majority of those voting on issues and that their non-profit organizations are run for and by people with disabilities. Their answer to the question of "what is independent living?" is the statement: "Consumer choice, autonomy and control define the Independent Living Movement. The independent living philosophy holds that individuals with disabilities have the right to live with dignity and with appropriate support in their own homes, fully participate in their communities, and to control and make decisions about their lives." ("About NCIL", 2001, 2) The national organization, NCIL, carries out a number of activities in support of this philosophy: (1) advocacy on issues before Congress and the Administration, (2) informing members of advocacy issues and the organization's stance on these issues, (3) carrying out a variety of training programs provided to SILCs and CILs, (4) holding annual conferences for over 700 people, (5) raising money from a variety of sources to carry out its mission, and (6) answering about 6,000 requests for technical assistance each year. ("NCIL Projects" 2001). In 1999-2000, NCIL was working on four major advocacy projects: (1) against a bill that would weaken the ADA's discrimination provisions, (2) for a bill, MiCASSA—Medicaid Community Attendant Services and Support Act, that would expand and modify access to attendant services, (3) modify social security legislation that would allow persons on SSI or SSDI to keep their health benefits even if they return to work, and (4) increase funding by $75,000,000 for CILs in order to extend services to underserved geographic areas in the United States. ("NCIL's Advocacy Priorities", 2001).

At the local level, a variety of services are provided although every CIL may not offer all of the following services. But it is these services that have made CILs a vital part of the lives of their members: (1)

housing referral and adaptation, (2) peer counseling, (3) advocacy on local and state issues and being represented in both SILCs and the NCIL, (4) transportation, (5) training in a variety of independent living skills, (6) wheelchair repair, (7) information and referral, (8) attendant care services. (Braddock, 2001; Pelka, 1997; Basnett, 2001), Attendant care services have been critical to many if they are to live in their own homes. While not a service per se, one of the central benefits of CILs is the sense of empowerment they confer by emphasizing the independence, autonomy and decision making ability of their disabled members.

One of the effects of the independent living movement has been to challenge the medical model which historically placed service providers (physicians, vocational rehabilitation counselors, case managers, etc) as the decision makers. Such "caregivers" variously carried out the diagnoses of a "patients'" needs, acted as gatekeepers in determining services needed and authorizing them in some health or other service system, and then evaluating the effectiveness of the services provided. Ian Basnett, who became a paraplegic after earning his M.D, reports on the learning experience he went through in understanding how little understanding many medical personnel had about disability and how they often made decisions for those who had experienced a "tragedy" often assuming their lives were somehow worth less. In reflecting about the independent living movement's importance, he writes,

The disability movement had a profound effect on society and access. It is a way of living, but it also proved to be the genesis and hub around which disabled people have organized and expressed themselves as part of the disability rights movement. In the more rights-based culture of the United States, this was partly reflected in the adoption of antidiscrimination legislation much earlier than in many other developed countries. (Basnett, 2001, 406).

Reflecting on how it impacted on him personally, he writes,

To what extent has this movement influenced the mainstream provision of health care and social support? As an individual, I became more involved, less excluded, more confident, and unwilling to accept the status quo. I had the practical support enabling me to participate. This reflects the disability movement more broadly, in which disabled people were less likely to be institutionalized, more confident, and better able to organize, and power is transferred from professionals. Thus, independent living became and remains a major potential change agent for health and social services—partly through its direct effect on community care services, enabling disabled people to have more control over their lives (e.g. via direct payments), and partly as the movement itself emancipated disabled people, leading them to challenge health policy. (Basnett, 2001, 460).

While the independent living movement has been very empowering to thousands, several limitations and criticisms of it exist. One is that it tends to be an urban program with many CILs too far from rural areas and small towns to serve them. A second is that since one of its funding streams has been the federal government, it has lost it fighting edge in advocacy for fear that one of the hands that feeds it may withdraw that support. A third is that while it claims to be a cross-disability organization, it mainly serves articulate, white, wheelchair users and provides few services to those who do not need personal assistance services or who have psychiatric or intellectual disabilities. (Pelka, 1997; "NCIL's Advocacy Priorities" 2001, 2)

An appraisal of the independent living movement finds that it has had multiple beneficial effects. While most of these effects are not subject to quantification they are hugely significant at the level of the lives of the disabled, their families, social policy, societal perceptions of those with disabilities, and in operation of many of the organizational and interpersonal processes sociologists define within institutional contexts. Some of the main effects are:

>More people with disabilities have been able to live in their own homes rather than in hospitals, nursing homes or other institutions.

>It has brought many people together into CILs. The operation of CILs have enriched their lives immensely by providing support groups, independence training, personal assistance services, advocacy, transportation, inclusion into community institutions and other services.

>Persons with disabilities have gained more power vis-à-vis professionals to direct their own lives in ways that are satisfying to them.

>More persons with disabilities have been employed in the provision of services as a part of the philosophy of the CILs.

>Persons with disabilities are more frequently involved in other community institutions and this contact with the nondisabled helps to reduce stereotyping and discrimination.

>The empowerment that comes with the training, advocacy, education and support endeavors of CILs improves the self-images of persons with disabilities.

>Persons with disabilities are having an increasing democratic say in federal, state and local policies that impact on them through the advocacy groups they populate.

>CILs lowers costs of providing services to persons with disabilities in two ways: (1) by allowing many more to work when they can live at home and thus becoming taxpayers rather than using

extensive taxpayer services, and (2) by reducing the numbers of persons living in costly institutional facilities.

SUMMARY

In this chapter we first discussed the variety of conditions that caused physical disabilities. While about 7% of disabilities stem from sensory impairments and another 7% from cognitive disorders, the remaining 86% involve some type of physical impairment of which 40% are due to orthopedic impairments, arthritis and heart disease. The most significant feature of disability is its diversity which in turn is responded to by a large variety of professionals with distinctive training and views of how they should respond to persons with disabilities.

Organized society has responded to physical disabilities with widening waves of services as the functions of the western welfare state have expanded in response to disabling conditions. The first wave in the 20th century was that providing workmen's compensation insurance to cover the cost of work related injuries. This insurance program was implemented at the state level to pay for loss of life and loss of income due to loss of work from job related accidents or diseases. Sometimes this money was used for vocational rehabilitation in order to return persons injured on the job to work. The next two large waves of extending vocational rehabilitation services to those with disabilities occurred after World War I and then again after World War II to restore persons injured by military service to work. After both wars vocational rehabilitation services were also extended to civilians but so underfunded that only a small fraction of those needing services actually received them. Starting in 1965 legislation was passed that enabled workers who became permanently and totally disabled while covered under social security to receive a lifetime assured income and to this was added certain lifetime medical benefits when Medicare was extended to SSDI beneficiaries in 1972. The Magna Carta of disability legislation was passed in 1973 under the title of The Rehabilitation Act of 1973. This act created a billion dollar a year vocational rehabilitation program in which the federal government supplied 80% of the funding and the states 20%. In 1977 key regulations of this act were finally released after many protests by the disabled. These regulations were the first to prohibit discrimination against the disabled by employers who were receiving federal funding. Much additional legislation has been passed in the 1980s and 1990s to extend the civil rights for those with disabilities. The most important of these acts was the 1990 Americans with Disabilities Act which extended protection from discrimination for those with disabilities.

An analysis of emergence of disability rights groups reveals that more such organizations were created in the 1970s than in any other decade. This decade also saw the new emergence of many cross-disability rights organizations whose focus was on advocating for persons with a variety of kinds of disability rather than for just one form of disability as had been the case before. Disability rights organizations have carried out there work using a variety of strategies from recruiting and educating their members and the public, to lobbying, filing court cases, to engaging in media attention-getting protest activities. Collectively these activities have been a powerful force in helping to reduce the stigma of disability and improving the rights of those with disabilities. The lobbying and protest activities of disability organizations changed the political climate so that increasingly those with disabilities were involved in framing legislation that impacted upon them. This was particularly the case where 180 national organizations supported the passage of the Americans with Disabilities Act of 1990. The protest of many organizations against the fund-raising telethons that depicted persons with disabilities as tragedies was another accomplishment as such telethons were ended.

One of the positive changes that occurred in the last 30 years is the increasing deinstitutionalization of persons with physical disabilities from long term care institutions some of which were rehabilitation hospitals where rehabilitation was often slow and infrequent. One of the most successful disability rights movements has been the Independent Living Movement which has enabled many persons to move out of chronic care institutions to their own homes, often enabling them to be employed, by providing personal attendant services, reducing architectural barriers and providing a range of other services allowing them to live fuller and richer lives in their community. A review of the functions of Centers for Independent Living show they provide a range of services that enable members to live in and be a part of their local communities. These services include information and referral, transportation, technical assistance, support groups, advocacy, housing referral and adaptation, training and attendant care services. While the Independent Living Movement arose mostly among younger persons with physical disabilities it is being extended to those with activity limitation associated with the aging process.

CHAPTER 7
THE GROWING WAVE OF SELF-DETERMINATION

THE ISSUES IN THIS CHAPTER

The disability rights movement is not something that began and ended but something that continues to evolve as self-advocacy groups, advocacy groups, professionals and policy makers at all levels of government continue to redefine disability and the ways in which participation in all aspects of life can be most meaningful and enriching. This chapter focuses on a reform movement that is attempting to restructure the disability "service system" by changing it from a supplier driven system to a consumer or participant driven system. In this chapter we first want to look at the conceptual or philosophical meaning of self-determination. Second we will note that while this new wave first involved those with physical disabilities, then expanded to those with developmental and cognitive disabilities and finally is growing bigger as the self-determination movement is being applied to a growing aging population with disabilities. Third, we will then contrast several approaches to implementing self-determination as they have evolved from the service system of the 1970s where "providers" managed a range of programs they controlled. But since the late 1970s there has been a growing demand-side approach to services that over the decades kept enlarging the areas of power and decision-making that were increasing centered in persons with disabilities and/or their families. This wave is expanding as many of the aged with disabilities are part of this cresting wave of change. Fourth, we will explore in some detail how the most fully developed model of self-determination works that involves individualized planning, individualized budgeting, the use of "service brokers", fiscal intermediaries, and individualized choice in selecting and deselecting services. Fifth, we will look at some issues that are likely to exist as tension points in policy making and policy implementation as this revolutionary change in resource allocation and service delivery impacts on all levels of government, many thousands of service providers and millions of individuals and their families upon whom these changes will impact so dramatically. Sixth, as part of our approach to understanding not only the waves of the disability movement but the social and economic forces behind them, we will look as some of the key persons and organizations that have had some impact on the self-determination movement. Last, we will review some of the forces that will impact on the future of the self-determination reform movement.

THE MEANING OF SELF-DETERMINATION

The concept of self-determination at its most basic level involves people controlling their own lives and determining what they want to do or not do. This approach would allow them to make decisions about all daily aspects of their life: where they live, how they dress and what they eat, what kind of work they would like to do, how they spend their time. While many persons with disabilities could make these decisions, those with increasing severities of intellectual disabilities may need assistance in expressing their wishes.

The Alliance for Self-Determination, an "association open to organizations and individuals who have demonstrated the capacity to contribute to research, dissemination and training in self-determination and the ability to advance the Alliance mission" says

> **Self-Determination** is broadly defined as the ability of individuals to control their lives, to achieve self-defined goals and to participate fully in society. Self-determination is used to describe a set of beliefs and behaviors adopted by people (individuals, families and communities) seeking to improve their own lives and by those who seek to help them. ("Current Projects" 2001)

One statement about self-determination developed by the delegate body of The Association of Retarded Citizens (now known as The Arc) in 1998 follows:

> *ISSUE*
>
> People want to take control of their own lives. This is often referred to as self-determination. This means individuals make choices based on their

preferences and beliefs. They participate in and take control over decisions which affect the quality of their lives. This means that people have the freedom and authority to plan their lives and have the support to build a life and contribute to their communities. They take risks and responsibility. They can advocate for themselves. The lack of such supports, learning opportunities and experiences denies children and adults with mental retardation the right to become participating, valued assume responsibility for their actions. Empowerment through self-determination increases the respect and values others have for the individuals and that one has for oneself.

Many people with mental retardation have not had the opportunity to learn the skills and have the daily experiences that will enable them to take more control and make choices in their lives. Instead, they are often over-protected and segregated, are not included in making decisions that have an impact on their lives and have limited opportunities to make choices as well as limited options from which to choose.

Research and practice have shown that when given adequate support, learning opportunities and experiences, people with mental retardation can improve the quality of their lives by assuming greater control and respected members of communities.

POSITION

The Arc believes:

>People with mental retardation must have opportunities to acquire skills and develop beliefs that enable them to take greater control over their lives. They must have the freedom to exercise control and self-determination in their lives with the support they need from friends, family and individuals they choose.

>All people with mental retardation, including individuals with the most significant disabilities, can express preferences and use those preferences to make choices. Individuals must be present at and participate when decisions are made about their lives.

> While a disability may make it more difficult, all people have the opportunity to learn decision-making skills, to express their decisions and have respect by others.

>People with mental retardation must:

- be treated with dignity and respect and have their dreams and desires acknowledged and acted upon;
- have a wide range of typical, community experiences to understand the options available where they learn, live, work and play;
- be provided with support and accommodations needed to make decisions that have an impact on their lives;
- have the opportunity to advocate for themselves, without fear of punishment, and with the knowledge that their

- demands and suggestions well be heard and given fair consideration;
- have control over financial resources, services and formal and informal supports.

>Professionals, family members and the public must support and enable people with mental retardation to have greater control over their lives. ("Self Determination" Position Statement #25, 2001)

Self-determination is an emerging concept that is often distinguished from "consumer direction". Consumer direction is typically seen as having a more delimited focus. In contrast to the medical model in which the professional makes most of the decisions, perhaps with client input, about a patient's condition or diagnosis, and a determination of what they need in the way of services, the consumer directed model says the consumer should be central in determining what services they need and where they are going to get those services. Consumer direction primarily focuses on decisions by consumers (not professionals) about the decisions of using and managing long-term care services. "Consumer direction as a philosophy emphasizes a consumer's capacity to 'assess their own needs, determine how and by whom these needs should be met, and monitor the quality of services they receive.'"(Scala and Nerney, N.D.1). In contrast, self-determination in the evolving literature does not refer just to the use of services and who decides on that but

represents a much broader concept related to individuals' overall control of their lives and ability to participate fully in society and rests on four basic principles: (1) freedom to exercise the same rights as other citizens, (2) authority to control the funding needed for services and support, (3) support through the organization of resources as determined by the person with the disability and/or their circle of supporters, and (4) responsibility to use public dollars wisely. (Scala and Nerney, N.D. 1).

These four principles, freedom, authority, support and responsibility have been seen as the heart of the philosophy which has been propelling efforts around the country to implement variations of self-determination. These "four basic American principles" are explained in the following way by the National Program Office on Self-Determination:

FREEDOM: the exercise of the same rights as all citizens. People with disabilities with assistance when necessary will establish where they want to live, with whom they want to live and how their time will be occupied.

They do not have to trade their inalienable rights guaranteed under the Constitution for supports or services.

AUTHORITY: the control over whatever sums of money are needed for one's own support, including this re-prioritizing of these dollars when necessary. This is accomplished through the development of an individual budget that "moves" with the person.

SUPPORT: the organization of these resources as determined by the person with a disability.   This means that individuals do not receive "supervision" and "staffing."   Rather, folks with disabilities may seek companionship for support and contract for any number of discrete tasks for which they need assistance.

RESPONSIBILITY: the wise use of public dollars. Dollars are now being used as an investment in a person's life and not handled as resources to purchase services or slots.   Responsibility includes the ordinary obligations of American citizens and allows individuals to contribute to their communities in meaningful ways. ("About Self-Determination: The Four Principles", 1998).

In a more recent internet publication, one of the leaders in the self-determination movement, Thomas Nerney, along with Eli Cohen (2001, 2) has argued that a fifth principle needs to be added to the above 4 principles. The fifth principle they add is: "CONFIRMATION. The valued role that individuals with disabilities must play in the design, creation and execution of all public policies affecting them." Historically, those with disabilities have often been excluded from meaningful participation in the development of policies that impact on them. When they are so included we will have *confirming* evidence that they are participating in self-determination.

DISABILITY GROUPS INVOLVED IN SELF-DETERMINATION

The first group to really pursue policies and programs under the rubric of self-determination were those with physical disabilities who were involved in the independent living movement described in the previous chapter. For them to be more self-determining of their lifestyles since they wanted to live outside of institutions like nursing homes or rehabilitation hospitals they needed a number of things. The things they needed were one or more (and usually more) of the following: homes that were accessible and useable given their mobility limitations, the ability to hire, pay and use personal assistants to help them with tasks of daily living they could not do independently, public transportation in the outside world and assistive devices that enable them to communicate with the outside world or enable them to do other tasks. The Centers for Independent Living Movement met those needs by training and/or assisting their participants learn about a range of services, get the services they needed and provide other services ranging from peer support groups to self-advocacy groups. In most ways the first group to seek and get some degree of self-determination were those with physical disabilities. Many were getting some of these services as early as the 1970s but many more had to wait until the 1980s, 1990s to get the support services they needed. And many of those are still hoping that in 2001 or soon thereafter that the MiCASSA bill will be passed to give them not only more support services but the right to control them to a much greater extent than now. While many of the principles and practices of self-determination were embedded in the CIL movement, the term "Self-Determination" was not used in the more formal sense listed in the four principles that emerged in the late 1980s and were progressively elaborated on in the 1990s.

Several other clusters of persons with certain disabilities were emerging in the late 1980s and into the 1990s whose advocates sought more independence for them. These clusters included persons who were being released from or no longer going to institutions for the mentally retarded. They included persons with traumatic brain injuries often maintained for long periods of time in nursing homes or rehabilitation hospitals. They included persons with mental retardation or mental illness who were transitioning from school to community programs who were capable of living on their own if they had sufficient supports. They included a few persons with mental illness even though the self-determination movement has been most centrally focused on persons with developmental disabilities.

The last cluster of persons being considered for self-determination approaches have been the aged and the HIV/Aids population who have chronic illnesses or limitations and who would often like to stay out of hospitals and nursing homes if they can get the communal supports they need and thereby not only control the costs of long-term institutional care but live in their own homes. While their language often uses consumer-direction and participant-direction rather than self-direction, the concerns are much the same—particularly as they focus on consumer supports like personal assistant services that will allow them to stay in their own homes rather than institutions. (Agosta, 1997; Cohen and Nerney, 2001; Simon-Rusinowitz, 1999).

THE EVOLUTION OF SELF-DETERMINATION

The evolution of self-determination occurred primarily in the 1990s first as a philosophy and subsequently implemented in varying degrees as operational principles by many states and entitlement programs. This evolution is still going on as the fifty states, the federal government and other organizations experiment with various elements of self-determination.   As we shall see, the full version of self-determination that includes individualized budgeting and individualized control of the use of resources requires a profound change in the system that has provided those resources in the past.   To transition to a system so different from the **supply side model** to the **demand side model** will require huge adjustments at four levels: the federal government level, state government level, the provider level, and at the level of those with disabilities and their supporters.

Table 7.1 provides comparative information on three models of service delivery in terms of the locus of decision-making.   We will first look at the **supply model** or the **professional service model** which has been the dominant model for many generations.   The number and size of providers of services in this model grew sharply as the deinstitutionalization process shrunk the number of persons with disabling conditions in institutions and served them in the community. This model typically started with a determination by a state agency of who needed services.   We will illustrate how this process worked for a person with a developmental disability.   Assume a person, John M., was moderately retarded.   A state agency, perhaps entitled the office of mental retardation or state department of social services, or its regional counterpart, makes a determination that as the state is reducing the numbers of persons in state training schools for those with mental retardation, that John M. should be released back to his home community.   Staff from the local authorizing agency and perhaps even from one or more provider agencies will visit John M. at the state institution where they will gather information from his "file" and the staff at his institution before he is released.   They are very likely to also talk to John M's family, if he has one, about their interest in having John M. return to his home community and perhaps live with them. They will file for Supplemental Security Income for him as this helps

Table 7.1 Comparison to three models of service delivery in terms of decision-making.

TYPE OF DECISION MADE	SUPPLY SIDE—PROFESSIONAL SERVICE MODEL (Medical Model)	DEMAND SIDE—SELF DETERMINATION MODEL WITHOUT CONSUMER BUDGET CONTROL	DEMAND SIDE—SELF-DETERMINATION MODEL WITH CONSUMER BUDGET CONTROL—**INDEPENDENT FUNDING**
Determination of eligibility for services	Either state or contractor with state determines diagnostic need for services.	Either state or contractor with state determines diagnostic need for services	Either state or contractor with state determines diagnostic need for services
Determination of kinds/amounts of services "needed"	**Caseworker with** either state and/or contractor with state makes determination of client or patient needs for **program services. Client** of their family may have some input into plan of services.	**Support broker** works with citizen and a circle of friends and family to determine consumer preferences interests and needs for **consumer supports. Person-centered planning** process is vital to self-determination	Same as to left
Who chooses provider(s)?	Typically the states contracts with provider agencies to offer services and then clients assigned to them based on availability of **slots** and funding for those slots.	The person with a disability (and sometimes with the family's assistance) makes the choice with the state being responsible for allowing choice among providers.	Same as to left

Who pays providers? (And how much?)	State pays provider directly or through regional funding organizations according to rate setting schemes	Same as to left.	**Fiscal intermediaries.** Banks or other independent agencies pay providers for services allowed in **individual budgets** with rates negotiated with or set by provider.
Who determine amount of services	The state largely determines after some "negotiation" of reasonable rates with providers. Funding caps often established by state.	Negotiated by support broker with state in light of availability of funds and changing needs of person with a disability.	Same as to left
Who monitors quality of services of providers?	State licensing system. Accreditation boards. State system for reporting of "unusual incidents" regarding neglect, abuse, etc. Sometimes caseworkers monitor care	State licensing system. Accreditation boards. State system for reporting of "unusual incidents". Support broker monitors quality of care	Person with disability is primary monitor and/or their chosen spokesperson; but other quality assurance measures used such as inspection of provider services and monitoring by support broker.
Who has authority to change providers?	Typically only the state or its delagatee can determine the most appropriate and cost-effective provider.	Individual may be given some choice of program slots with different providers if slots are available.	Person with disability or spokesperson.

pay for a small portion of the costs of his living in the community and benefits the state by transferring some of his upkeep costs to the federal government. The staff will determine what level of supports John M. needs. A key decision is where he will live—in a group home for six residents or maybe three residents which is staffed by paid employees of some non-profit or for-profit agency that provides these services, or with one family that provides board and room and other services to him for a monthly stipend or with his own family of origination. Typically these families also provide some recreation outlets for John M. Since these agencies run on annual contracts with the county/municipal authority, John M. will be assigned to one of the available "slots" or vacancies that exist. If the residential program is expanding in numbers served because of deinstitutionalization, various providers may compete for expanding their residential program by making proposals to the authorizing county/municipal agency. The provider organization that gets the contract may be chosen on the basis of past performance, or the best written proposal judged by qualitative and/or costs elements in the proposal. A second type of service may be medical services. While medical services will be paid for by Medicaid, the provider agency must make arrangements with local doctors and hospitals for the services that John M. needs. A third type of service will be what John M. will do during the day. He may go to a pre-vocational day treatment program, a sheltered workshop, or some type of sheltered employment or supported competitive employment based on the best judgments of the staff who make this decision. In this professional service model we see that the decisions of whether John M. needs or gets services is located with a case manager who manages his "case" for the state and service providers who work with the state's case manager for John M. The state's local administrative agency will typically determine where John M. gets these services. He or his support group will have no choice in this matter. To ensure the safety and acceptable quality of residential and other services, the state will implement a number of quality assurance programs that typically involve state licensing of provider agencies and their homes or other programs. State licensing involves annual inspections of residential and day-activity facilities, staff credentials and training, and extensive information relative to the quality of programming that contracted agencies provide. This may include such things as frequency of activities in the community, contacts with friends, reports of gains in behavior and skill performance. There may be accreditation processes involved for some agencies like rehabilitation agencies. There will be reporting requirements to state agencies on "unusual incidents" where "client" lives are put at risk for health or safety due to such things as injuries, fights, neglect, abuse, medication errors, and accidents.

While such a system has provided persons with developmental disabilities a range of services that often enriched their lives over what they were or might have been in institutions, it has frequently been criticized on a number of grounds. First, the person with the disability (or in combination with their advocates or support group if they have severe disabilities that may limit communication) is not given a significant say in decisions being made about them—housing, support services, daily routines, and so on. This takes away a basic right—of deciding for them-selves what they want. This limits their growth if they do not have to make decisions and undermines their self-identity. Furthermore, this system of decision-making does not assure that case managers or persons who decide what is best for a persons with disabilities will be required to really get to know the likes and dislikes, dreams and hopes, strengths and limitations of the person for whom they are deciding. Furthermore, case managers in the professional service model are typically employees of the state or perhaps a specialized agency that does only intake, assessment, service planning and/or case management. But they are not employees of the disabled person. They often have a conflict of interest to serve the interests of their employer rather than the person whose "case" they are managing. Often such case managers have ambiguous and/or conflicting duties that may involve managing resources in a "cost effective manner" for the managing agency they represent (their employer), being a friend and advocate for their "case", sometimes providing direct service and support during times of crises and staff shortages, and engaging in assessment and planning the delivery of supports. (Kane, Kane, and Ladd; 1998; "'I'm Not Case and I Don't Want to be Managed!'" 1998). In some rural communities there may be only one provider agency who provides both case management and a range of services within that agency. In this case, there are no options for the case manager. Or there might be a situation where two provider agencies exist, but only one of them provides case management services. In such a situation the case manager will be under pressure to refer their "cases" for additional services to the agency for which they work.

The supply model is also called a **program-funded** model. State agencies contract with providers to offer a "program" such as residential services, or transportation or day activities for persons. Persons with disabilities fill "slots" in such programs where the funding amount is based on providing services for a certain number of persons for so many hours a day and a stipulated number of days per year. In this way per person charges can be calculated and rate-setting formulas developed to fund relatively similar programs at about the same rate. The criticism of program-funded services is that individuals with disabilities need to match the services offered for them rather than having services tailored to their very particular needs and desires. A later philosophy called "wraparound services" involved designing services to wraparound the needs of a specific individual rather than enrolling him in a program for persons with a wide range of disabilities that are not tailored to his unique interests. Other criticisms of program-funded programs include that they are not very flexible in response to the changing needs of individuals, supports tend to be bundled into provider packages that meet the interests of the provider, quality assurance measures are implemented primarily by the provider who wants to report doing excellent work, providers sometimes engage in "creaming" in order to work with clients who are the easiest to manage, and there is a reliance on paid supports rather than unpaid natural supports.

In the evolution of the self-determination movement, the self-determination model without consumer budget control emerged first followed in quick succession by the model with budget control. A new vocabulary continues to emerge to identify the roles of different intermediaries in the determination of social supports needed, and the management of money. The use of the term consumer instead of "patient", or "client", or "case" was thought to be a step toward recognizing that the person with a disability was in control inasmuch as typically consumers and not others decide how to spend their money. However, some persons are wary of using this term because it conjures up images of a medical model consisting of unwary consumers buying services available from self-interested "providers". Others search for more neutral terms such as "participant" or "citizen" that do not carry the pejorative connotations of past concepts. The consumer concept implies economic decisions only while the concept of participant or citizen suggests equality of decision-making in many different social roles. (See "'I'm Not a Case and I Don't Want to be Managed,'" 1998).

One of the big steps in self-determination for those primarily with moderate to profound cognitive disabilities came with the publication of *Everyday Lives* in 1991 and *Finding A Way to Everyday Lives* in 1993 in Pennsylvania with similar publications in other states setting the conceptual groundwork for beginning the transformation of state systems from supply to demand side principles. These monographs were widely used among state agencies and providers and families to assist in the shift from planning **for** persons with disabilities to planning **by and/or with** them. The 1991 document listed 15 things "to do next" to change toward a consumer directed system. These included:

> PROVIDE CHOICES in living, working and having fun. GIVE OVER CONTROL rather than managing and directing. ENABLE AND SUPPORT THE INDIVIDUAL to make decisions. . . . REWORK THE WAY MONEY IS ALLOCATED by providing for more local control. Put money in the hands of individuals and families and give them the knowledge and the flexibility to make their own decisions. *(Everyday Lives.* 1991, 13).

The 1993 document espoused two things—that **person-centered planning** ought to be the **moral philosophy** of centering planning on the needs of a person as they were able to express them by themselves or with the help of others who know them well and a **process of how to do person-centered planning.** That it should be done was supported by the feasibility of doing it better with detectable positive outcomes than it had been done in the past. And new processes of how it could be done emerged that demonstrated that by closely involving both the person with the disability and the people who know that person well such as parents, siblings, close friends, professional advocates, teachers, service providers and others as appropriate the person's real needs and interests could be determined. The philosophy of person centered family squared with individual freedom. Several different models within person-centered planning emerged—one came from the field of planning and community development and was called "personal futures planning". This focused on helping two different groups: (1) individuals with disabilities and their families who have not had much experience of working with the service system up to that point, and (2) service providers who want to transform the system they work within to make it less program focused and more person-centered focused. In contrast, "essential lifestyle planning" emerged from efforts to assist individuals who were moving from state development centers back to home communities. Both focused on assembling persons who knew the person well and determining such things as their likes and dislikes, friendships, preferences in housing, friends, activities, food, their hopes for the future and the range of paid and unpaid supports that would make their lives richer and more socially included in the community. Very often this process also yielded information that supports were unavailable or inadequate. Some believed that this uncovering would set processes in motion that would expand services in a competitive service system. ("Finding A Way Toward Everyday Lives", 1993).

One of the language changes that occurred with the self-determination movement was the shift by some proponents to the concept of "support" and away from services because the latter term implies a provider who offers "services" to a client.   The use of a "support broker" occurs under the self-determination model. According to Nerney (2001, 2) functions provided by support brokers may also be called "independent support coordination, personal agents, or independent brokering."   While a support broker could occur with the self-determination model without consumer budget control, the term is most closely aligned with the model where the consumer has budget control and, as we shall discuss shortly, is one of three key parts of the consumer budget control model along with the "individual budgets" and "fiscal intermediaries".   The California Department of Developmental Services in their California Self-Determination Pilot Projects gives this "general definition" of **support broker:**

> A support broker is the individual or agency who arranges for the specific services and supports a consumer and/or family needs.   The broker acts on behalf of the consumer as his or her personal "agent" to arrange these services and supports. The broker helps define the needs and life dreams, provides information about resources, identifies potential providers (regardless of funding source), arranges contracts for services, and evaluates the effectiveness of the services and supports. ("Support Broker", 2001)

Most discussions of support brokers argue that ideally the support broker should be independent of any of the service providers that are contracted with on behalf of the consumer in order to avoid conflicts of interest. (Nerney, 1998; Mosely and Nerney, 1998; "Moving to a system of Support", 1994).   In New Hampshire two variations in service brokerage are available in meeting the varying needs of individuals.   One variation involves a nonprofit agency that is independent of any service provider simultaneously providing both service coordination and support brokerage functions.   This support broker is one of the services purchased by the consumer from resources allocated in their individual budget.   The service broker helps the consumer develop an "Individual Program Plan", negotiates specific hours of service and hourly rates on behalf of the consumer with service providers.   If a plan needs periodic readjustment, the service broker can be rehired to rework the plan and the consequent adjustment in purchased services. In this case the consumer uses some of the budgeted funds for brokerage/planning services. This approach is particularly used by consumers who have non-traditional service needs. The second variation in New Hampshire is where a state department staff person acts as service coordinator and support broker. This model is used more by persons wanting a more traditional array of services. ("Support Broker", 2001).

The support brokerage in Oregon is consumer directed. That state uses a non-profit, tax-exempt organization specifically designed to act as a support broker. The board of this agency is composed entirely of persons with developmental disabilities and family members. This agency in that state carries out multiple functions: service brokerage, "person-centered planning, consumer education, technical assistance, community development, quality monitoring, fiscal intermediary, and administrative employment supports."("Support Broker", 2001, 2). In Canada, many of the provinces have experimented substantially with support brokerage and independent budgeting and management. They use the term "Microboard" to refer to small groups of persons of 5, 7 or 9 individuals in a community that assist persons with disabilities do the planning, supports brokerage and resource management that is needed to deal with individualized budgets. These "microboards" are non-profit entities that negotiate with the government for money needed for supports and then arrange those supports in line with the wishes of the individual. These microboards are chosen by or on behalf of the person with disabilities. ("Self-Directed Support Corporations (Microboards))" 2001; National Union Research, "The Hard Truth About Individualized Funding," 1998).

In the field of aging disability, a somewhat new concept and practice has emerged called the **geriatric care manager** who provides much the same function as support brokers for persons with cognitive disabilities. Geriatric care managers assess an older person's needs in their particular location, develop a plan of care that the older person will need to assent to, find and secure services needed from legal care, home care and nursing care to home maintenance, and personal supports, and counsels family members who often live some distance from an aging parent. In 2001 the hourly fees of **geriatric care managers** were ranging between $80 and $150 an hour. The National Association of Professional Geriatric Care Managers has emerged to promote quality in the field by requiring members to be licensed in their fields, trained in geriatrics, and abide by professional guidelines and ethical standards. The geriatric care manager service is often able to keep a person out of a nursing home and its substantial costs—often at substantial savings by arranging for a person to stay in their own home by using services relevant to their needs. (Greider, 2001)

The second element in the self-determination model where the individual has budget control is the **development and control by consumers of individual budgets.** In this model either the consumer and/or their family and/or a "microboard" controls the specific amount of funds that they can spend for services from a variety of sources. The arguments for this element is that this gives those with disabilities and/or their circles of support the experiences of making personal choices, it engages them in relationships with others about making choices now that will enable them to make better choices in the future if they learn from their experiences, and that they enjoy the same rights to spend money as others. In some cases state staff are involved in developing the individual budget. Ideally such a budget is based on a well-designed **"person-centered plan"** that identifies consumer strengths, needs and resources. Often a person with a disability and/or their family will need the assistance of an independent support broker discussed earlier to provide them information about the range of options about services available and their costs. The support broker may help them arrange for services, monitor the quality of services, negotiate problems with service providers or the need for a revised person-centered plan and budget changes that may flow from that. Having budget control is seen as empowering to individuals with disabilities and their families. A "best practices model" of individual budget management gives control of hiring and firing support personnel to the participant, some flexibility in making reasonable adjustments to line items in budgets and having budgets tailored to the unique needs and dreams of each person. (Nerney, 2001; Bach, 1998). The last column in Table 7.1 shows the key elements in this model which is most frequently referred to as the **independent funding** model. Nerney (2001b) has argued that ideally the support circle that creatively develops a plan should also have the power to construct an individualized budget around the supports a person needs. But to do this they need to be free of any relationship with historic service agencies.

How does the state determine what is a "just" dollar amount for an individualized budget? This remains a thorny question for many states who fear three problems. One fear is that of runaway costs if there are no controls on costs exerted by the state. A second fear is that of developing a costly bureaucracy to oversee the implementation and monitoring of such a system. The third fear is that substantial differences in funding could develop for individuals with about the same kind and level of disability that would be judged as inequitable and therefore a political liability.

Three recognizable different approaches have been taken to individualized budgets: (1) a quantitative approach, (2) a needs/assessment planning approach, and (3) a historic cost approach according to research carried out by the California Department of Disabilities as it initiated "The California Self-Determination Projects" (2001). The **quantitative approach** uses a detailed formal assessment procedure that yields an individual "score" based on a person's "need" for services. These needs will be defined using: the nature and severity of their diagnostic disability, their skills in ADL and IADL, their need for assistance, special medical, physical or behavioral challenges they have, their age, lifestyle, family and unpaid supports, and the availability and costs of both generic and specialized services in their community. The advantage of this system is that if the scoring system is valid and reliable it will enable the state to measure the amount of resources needed with some accuracy, allocate about the same level of resources to individuals with similar levels of need all the while making individual budgets available to empower individuals to use them as other citizens spend their resources. However, this functional model that measures a person's "deficits" is sometimes criticized because it focuses on needs and not a person's dreams. (Nerney, 2001b)

The **planning approach** is more qualitative in that it is based on a **person-centered plan** developed by a team including the person with the disability. This approach also assesses a person's disabilities, strengths, existing supports, and life plan goals with regard to residence, work, activities. Historic costs of services in that person's community may be used as benchmarks against which comparisons and adjustments can be made in light of the person's array of needs, dreams, and local community costs. Some agencies may have to review all such budgets to determine if their aggregate costs exceed the funds available or allocated. One of the leaders in the independent funding movement, Tom Nerney (2001b) from the Center for Self-Determination believes that person centered planning and individualized budgeting need to go together and not assume anything about costs based on the current system of costs determined largely by providers in negotiation with state administrative agencies

The **historic cost** approach is mainly available for startup programs that are transitioning from program budgeting to individualized budgeting. This method will look at the previous year's "program" budget where the individual was allocated a set amount of money to be given to the provider in a POS—purchase of service contract. Using a person-centered planning process the prior year's budget will be adjusted up or down according to the changes in costs for housing, recreation, special needs and the costs of other support services this person will need. Of course, this process can be extended beyond the initial year. Other adjustments may be made in lieu of how comparably situated individuals are funded. Other states are using various combinations of these methods as they devise methods to allow individual budgeting while trying to manage aggregate costs. Wyoming, for example, has an IRA—"Individual Resource Allocation" process that combines needs assessment of the person along both qualitative and quantitative dimensions of their disability, his/her historic costs, community and provider variations in costs and family/consumer wishes. Wisconsin's Dane County has developed an individualized funding mechanism that calculates an individual's rate of funding based on their costs for four services: (1) the number of hours out of each 24 hour period a person needs supports, (2) the number of hours of service they need from a support broker to plan, coordinate and monitor their services, (3) the cost of their housing, and (4) their personal needs funding component. They allow an individual to go above or below this "standard rate" according to special needs they do or don't have. ("Individual Budgets", 2001).

A demonstration program funded by the Robert Wood Johnson Foundation and the Office of the Assistant Secretary for Planning and Evaluation in the Department of Health and Human Services was begun 1996 in four states in order to test a variation in independent funding for older persons. The four states where this demonstration program is being tried are Arkansas, Florida, New Jersey and New York. In 1998 these four states got Medicaid waivers to give eligible Medicaid recipients a choice between traditional services or the new approach called "**cash and counseling**". In it disabled persons over 18 years of age get cash benefits directly from the government to purchase a wide range of services. In addition, they may choose to get "counseling" to assist them in making wise decisions about purchasing services, fiscal management, and training personal assistants. The amount of counseling they get will depend on their level of disability, their prior experience in purchasing services, and the variety of needs they have. (Lagoyda, et al, 1999; "Consumer-directed personal assistance services", 2001; "A National Personal Assistance Demonstration—Cash and Counseling", 1999)

The third component of the consumer budget controlled self-determination model is the use of a **fiscal intermediary.** The fiscal intermediary manages the funds in the individual budget for the person with a disability. This will involve making payments to agencies or persons authorized by the participant, family or circle of support. The fiscal intermediary not only pays invoices for services but keeps records of these while acting as the "employer of record". As employer of record the fiscal intermediary will deduct social security withholdings, file tax documents, manage workmen's compensation and health and disability insurance, and verify the citizenship/legal alien status of support providers. Such fiscal intermediaries should be able to isolate the budget of each person whose account they handle and should be conflict free in that they provide no other service to the person who uses them. Ideally, the fiscal intermediary should be in the same community so that they can be accessible. The fiscal intermediary is not considered a direct support service provider even though they may charge a fee for their services whether they be a for-profit bank or a nonprofit organization that has the capabilities of paying bills, managing funds, providing payroll functions, administering benefits, keeping relevant records and sometimes negotiating with contractors. (Nerney, 2001). States vary in how the fiscal intermediaries are labeled and operate. In Massachusetts, "Family Governing Boards" not only act as fiscal intermediaries but also carry out the functions of the support broker as well--from helping individuals develop life plans, supports and individual budgets to monitoring the quality and quantity of services provided to the participant. In Wisconsin's Dane County, nonprofit "Fiscal Management Agencies" provide fiscal services only but not support brokering. ("Fiscal Intermediaries", 2001).

ISSUES OF CONTENTION IN FISCAL SELF-DETERMINATION

A number of issues have developed about the implementation of fiscal self-determination where the individual with a disability has a "microboard" or some form of support broker services, an individualized budget and a fiscal intermediary. Already some 30 states are experimenting with self-determination projects and so are the provinces of Canada. The major system transformation involved in moving from a supply/provider dominated model to a demand/user dominated model is twofold and centers heavily around the use of resources. The first is who controls the money for planning and second is who controls the money for purchase of supports. In the supply side model, case managers working for providers made most of the planning decisions. And providers had to meet state criteria to provide services the state paid for. In both cases the money went from the state to planning providers (caseworkers) and service providers to benefit the recipients. In the supply side model—the disabled individual stands between the government and the service providers and uses his/her allocation to buy the supports believed needed from service providers which can be changed if they are unsatisfactory. (Salisbury and Collins, 1998).

Since the self-determination movement is in its early stages, no one is certain how well each of its many variations will work. We will look at several research studies that suggest the self-determination projects they investigated worked well. In the next paragraph is a list of issues that have been raised but not answered fully yet as many self-determination pilot and demonstration projects are being initiated and/or evaluated around the country. Historically social scientists sometimes find that "new" programs often run well when they are first operated with high enthusiasm and new funding. However, over time, the novelty of a new program becomes bureaucratized, the enthusiasm of a fresh start fades, and the extra funding used in the startup program erodes over subsequent years. (See, e.g., Uditsky, 2001; Bach, 1998; National Union Research, "The Hard Truth about Individualized Funding, 1998).

The key issues of contention often come from persons who have social and financial investments in the supply side approach to dealing with disabilities and who would be affected by the transition from that approach to self-determination that includes individualized funding. Some of the key issues we have identified are:

>Is exclusion from self-determination or entrance to it founded on a skills approach or a rights approach? Self-determination will not likely become a reality if people with intellectual disabilities are tested to see if they have the capacity or skills to make the decisions involved in self-determination by themselves. Those who argue well-informed professionals should make the decision take the skills approach while legal rights advocates argue that while skills training should be undertaken, this is finally a legal and human rights issue. They argue that it is the support circle which includes the disabled person who makes this decision if the person's disability keeps him from making it

solely on his own. But current professionals working in the area of supports question whether persons with disabilities or their guardians working alone are the best persons to make decisions about support since they are often unfamiliar with the continuum of services that exists in a community, may not know how to access them or evaluate their quality of service. (National Union Research, "The Hard Truth About Individualized Funding", 1998)

>A second issue is whether the state can surrender some of its power to individuals. While the state has long institutionalized those with intellectual disabilities, it did so by taking power away from them to make the decision of where they wanted to live. Can that power and decision making that is embedded in state structures be returned to citizens and their families?   Bach (1998, 2) points out that the Independent Living Movement in both the U.S. and Canada demonstrated that those with physical disabilities could successfully use independent funding. "A body of experience, policy developments, and program evaluation demonstrates both the viability of this approach to funding, and its necessity in ensuring that people are able to guide their lives toward the personal and collective aims they choose."

> One of the barriers to self-determination is the legal distinction between competence and incompetence and whether people who have guardians and are judged to be incompetent can enter into legal contracts involving the hiring of support services. But the supporters for self-determination say this problem is solved by vesting legal authority in support brokers, person-centered planning circles, and fiscal intermediaries. (Bach, 1998)

>Perhaps one of the biggest barriers to self-determination is the huge social, psychological and financial investment that tens of thousands of providers and their employees have in their jobs and agencies that are in the disability services businesses. What will happen to these agencies and their employees. How can such workers be transitioned to be being employed by those with disabilities? What will happen to unions of employees and collective bargaining agreements? Will wages of support workers be depressed as employer practices become atomized among tens of thousands of persons with disabilities becoming employers? Current providers may be resistant to the impacts individualized budgeting will have on their agencies. (Bach, 1998;   National Union Research, "The Hard Truth About Individualized Funding", 1998).

>The assumption that the person with a cognitive disability has a loving family and supportive circle of friends that will assist him/her in

becoming more self-determining may be true for many but not all. Even if such a circle of supporters exist, will they have the interest and skills to operate and oversee the process of acquiring and administering a individualized budget? "How can the control over dollars and decision making be transferred to individuals and families without over-burdening them with the administration of those dollars and the management of the services they purchase?" (Bach, 1998, 4) Nerney (1998, 7-8) answers that person centered planning without control of individualized funds simply leaves providers in control and does not contain the "electricity that individual budgets inject into the planning and budgeting process. Person-centered planning takes on new meaning when individuals know how much they can spend, are free to prioritize budgets and can purchase wherever the dollars will bring the most value."

>A major issue is that there are not enough dollars to fund all the community supports that could be utilized but remain unmet. With an aging population, growing waiting lists for disability supports and relatively flat financial resources, how can supports be rationed that various constituencies feel is fair? (Agosta, 1997) However, this was also the situation whether the funding approach was supply side or either of the two variations in demand side models.

> Another question is whether the IF—Independent Funding model will be able to adjust to the changing needs of persons with disabilities as does the model where professionals have more surveillance over the evolution of change and greater awareness of a continuum of services in the community. (National Union Research, "The Hard Truth About Funding", 1998).

>Another issue is what kind of services will be available under the highly individualized demand model of individualized funding. When this model started in many communities there was an array of providers who provided a continuum of services from agencies who had trained staff. But if the transition is made to a highly individualized hiring market of supports, will trained support services be available? Who will provide the training that may more easily be achieved with program funding than individualized funding? Who will monitor the quality of services that are provided? Will there be training available to meet the needs of an atomized market of support services? (National Union Research, "The Hard Truth About Individualized Funding," 1998; "Consumer Direction" 2001).

>A survey of state administrators who direct programs that provide benefits to long term care persons under federal aging, MR/DD, vocational rehabilitation and Medicaid found that they had concerns in several areas. Fifty one percent felt individualized funding programs lacked oversight and quality control, 32% felt they would be subject to fraud and abuse while 27% thought they would be hard to implement. But a large majority of them felt that consumer control would be enhanced in them and that there would be cost savings in such programs. (Lagoyda, et al, 1999).

Many of these contentious issues cannot be solved in theory but must await the unfolding of many experimental approaches to independent funding within self-determination to see what works best. It may be that multiple models may work well if they are tailored to the special circumstances of communities and the person with disabilities in them.

KEY ACTORS AND ACTIONS IN THE SELF-DETERMINATION MOVEMENT.

This section of the chapter is not a precise historical accounting of what persons, advocacy and self-advocacy groups, and governmental agencies did what things in what sequence to shape the self-determination movement. Rather it is a listing of some of the major actors and some of the activities they engaged in that kept the self determination wave moving and gathering momentum over time. The most important, in the author's mind, is the Robert Wood Johnson Foundation which provided or is providing somewhere in the vicinity of 100 million dollars to explore the meanings of self-determination, to hold national meeting to promote its study and to fund many demonstration programs to gain information on how to make it work effectively for a range of persons with disabling conditions.

The Robert Wood Johnson Foundation's Support of Self-Determination Initiatives and Demonstration Programs. A number of private foundations have provided money to explore the philosophy and particularly the implementation of programs to check on the feasibility of participant driven control of supports. But by far the major financial support has come from the well-endowed Robert Wood Johnson Foundation which funds programs only in the general field of health care research. While I have been unable to locate all the programs they have funded in the area of testing the feasibility of self-determination initiatives, following are some major ones that have been critically important in moving self-determination from an idea to a policy:>In 1993 the Robert Wood Johnson Foundation funded a two-year program in California to the Corporation for Supportive Housing to develop a nationally replicable model of blending multiple government funding sources to provide housing and other services to homeless persons with disabilities. ("Integrating Financing and Services for Disabled Persons in California", 1997)

>In 1993 the Robert Wood Johnson Foundation (hereafter RWJF) awarded a three year demonstration grant to Monadnock Developmental Services of Keene, New Hampshire, to determine how services would operate if people with disabilities and their circle of friends could be truly in charge of their own services—that is if they achieved self-determination in its fullest sense including what is now called "independent funding". James Conroy and Anita Yuskauskas (1996) did a thorough study of the outcomes of this program. They found that overall the project held great promise based on their findings. Using the "Decision Control Inventory" that measures 26 elements of self-determination such as choice of home, foods, visiting friends, they found positive gains in 24 areas of which 11 were statistically significant and negative changes in only 4 areas of which 1 was statistically significant. Participants were interviewed before and during the program about their satisfaction with nine quality of life measures. All nine of these indicators showed positive gains of which 8 were statistically significant. The authors also found that participants had more choice in the composition of their planning teams, showed gains in productive behaviors, a reduction in "challenging behaviors", and, using other measures, found that their home environments had become more individualized during the course of the study. Of substantial significance to many policy makers was that for the 40 study participants, costs were reduced by 12.4% or $7,698 per person for a total savings of $307,920 using the most conservative method of calculating costs. These findings led RWJF to fund many related projects in succeeding years. Starting in 1996, the RWJF funded a "Self Determination for Persons with Development Disabilities" initiative to help 19 states implement changes in their service delivery systems to enable people with disabilities to directly control the services they receive and the resources provided to them for that purpose. Nearly $5 millions dollars was given to those states to implement demonstration programs over anywhere from one to three years to experiment with and to transition to new delivery systems. (Mosely, 1999; Conroy, 2001). Subsequently, ten states received technical assistance funding grants to enable local communities to

better implement system changes required under participant driven programs. (Simon-Rushinowitz, 1999). Starting in 1997, Ohio was one of the states to participate in the "self-determination initiative." In the first wave of this experiment, four of Ohio's 88 counties engaged in person centered planning for 160 persons with disabilities that resulted in 100 individualized budgets implemented. Each of the counties had to redesign its local delivery system, streamline policies and funding systems. Starting in 1999 an additional 21 counties in Ohio were to be included in the systems change initiative with the state committing $700,000 to expand the self-determination project. ("Next Steps: Ohio's Expansion of Self-Determination," 1999.)

>RWJF funded the "Independent Choices Initiative" that supported thirteen demonstration and research projects designed to expand knowledge about consumer directed programs for the aged. In 1996 RWJF along with the U.S. Department of Health and Human Services began the funding of a multi year-multi state research project to see how Medicaid recipients who were allowed to use their money with the assistance of service brokers and fiscal intermediaries, if needed, compared in outcomes to those who were to get services under the traditional medical model. Originally four states, New York, Florida, Arkansas and New Jersey were to participate in this experiment, but New York dropped out. The CCDE—"Cash and Counseling Demonstration/Evaluation is a large scale policy experiment designed to determine the advantages and disadvantages of a participant driven approach in using personal assistance services compared to the demand-side medical model. (Doty, 1998). The early experience in Arkansas showed 93% said they would recommend the program to others while 80% reported it helped their lives. (Brown and Foster, 2000). Such sizeable and costly social experiments probably would never have been tried without the vital support of the RWJF.

>The RWJF "Community Partnership for Older Adults" is one of the latest initiatives of this foundation to help communities develop and sustain comprehensive long-term care and supportive service systems for two target populations of older people—those "who are at increased risk of disability due to poverty, race or ethnicity, chronic illness or advanced age; and older adults with physical or cognitive impairments who require long term care and supportive services." ("Community Partnerships for Older Adults", 2. 2001). This new initiative was designed to support 30 grantee community partnerships over a period of eight years with a cost ranging up to $20 million.

>In 1997 RWJF gave SABE $74,393 to build "Self-Determination Among People with Disabilities" by supporting a number of activities including: a web site with links about disability organizations, money for two years for a hot line about closing institutions for those with mental retardation, development of a *Self-Advocacy Tool Kit,* and leadership training tool kits among other program supports. ("Building Self-Determination Capacity Among People with Disabilities", 2001)

>In 1999 the Oregon Health Sciences University received a RWJF grant for $29,989 to hold a "National Leadership Summit on Self-Determination, Consumer-Direction and Consumer Choice" for 120 leaders of disability related agencies both within and outside government to develop a national consensus agenda to promote the cause of self-determination. ("National Leadership Summit on Self-Determination, Consumer-Direction, and Consumer Choice Among People with Disabilities", 2001). This conference led to the release of a publication, *Foundation for Freedom* (Dowson and Salisbury, 2001) that showed an emerging international consensus on the principles and operation of "Self-Determination and Individualized Funding". The RWJF has truly been a consistent leader in promoting the exploration of self-determination in its many facets for persons with a variety of disabilities!

The Responsiveness and Initiatives of Government. The federal government and most state governments and many local levels of government have not only shown a responsiveness to try new ways of doing things under the self-determination label but often have taken the initiative to test new approaches to meeting the needs of those with disabilities. The Cash and Counseling experiment described earlier is an example of three states and the federal government cooperating in a complex program to be monitored and evaluated through contracts with the University of Maryland and Mathematica Policy Research Inc. Most of the funding for this experiment came from the Robert Wood Johnson Foundation but some from the federal government. To test whether cash with counseling would work and work better than traditional services for Medicaid recipients required several federal government departments waiving some of their usual requirements about accounting for Medicaid services, food stamps, and HUD subsidized housing.   And the states under the direction of the University of Maryland Center on Aging had to design and implement new outreach, counseling, fiscal intermediary and quality management components. (Mahoney, Simone, and Simon-Rusinowitz, 2000). Dozens of other research/demonstration projects have been funded by other federal agencies such as the "National Center For Family Support" which involves federal funding by the U.S. Administration on Developmental Disabilities to the Human Services Research Institute to provide technical and research assistance on family support to 38 states, three U.S. territories and the District of Columbia. ("National Center for Family Support," 2001). Another illustrative project by the federal government focuses on determining current knowledge about the best practices related to training people at the school level for self-advocacy and self-determination. The University of North Carolina at Charlotte received a grant from the Office of Special Education Projects located within the U.S. Department of Education to review and synthesize the knowledge base in these areas that teachers and other professionals should be aware of who serve children and youth with disabilities and their families. ("Welcome to the Self-Determination Synthesis Project Homepage. 2001).

The Supreme Court *Olmstead v. LC (1999)* decision has been very instrumental in moving the federal government to begin programs to deinstitutionalize persons in long term care facilities. In this decision, "The Court ruled that it is a violation of the Americans with Disabilities Act to discriminate against people with disabilities by providing services only in institutions when they could be served in a community-based setting, and certain conditions are met." ("The *Olmstead* Decision," 1, 2001). President Bush announced a "New Freedom Initiative" by executive order on June 19, 2001, to implement the *Olmstead* decision. In 2001 the federal HHS announced a $64 million grant to 37 states and one territory to develop programs for people with disabilities and long term illnesses that will provide support services in the least restrictive environments. By late 2001, 36 states had task forces or commissions to seek ways to integrate more persons with disabilities into their home communities by the means of individualized supports. (Fleischer and Zames, 2001; "The Olmstead Decision", 2001; "What's New", 2000.

The National Program Office for Self-Determination. This national office was funded by the Robert Wood Johnson foundation from 1998 through June of 2001. The office was located in Durham, New Hampshire where Charles Mosely was co-director. Their web site, with much of the information developed during its existence, is still available even though this office's funding ran out in June of 2001. This office promoted self-determination in all its dimensions by means of a national newsletter, *Common Sense,* (also available through its website at www.selfdetermination.org), a list of publications and videos available for purchase (now available from the

Institute on Disability), a calendar of events available for those working on or interested in self-determination, and a list of websites carrying information relative to self-determination including independent funding. The information made available through this National Office was instrumental in spreading information about both the principles and implementation of self-determination. New Hampshire has been a leader in deinstitutionalization and the self-determination movement. New Hampshire and five other states and the District of Columbia no longer have state institutions for those with developmental disabilities.

The Center for Self-Determination. While this "group" does have an office location at Metroplace Center in Wayne, Michigan, it describes itself as "a highly interactive working collaborative of individuals and organizations committed to the principles of self-determination. The purpose of the collaborative is to change the nature of the support and service system for individuals with disabilities, using the principles of self-determination to help all persons create the lives they want, connected to and with their communities." ("About CSD", 2001, 1). The Center sees itself as having two initiatives: one is supporting the grassroots movement for self-determination that is spreading across the country while the second is to provide technical assistance to individuals, groups, and organizations as they gear up to provide individualized funding, support brokerage, and fiscal intermediates in the drive to implement self-determination with individualized funding. It also sees itself as pushing efforts to "support the development and recognize the leadership of self-advocates". The work of the center is carried out by providing a newsletter, a web site containing publications and ways to connect with other organizations in the self-determination movement, technical consultation with individuals and governmental and non-governmental agencies, lists of "experts" in various areas, and "state pages" which show what some of the states are doing in the area of self-determination. Tom Nerney, the Director of The Center for Self-Determination, has written and consulted extensively on the principles of self-determination and the need for systems change if individualized funding is to be implemented. (Nerney, 1998; Mosely and Nerney, 1998)

TASH: Lobbying for and Reporting on Self-Determination Initiatives. TASH has been one of the major advocacy/self-advocacy groups pushing for deinstutionalization, inclusion in education and the community, and self-determination. It operates a rich website with a member chatroom, publishes a newsletter, *TASH Connections,* and publishes the *Journal of the Association for Persons with Severe Handicaps.* This international advocacy organization with its home office in Baltimore, has 32 chapters in the United States, and lists an array of publications that persons can purchase as well as connections to many other websites with information about disabilities. It has over 8,000 individual, chapter and organizational members. Its 25 operating committees develop position documents on persons with severe disabilities and take stands on national issues impacting all people with disabilities. In 2001, for example, as in several preceding years, it has lobbied for the passage of MiCASSA—the Medicaid Community Attendant Services and Support Act. This act would allow people who now receive Medicaid funding to pay for their care in nursing homes and Intermediate Care Facilities for the Mentally Retarded to instead use this funding to live in the community in their own homes by using that funding instead for personal attendant services and the like. ("America's People with Disabilities-- . . .", 1998)

In 2000 it sponsored the "First International Conference on Self-Determination and Individualized Funding" attended by over 1200 people from 21 countries. It published information from this conference about its concluding 35 principles under the title, "The Seattle 2000 Declaration on Self-Determination and Individualized Funding" on its web site at *www.tash.org*. This well-organized group has argued that the oppression of persons with disabilities is due to poverty, public attitudes and systems of publicly and privately funded support that deny control to those it services. It argues that "Without accountability to those who require their assistance, these systems decide how, where and with whom people shall live and spend their days." ("Seattle 2000 Declaration", 2000, 4). Like many self-advocacy organizations in the disability movement, it calls for many reforms at the federal, state and local level that will implement self-determination/independent funding for persons with disabilities. The principles of the Seattle 2000 Declaration are firmly committed to the principles of self-determination and individualized funding as the following quotes powerfully suggest: ("Seattle 2000 Declaration", 2000, 5,6)

10. People with disabilities and their families must be present and central at all planning and decision-making tables in policy development.

11. Citizens with disabilities and their supporting networks and organizations must be in charge of developing and promoting public policy which is related to the provision of supports.

17. Individualized funding arrangements must allow for flexible practice within consistent guiding principles.

21. Individual funding systems must include arrangements to provide assistance, where required, in the management of funding and supports, and not limit eligibility on the basis of judgments of 'capacity'.

30. Service providers and agencies must be encouraged to endorse and apply the principles of self-determination and individualized funding; and, in an expanded organizational role, to deliver supports that minimize dependency and strengthen partnerships with the larger community to address barriers to freedom and opportunity.

Brian Salisbury and Steve Dawson from Canada and Great Britain respectively have been very active in the international independent funding movement. They write and consult about both the principles and operational details of independent funding. They operate Emprise International Training and Consultancy for consulting purposes and they support their own website at "http://members.home.net/tsalisbury" that had about six dozen articles in 2001 about individualized funding that can be downloaded as well as an extensive list of web sites containing related material. This web site says it is "a site dedicated to providing comprehensive information about the development of ways that people with disabilities can gain control over the funds to pay for needed community services & supports—a crucial step towards self-determination and citizenship." Their work also illustrates the importance of the internet in helping to keep the self-determination alive. ("Welcome to the Home of Individualized Funding Information Resources", 2001, 1).

The Center on Self-Determination and the Alliance for Self-Determination. The Center on Self-Determination is a program of the Oregon Institute on Disability and Development that is located at the Oregon Health Science University. This Center was staffed by 17 people in 2001 with a mission "to identify, develop, validate and communicate policies and practices that promote the self-determination of people with and without disabilities." It was the lead agency to apply for and get a Robert Wood Foundation Grant of $29,989 for a 120 person "summit conference" entitled "National Leadership Summit on Self-Determination, Consumer-Direction, and Consumer Control Among People with Disabilities" in 1999. Some 15 of the participating agencies contributed another $77,500 to focus on emerging policy, training, and research issues in the self-determination movement.

Twenty-one brief commissioned papers were presented to focus the agenda of this meeting of cross-disability leaders. ("Grant Results Brief: National Leadership Summit on Self-Determination, Consumer-Direction and Consumer Control Among People with Disabilities," 2001; "The Center on Self-Determination", 2001). The Alliance for Self-Determination states that its mission "is to promote the sharing, development, and application of knowledge about self-determination to policies and practices". ("Mission and Key Principles, 1997, 1). The Alliance is a national partnership of individuals and organizations who "have demonstrated the capacity to contribute to research, dissemination and training in self determination. . ." ("Alliance for Self-Determination", 1997, 1).

Other Groups Involved In Promoting Self-Determination. There are too many groups involved in promoting self-determination including independent funding to name them all. However, several should not be left out of this effort. One of these is SABE—Self-Advocates Becoming Empowered. The basis for this organization had its roots in Sweden in 1968 and then in Oregon in 1974. At that Oregon meeting one of the seeds for organizing a self-advocacy movement began in the United States when one person with mental retardation said at a meeting, "I am tired of being called retarded—we are people first". (Quoted in Ward, 1999). The "People First" name struck a powerful chord and became organized nationally as SABE in 1991. SABE has advocated for such things as closing all institutions, including persons with cognitive disabilities in all decisions impacting on them, and improving self-advocacy skills. In 2000 the Administration on Developmental Disabilities provided a grant to SABE under the rubric, "Project Leadership" to help self-advocates and family members learn about things going on in Washington and have a say in those things. (Meadours, 2001). On Nov 1, 1997, delegates to SABE's national meeting in Nashville adopted a "Declaration of Self-Determination". In part this declaration read, "We believe self advocates are the professional, as us first, and we should be the decision makers and planners in all our daily living activities such as working, voting, conferences, leadership development, and taking financial control of our service and personal dollars." (Ward, 1999, 2)

Another organization, the Consortium for Citizens with Disabilities, with over 100 member organizations has provided an important coordination and information resource service for not only disability advocacy groups but for persons with disabilities, their families and professionals working in the field. This group has also been developing policy statements and lobbying for the rights of persons with disabilities including increased funding for personal care supports, improved monitoring of deinstitutionalization after the Olmstead decision, and greater fiscal self-determination for persons using personal support services. ("Report of CCD: Long Term Services and Supports Task Force", 2000). Freedom Clearing House, a web site project of Free Hand Press and a nationwide network of dedicated advocates, has been an important source of information for those working in the disability rights movement. ("What is Freedom Clearing House", 2001). Information over the web has replaced much mailed information. Another source of such information for persons with disabilities who live in the community or who move from institutions to the community is the Home and Community-Based Services Resource Network that provides a wide range of information on federal and state policies and services that impact on those working for community inclusion. ("Welcome to the Home and Community Based Services Resource Network", 2001). The Roeher Institute located at York University in Ontario is Canada's institute for education, information and the study of public policy impacting people with intellectual and other disabilities. It has promulgated many studies and reports that report on the processes and outcomes of deinstitutionalization and self-determination. This organization is significant because of the growing globalization of ideas that are shared as the disability movement is internationalized. (Crawford, 1996; The Roeher Institute, 1997).

ADAPT Supports Rally and March to Move from Institutionalization to Self-Determination. While much of work in developing independent funding programs involves demonstration programs with careful research to see if they work well, part of the motivation in social movements comes from capturing the public imagination to put some pressure on federal and state governments to make the policy moves necessary to implement self-determination. ADAPT put out a call for supporters to join that organization along with thirteen other disability rights group for a rally and march in Washington the week June 17-22, 2000. The rally was aimed at speeding up the slow process of deinstitutionalizing people from human warehouses and of changing the failed system of long-term supports for community living. At the rally speakers were heard who denounced policies that kept them in institutions. One of the speakers was a 60 year woman from Bethlehem, Pa, who told the rally, "I spent 6 years in 2 nursing homes against my will and while there I was overly drugged, left in a pool for over 2 hours, hit, and put to bed without dinner—all on more than one occasion" ("Rally and March Demand End to Forced Institutionalization", 2000. 2). The week long rally also aimed at rallying support for MiCASSA, the Medicaid Community Attendant Services and Support Act, that would allow individuals to choose to live and receive services in their own homes rather than in nursing homes and other institutions which Medicaid supports. The rally speakers argued that Medicaid follows a medical model of institutionalizing people in order to get services they need rather than letting them stay in their homes and use even less money than institutional services cost. They argue that three quarters of Medicaid dollars goes for institutional care rather than home and community based services. ("Rally and Action Events", 2000, 1-2). Such rallies help put a media face into the self-determination movement.

SOCIAL CHANGE AND THE FUTURE OF THE SELF-DETERMINATION MOVEMENT.

Uncertainty exists on how fast and in what directions the reform movement we are calling the wave of self-determination will move. Many authors (Agosta, 1997; Simon-Rusinowitz, 1999; Doty, 2000; Nerney, 2001b; Fox-Grage, et al, 2001; Bradley, 2001) see a growing crisis between the demand for and the supply of a variety of services for those with disabilities. Table 7.2 shows the two sides of the supply/demand equation but does not show the immense changes that would be needed to change from our provider driven/supply side model to a participant/demand driven model that the self-determination philosophy supports. The key components in this model are three—the "**need**" or demand for more services for those with disabilities is going to increase fast, the **supply** of such services is in short supply and may grow worse because of the low wages paid to many persons in the human services—particularly those who provide the direct services to those with disabilities, and the **dollar resources** for these services appear to be flat in the future unless funding allocations are greatly increased and/or participant driven funding provides more and/or less costly services for the dollar resources available. As the nation moves from 13% of the population that is over to 65 to 20% with those over 85 growing fastest and having the most disabilities services for them will expand substantially if there needs are to be met. While many services for the aged disabled and physically and cognitively disabled are given by family members now, many of them will need new and often paid supports in the future. The low status, hours of work and low pay of many direct service providers makes it difficult to attract and keep them. Many individuals and families want home and community based supports rather than institutional residential care

TABLE 7.2   CHANGES IN THE DEMAND FOR AND SUPPLY OF HUMAN SERVICES FOR THOSE WITH DISABILITIES

CHANGES IN DEMAND FOR SERVICES	CHANGES IN SUPPLY OF SERVICES
Rapid increase in older population, especially those over 85 who have the most disabling conditions.	Shortage and high turnover of many persons in low wage direct care services.
Increased number of persons defined as having disabilities.	Smaller families and a growing percent of two wage-earner families less able to provide home care to their parents whose disabilities require services beyond what they can provide.
Phasing out of some institutions which translates into a demand for more community care.	A relatively flat resource base, especially if managed care expands into chronic care services.
Growth in advocacy/self advocacy groups who want greater self-determination and individualized funding.	A system hard to change because it is a very complex service system oriented to the medical model of providers determining needs based on individual deficits rather than the responsible dreams of participants.
Many states are experiencing growing waiting lists of persons needing chronic care services.	There will likely be competition for resources among different providers and types of providers and among persons with different types of disabilities.

programs. This is seen in the changing pattern of expenditures under Medicaid. In 1988, under 3% of all expenditures for chronic care under Medicaid went for Home and Community Based Services. But by 1999 this was up to 16.5% of all chronic care expenditures and the pattern of annual increase in the last five years or personal care services ranged from 12.2% to 44.6%. (Fox-Grage, 2001). What does the future hold for participant driven supports and funding? I believe that there will be a growing transition to this type of system but it will create tensions among state agencies, between federal and state systems, among providers, and between providers, families and those with disabilities. I believe there will be substantial experimentation on how to make transitions to new systems of individualized planning, participant driven supports and budgets, the use of support brokers or care managers and fiscal intermediaries. While different state/federal agencies—DD/MR, Independent Living Centers, Mental Health, Aging, have different experiences with such programs, a growing cross-fertilization of philosophies and implementation experiences will be shared and evaluated. Different states may devise equally effective but quite different approaches. Some of the biggest changes will be to transition current agency providers into providing support brokerage **or** direct care services **or** fiscal intermediary services but keep them from having conflicts of interests by not allowing two or more of these services to be provided by the same agency. There will substantial resistance by some federal, state and provider agencies to the demands of the self-determination movement, yet a humanitarian concern for devising the best administrative structures will need to be a universal constant to make transitioning to new systems possible. What needs to be the central focus here is devising a system driven by persons with disabilities and their close allies who are fiscally responsible to the larger community. Much of the earlier research shows that in most cases money can be saved, substantial gains made in the quality of life of persons with disabilities and their circle of supporters, and significant steps toward freedom, equality, dignity and responsibility made.

SUMMARY

The self-determination reform movement is the current wave of change both impacting upon and substantially driven by persons with disabilities and their supporters. The self-determination movement has been the social movement to allow those with disabilities to have the same choices as other citizens—choices about where and how to live, work, recreate, worship, and get health care, educational and other services. This movement for persons with disabilities to be in charge of their lives first emerged in the late 1970s for persons primarily with physical disabilities who pushed for the control of services that Centers for Independent Living were advocating for. It spread to those with cognitive disabilities in the late 1980s and the momentum for system change was expanded in the 1990s with the support of foundations like the Robert Wood Johnson Foundation and the vigorous promotion by many advocacy/self-advocacy agencies. Starting in about the mid 1990s, the aging community began to see the implicit values of self-determination for those with disabling conditions in the aging population.

The move toward self-determination has involved two fundamental changes in the use of resources. First, resources for planning were increasingly focused around the needs and interests of persons with disabilities as they and their allies saw them rather than through the eyes of professional providers. Second, decisions regarding resources for the purchase of supports were increasingly moved to the persons who used them rather than under the control of agencies providing those services. This movement from a supply side control approach to a demand side control approach is immense as it involves complex changes that ripple back and forth among multiple levels of government, providers, persons with disabilities and their allies and advocates. Such major system transformations have been gaining momentum for about a decade and will likely continue as new methods and combinations of service planning, service brokering and fiscal intermediation are experimented with by the states, federal government, providers, and those with disabilities. Tensions among the parties listed above may continue as self-interest and bureaucratic rigidity compete with systems to expand values fundamental to the self-determination movement (freedom, authority, support, responsibility, confirmation). The wave of self-determination is not over. It is a wave that will roll on and will enter the shorelines of millions of organizations and individuals and change them in ways that cannot be fully imagined yet.

REFERENCES

"A National Personal Assistance Demonstration—Cash and Counseling" 1999, 1-7. Retrieved from http://www.inform umd.edu/EdRes/Colleges/HLHP/AGING/CCDemo/NCIL .memo.html on 11-26-2001.

"About CSD", 2001, 1-3. Retrieved from "http://www.self-determination.com/about/ aboutCSD.htm" on 8-10-2001.

"About NCIL" 2001. Retrieved from http://www.nicl.org/ aboutncil.htm, pp. 1-4 on10-25-2001.

"About Self-Determination: The Four Principles" 1998. Retrieved from http://www.self-determination.org/inform...248/ information_show.htm-doc_id=1507.htm on 7-20-2001.

"About The Arc," 2001 pp. 1-2. Retrieved from http://www.thearc.org on 10-12-2001.

"About Us", (2001). Retrieved August 10, 2001 from http://www.self-determination. com/index-include.cfm?ID=39.

Agosta, J. 1997. "Developmental Disability Services at the Century's End: Facing the Challenges Ahead", 15 pages. Retrieved from "http://www.mcare.net/briefs/ pbrief2.html" on 11-15-2001.

Albrecht, Gary L. 1992. *The Disability Business: Rehabilitation in America.* Newbury Park: Sage Publications.

Albrecht, G. L., et al. 2001. *Handbook of Disability Studies.* Thousand Oaks: Sage Publications, 663-692.

Altman, B. 2001 "Disability Definitions, Models, Classification Schemes, and Applications," in Albrecht, G.L. et al. *Handbook of Disability Studies.* Thousand Oaks: Sage Publications, 97-122.

"Alliance for Self-Determination" 1997, 1-2. Retrieved from http://cdrc.ohsu.edu/selfdetermination/alliane.html on 7-26-2001.

American Association On Mental Retardation. 1992. *Mental Retardation.* (9th Ed.) Washington, D.C.: AAMR.

"Americans with Disabilities" 1994. Bureau of the Census: Statistical Brief. Retrieved from http://www.sipp.census. gov/sipp/sipphome,htm on 11-9-2001.

"Americans with Disabilities: Table 2." 1997. Retrieved from http://www.census.gov/hhes/www/disable/sipp/disable97/ds97t2.ht ml on 9-17-2001.

"Americans with Disabilities: Table 5" 1997. Retrieved from
    http://www.census.gov/hhes/www/disable/sipp/disable97/ds97t5.ht
    ml_on 9-17-2001.
Anderson, M.L., and Taylor, H.F. 2000. *Sociology.* Belmont, Ca.
    Wadsworth.
Braddock, D.L. & Parish. S.L. 2001. "An Institutional History of
    Disability", in Albrecht, et al (Eds.) *Handbook of Disability
    Studies.* Thousand Oaks: Sage Publications, 11-68.
Barnartt, S. Schriner, K., Scotch, S. 2001. "Advocacy and Political
    Action" in Albrecht, G. et.al. *Handbook of Disability Studies.*
    Thousand Oaks: Sage Publications, 430-459.
Barnes, C. 1992. *Disabling Imagery and the Media: An Exploration of
    Media Representation of Disabled People.* Belper: British Council
    of Organizations of Disabled People.
Barnes, C & Mercer, G. 2001 "Disability Culture: Assimilation or
    Inclusion?" in Albrecht, G.L. et al. *Handbook of Disability
    Studies.* Thousand Oaks: Sage Publications, 515-534.
Baroff, G.S. 1974. *Mental Retardation: Nature, Causes, Management.*
    Washington, D.C. Hemisphere Publishing Corp.
Basnett. I. 2001. "Health Care Professionals and Their Attitudes
    toward Decisions Affecting Disabled People." In Albrecht, et al
    (Eds.). *Handbook of Disability Studies.* Thousand Oaks: Sage
    Publications, 450-467.
Baumeister, A.A. 1977. "The American Residential Institution: Its
    History and Character." In A.A. Baumeister & E. Butterfield
    (Eds.). *Residential Facilities for the Mentally Retarded.* Chicago:
    Aldine Publishing Co.
"Before You Label People, Look At Their Contents", 2001. Retrieved
    from http://www.mentalhealth.org/publications/allpubs/SMA96-
    3118/Stigmanew.htm
    on 10-2-2001.
Bercovici. S.M. 1983 *Barriers to Normalization: The Restrictive
    Management of Retarded Persons.* Baltimore: University Park
    Press.
Blasiotti, E.L., Westbrook, J.D., and Kobayashi, I. 2001. "Disability
    Studies and Electronic Networking." In Albrecht, G.L. et al.
    Handbook of Disability Studies. Thousand Oaks: Sage
    Publications, 327-347.
Braddock, D, 1986. *Deinstitutionalization in the Eighties: Trends in
    Georgia, the South and the United States.* Chicago: University of
    Illinois: Institute for the Study of Developmental Disabilities;
    Public Policy Monograph #25.

Braddock, D. et.al. 1990. *The State of the States in Developmental Disabilities.* Baltimore: Paul H. Brookes Publishing Co.

Braddock, D. et.al. 2000. *The State of the States in Developmental Disabilities: 2000 Study Summary.* Chicago. Dept. of Disability and Human Development, University of Chicago.

Brown, R. and Foster, L. 2000. "Cash and Counseling: Early Experiences in Arkansas." Retrieved from "http://www. mathematica-mpr.com/PDFs/cashcounsibrak.pdf" on 11-29-01.

"Building Self-Determination Capacity Among People with Disabilities", 2001. Retrieved from "http://www.rwjf.org/app/health/030917s.htm" on 11-5-2001.

"Census Brief" 1997. pp. 1-2. Retrieved from http://www.census.gov/prod/3/97pubs/cenbr975.pdf on 9-17-2001.

"Census 2000 Supplementary Survey Summary Tables". 2001. 1-4. Retrieved from http://factfinder.census.gov/servlet/QTT ...id= 01000US&qr_name=ACS_C2SS_EST_G00_QT02 on 9-18-2001.

Chamberlin, J., & Rogers, J.A. 1990. "Planning a community-based mental health system: Perspective of service recipients." *American Psychologist* 45, 1241-1244.

Chamberlin, J. 1990. "The ex-patients' movement: Where we've been and where we're going." *Journal of Mind and Behavior,* 11-323-336.

Charlton, J.I. 1998. *Nothing About Us Without Us.* Berkeley: Univ. of Calif. Press.

Cockerham, William C. 1996. *Sociology of Mental Disorder.* 4th Ed. Upper Saddle, Prentice Hall.

Cohen, E and Nerney, T. 2001. "The Right to Flourish: Self-Determination and People Who are Elderly." pp. 1-4. Retrieved from http://www.self-determination.com/publications/aging.html on 11-15-2001.

"Community-Based Mental Health Services Improve Lives and Save Dollars", 2001, Retrieved from http://www.nmha.org/federal/appropriations/factsheet.cfm on 10-3-2001.

"Community Partnerships for Older Adults." 2001. Retrieved from http://www.cpfoa.must.ums.main.edu/cfp.htm on 12-10-2001.

Conley, R.W. 1965. *The Economics of Vocational Rehabilitation.* Baltimore: Johns Hopkins Press.

Conroy, J., & Yuskauskas, A. 1996 "Independent Evaluation of the Monadnock Self Determination Project". Unpublished manuscript. 33 p.

Conroy J. 2001. Personal communication to the author. 12-4-2001.

"Consumer-Direction", 2001, 1-3. Retrieved from http://www. freedom clearinghouse.org/know/consumerdir.htm" on 11-26-2001.

"Continental Charged With Discrimination Against Disabled", 2001. Retrieved from http://www.airwise.com/stories/99/08/ 394966417.html on 9/25/2001.

Crawford, Cameron. 1996. *From Institutions to Community: Services and Fiscal Commitments to People with an Intellectual Disability in Canada.* North York: The Roerher Institute.

"Current Projects", 2001. Retrieved from "http://cdrd.ohsu.edu/ selfdetermination/alliance.html" on 7-26-2001.

Davis. L.J. 2001. "Identity Politics, Disability, and Culture," in Braddock, et al (Eds.), Thousand Oaks: Sage Publications.

"Definition of disability for disabled worker's benefits" 2001. Retrieved from http://www.ssa.gov/OP_Home/ handbook/handbook .05/handbook-0507.html on 9-18-2001.

DeJong, G. 1979. "Independent Living: From Social Movement to Analytic Paradigm", Archives *of Physical Medicine and Rehabilitation.* Vol. 60, October, 435-446.

DeJong, .G. 1984. "Independent Living: From Social Movement to Analytic Paradigm" in Marinelli, R. and Dell Orto, A. (Eds.) *The Psychological and Social Impact of Physical Disability.* New York: Springer Publishing Co. pp. 39-63.

"Demographics", 1997, 1-6. Retrieved from http://dsc.ucsf.edu/ UCSF/pic.taf?_UserRe...4AC2BF4240D3&_function=search&url =BOO1X3 on 9-7-2001.

"Developmental Disability" 2001. Title 1-- Programs for Individuals with Developmental Disabilities. Section 102—Definitions. Retrieved from http://www.acf.dhhs.gov/programs/add/DDA,htm on 10-9-2001.

"Did You Know?" 2001. Retrieved from http://www.nmha.org/infoctr/ didyou.cfm on 10-3-2001.

DiNitto, Diana, 2000. *Social Welfare.* (5th Ed). Boston: Allyn and Bacon.

"Disabled Most Likely to be Victims of Serious Crime, 2001, pp. 1-3. Retrieved from http://www/projectcensored.org/c2001 stories/20.html on 9/25/2001.

"Disabilities Affect One-Fifth of All Americans" Census Brief. Retrieved from: http://www.census.gov/prod/3/97pubs.cenbr975.sdf on 9-17-2001.

"Disability". Census Bureau Data on Disability. Retrieved from
    http://www.census.gov/hhes/www/disable/intro.html on 9-17-2001
Donnelly, Joseph W.; Eburne, Norm; Kittleson, Mark, 2001. *Mental
    Health Dimensions of Self-Esteem and Emotional Well-Being*.
    Boston: Allyn & Bacon.
Doty, P.J., 1998. "The Cash Counseling Demonstration: An
    Experiment in Consumer-Directed Personal Assistant Services" pp
    1-7. Retrieved from http://www.inform.umd. edu/EdRes/
    Colleges...AGING/CCDemo /Publications/dotyRehab.html on 11-
    29-2001.
Dowson. S., and Salisbury, B. 2001. *Foundation for Freedom:
    International Perspectives on Self-Determination and
    Individualized Funding*. Baltimore: TASH.
Drake, R.F. 2001 "Welfare States and Disabled People" in Albrect,
    G.L., Seelman, K.D., Bury, M, (Eds) *Handbook of Disability
    Studies*. Thousand Oaks, Ca. Sage Publications, 412-429.
Dybwad, R.F. 1990. *Perspectives on a Parent Movement: The Revolt
    of Parents of Children with Intellectual Limitations*. Boston:
    Brookline Books.
Eaton, William A. 1974. "Medical hospitalization as a reinforcement
    process." *American Sociological Review*. 39:252-60.
"Educational Level of People with Disabilities," 2000. Retrieved from
    http://www.nod.org/cont/discont item vi...1&StartRow-
    1&timeStamp on 10-31-2001
"Employment Rates of People with Disabilities", 2000 Retrieved from
    http://www.nod.org/cont/dspcont item vi...
    1&StartRow=1&timeStamp on 10-30-2001.
Fine, M. & Asch, A. 1988. *Women with Disabilities: Essays in
    Psychology, Culture and Politics*. Philadelphia: Temple
    University Press.
"Fiscal Intermediary", 2001. pp. 1-4. Retrieved from "http://www.dds.
    cahwnet.gov/DSPP/main/SDPilotHome.cfm" on 9-24-2001.
Fleischer, Doris. and Zames, Frieda. 2001. *The Disability Rights
    Movement: From Charity to Confrontation*. Philadelphia: Temple
    University Press.
Fox-Grage, W., Falkemer, D., Burwell, B., and Horahan, K., 2001.
    "Community-Based Long-Term Care", 12 p. National Conference
    of State Legislatures: Forum for State Health Policy Leadership.
French, S., and Swain, J. 2001. "The Relationship between Disabled
    People and Health and Welfare Professionals" in Albrecht et al
    (Eds.) *Handbook of Disability Studies*. Thousand Oaks: Sage. pp
    734-753.

Frese, F.J. 1998. "Advocacy, recovery and the challenges of consumerism for schizophrenia." *Psychiatric Clinics of North America*, 21: 233-249.

Funk, Robert. 1984. *Challenges of Emerging Leadership: Community-Based Independent Living Programs and the Disability Rights Movement.* Washington: Institute for Educational Leadership.

Garland, R. 1995. *The Eye of the Beholder: Deformity and Disability in the Graeco-Roman World.* London: Duckworth.

Goffman, E. 1961. *Asylums..* Garden City, N.Y.: Doubleday Anchor Book.

Goldenson, R. M.(Ed.) 1978. Disability and Rehabilitation Handbook. New York: McGraw-Hill.

Gooding, Caroline. 1991. *Disabling Laws, Enabling Acts.* Boulder: Pluto Press.

Greider, L. 2001. "Care Managers Emerge as New Force in Helping". *AARP Bulletin.* Dec, 2001, 9,12-13.

Gritzer, G. & Arluke, A. 1985. *The Making of Rehabilitation.* Berkeley: University of California Press.

Grob, Gerald. 1973. *Mental Institutions in America.* New York: Free Press.

Hahn, Harlan, 1985. "Toward a Politics of Disability Definitions, Disciplines and Policies." *Social Science Journal* 22 (October): 87-105.

Hall. L. 1996. "How NAMI won parity." *NAMI* Advocate. 18: 1,4.

Halpern, A, Close, D, Nelson, D. 1986. *On My Own: The Impact of Semi-Independent Living Programs for Adults with Mental Retardation.* Baltimore: Paul H. Brookes Publishing.

Halpern, Joseph, Et al., 1980. *The Myths of Deinstitutionalization: Policies for the Mentally Disabled.* Boulder: Westview Press

Hanson, S., and Temkin, T., 1999. "Collaboration Between Publicly-Funded Rehabilitation Programs and Community-Based Independent Living Centers," *Issue Brief.* Vol. 1, Issue 1, Mar., 1999, 1-4.

Hash, M. 1999. "Testimony of Michael Hash, Deputy Director, Health Care Financing Administration before the Senate Finance Committee on Patient Treatment in Mental Hospitals," retrieved from http://www.hcfa/gov/testimony/1999/991026htm on 9-26-2001.

Henslin, J. 1999. *Sociology: A Down to Earth Approach.*(4th Ed.) Boston: Allyn and Bacon.

Higgins, P. C. 1985. *The Rehabilitation Detectives.* Beverly Hills: Sage Publications.

Higgins, Paul C. 1992. *Making Disability: Exploring the Social Transformation of Human Variation.* Springfield: Charles C. Thomas Publisher.

Horner, R., Stoner, S. Ferguson. D. 1988. *An Activity-Based Analysis of Deinstitutionalization: The Effects of Community Re-Entry in the Lives of Residents Leaving Oregon's Fairview Training Center.* Salem, OR.: Developmental Disabilities Program Office, Mental Health Division, Department of Human Resources.

"How Does DREDF Carry Out its Mission?" pp. 2 (2001) Retrieved, August 3, 2001, from http://www.dredf.org/what.html

"How many Americans use wheelchairs and other assistive devices or technologies?" 2001. Retrieved from http://www.dsc.ucsf.edu/ UCSF/ pub.taf?_UserReference=126B5AOCCFEE8735BF913654 &_function=other&_array=OTH6&gr... on 11/6/2001.

"'I'm Not a Case and I Don't Want to be Managed!'", 1998 Retrieved from http://www.selfdetermination.org/newslet...249 newsletter_show.htm-doc_id=32214.htm on 7-23-2001.

"Individual Budgets" 2001. Pp. 1-6. Retrieved from "http://www.dds. cahwnet.gov/SDPP/main/SDPilotHome.cfm" on 9-24-2001.

"Integrating Financing and Services for Disabled Persons in California", 1997, 1-4. Retrieved from "http://www.rwjf.org.80/health/021883s.htm" on 7-26-2001.

"International Classification of Functioning, Disability and Health", 2001. 1-20. Retrieved from http://www.who.int/whosis/icidh.index.html on 8-12-2001.

Jans, L, and Stoddard, S. 1999. *Chartbook on Women and Disability In the United States.* Berkeley: *InfoUse.*

Kane R.A., Kane, R.L. & Ladd, R.C. 1998. *The Heart of Long-Term Care.* New York: Oxford University Press.

Kelley, L.C., 1990. *Federal Indian Policy.* New York: Chelsea House Publishers.

Kennedy. J, Laplante. M.P. and Kaye, H.S. 1997. "Need for Assistance in the Activities of Daily Living" *Disability Statistics Abstract.* No. 18, pp. 1-4.

Kent, Deborah. 1996. *The Disability Rights Movement.* New York: Children's Press.

Kugel & A. Shearer (Eds). *Changing Patterns in Residential Services for the Mentally Retarded.* Washington: President's Committee on Mental Retardation, 35-82.

Lagoyda, R., Nadash, P., Rosenberg, L., Yatso, T, 1999. "Survey of
   State Administrators: Consumer-Directed Home and Community-
   Based Services". National Institute on Consumer-Directed Long-
   Term Services. Retrieved from "http://www.freedomclearinghouse
   .org/documents/finalreport96.htm" on 11-27-2001.

Lakin, K.C. et.al. 1982. "One Hundred Years of Data on Populations
   of Public Residential Facilities for Mentally Retarded People."
   American Journal of Mental Deficiency. 87:1; 1-8.

Larana, Enrique, Johnston, Han, and Joseph R. Gusfield (Eds). 1994.
   New Social Movements: From Ideology to Identity. Philadelphia:
   Temple University Press.

LaPlante, M.P. Rice, D.P., Wenger, B.L. 1995 "Medical Care Use,
   Health Insurance and Disability in the United States. Disability
   Statistics Abstract. No. 8. pp. 1-4.

Leal, Linda. 1999. A Family-Centered Approach to People With
   Mental Retardation. Washington: American Association on
   Mental Retardation.

Litvak, S and Enders, A. 2001. "The Interface between Individuals
   and Environments", in Albrech et al (Eds), Handbook of Disability
   Studies. Thousand Oaks: Sage. pp. 711-733.

Long, L. & Van Tosh, L. 1988. Program descriptions of consumer-run
   programs for homeless people with mental illness. Rockville, MD:
   National Institute of Mental Health.

MacAndrew, C and Edgerton, R. 1964. "The Everyday Life of the
   'Institutionalized' Idiots". Human Organization. 23:312-318.

Mahoney, K.J., Simone, K., and Simon-Rusinowitz, L. "Early Lessons
   from the Cash and Counseling Demonstration and Evaluation,"
   Generations. Vol. XXIV, No. III, Fall, 2001, 41-46.

Marks, Deborah. 1999. Disability: Controversial Debates and
   Psychosocial Perspectives. London: Routledge.

Max. W, Rice, D.P., Trupin, L. 1996. "Medical Expenditures for
   People with Disabilities." Disability Statistics Abstract. No. 12.
   pp. 1-4.

McNeil, J. M., 2001a "Disability" Retrieved from
   http://www.census.gov/ population/www/pop-profile/disabil.html
   on 8-21-2001.

McNeil, J. M. 2001b. "Employment, Earnings, and Disability",
   Retrieved from
   http://www.census.gov/hhes/www/disable/emperndis.pdf on 9-17-
   2001.

McNeil. J.M. 2001c. "Disability", 1-4. Retrieved from http://www census.gov/population/www/pop-profile/disabil.htm on 8-21-2001.

Meadours, J., 2000. "Project Leadership," pp. 1-6. Retrieved from "http://www.sabeuse.org/sabenews/spring.2000.html" on 7-30-2001.

"Mission and Key Principles", 1997, 1. Retrieved from "http://cdrd. ohsu.edu/selfdetermination/mission.html" on 7-26-2001.

Moseley, C., 1999. "Making Self-Determination Work" Retrieved from "http://www.self-determination.org" on 8-4-2001.

"Moving to a System of Support". 1994. pp. 1-7. Retrieved from http://www.self-determination.org/newle...1249/ newsletter_show. htm-doc_id=1698.htm on 7-23-2001.

NAMI, 2001. "The Criminalization of People with Mental Illness" pp. 1-5. Retrieved from http://www.nami.org/update/unitedcriminal.html on 10-1-2001.

"National Health Interview Survey on Disability", 1995. Retrieved from http://www.icpsr.umich.edu:8080/ABSTRACTS /02578.xml?format:ICPSR on 9-17-2001.

National Institute of Mental Health. 1967. *Patients in Public Institutions for the Mentally Retarded,* Chevy Chase, MD: U.S. NIMH.

National Union Research. "The Hard Truth About Individualized Funding" 1998, 1-14. Retrieved from "http://www.members.hom.net/tsalisbury" on 10-27-2001.

"NCIL's Advocacy Priorities", 2001. Retrieved from http://www.ncil.org/advocacy.htm on 10-25-2001, pp. 1-3.

Nerney, T. 1998. "The Poverty of Human Services: An Introduction" in Nerney, T and Shumway, D.(Eds). *The Importance of Income.* Concord Center: The Center for Self-Determination, pp. 1-14.

Nerney, T. 2001b. "Filthy Lucre: Creating Better Value in Long Term Supports", 39 p. Unpublished manuscript. Emailed to me by the author on 11-30-2001.

Neufeld, G.R. 1979. "The Advocacy Role and Functions of Developmental Disabilities Councils." In R. Wiegerink and J.S. Petosi (Eds.) *Developmental Disabilities: The DD Movement.* Baltimore: Paul H. Brookes, 45-60.

"Next Steps: Ohio's Expansion of Self-Determination," 1999. 1-2. Retrieved from "http://www.self-determination.org/newsle" ...249/newsletter_show.htm-doc_id=20729.htm on 11-26-2001.

Noble, J.H., Honberg, R.S., Hall, L.L., and Flynn, L.M. 1997. "A Legacy of Failure: The Inability Of The Federal-State Vocational Rehabilitation System to Serve People With Severe Mental Illness." Retrieved from http://www.nami.org/update/legacy.htm on 10-20-2001.

Oberschall. A. 1993. *Social Movements: Ideologies, Interests and Identities.* New Brunswick: Transaction Publishers.

"Our goals", 2001 pp. 1-2. Retrieved from http://www.sabeusa.org/ on 7-23-2001.

Pa. Department of Welfare. 1991. *Everyday Lives.* Harrisburg: Office of Mental Retardation.

Pa. Office of Mental Retardation, 1993. *Finding a Way Toward Everyday Lives.* Harrisburg: Office of Mental Retardation.

Pelka, Fred. 1997. *The ABC-CLIO Companion to The Disability Rights Movement.* Santa Barbara: ABC-CLIO.

"People First of Oregon", p. 1. (2001). Retrieved August 1, 2001from http://www.open.org/~people1/whatis.htm.

Pope, Andrew M. and Tarlov, Alvin R. (Eds.), 1991. *Disability in America: Toward A National Agenda for Prevention.* Washington: National Academy Press.

Purdy, R. 1996. "The Campaign to End Discrimination in light of partial parity." *NAMI Advocate.* 18: 8-9"Rally and Action Events", 2000, 1-2. Retrieved from "http://www.libertyresources.org/mc/ca-49.html" on 11-26-2001.

"Rally and March Demand End to Forced Institutionalization", 2000, 1-2. Retrieved from "http://www.libertyresources.org/mc/ca-52.html" on 11-16-2001.

Ravaud, J and Stiker, H. 2001. "Inclusion/Exclusion: An Analysis of Historical and Cultural Meanings" in Albrecht et al (Eds.) *Handbook of Disability Studies.* Thousand Oaks: Sage. pp. 490-514.

"Real Homes Not Nursing Homes", 2001. Retrieved from http://www. adapt.org.back.htm on 7-23-2001.

"Rehabilitation Services" 2001. Retrieved from http://www.wfubmc edu/rehab/in/programs; on 10-23-2001, pp. 1-5.

Renzetti, Claire M. & Curran, Daniel J. 2000. *Living Sociology.* (2nd Ed.) Boston: Allyn and Bacon.

"Report of CCD Long Term Services and Supports Task Force", 2000, pp 1-2, Retrieved from "http://www.c-c-d.org/report_LTSS.htm" on 11-26-2001.

"Research and Statistics" 2001 retrieved from http://www.ed.gov/offices/Osers/RSA/Research on 12-4-2001.

Rivera, Geraldo. 1972. *Willowbrook: A Report on How It Is and Why It Doesn't Have to Be That Way.* New York: Random House.

Roeher Institute. 1997. *Evaluation of the Choices Project in Thunder Bay, Ontario.* North York: The Roerher Institute

Rose, David. 1996. "AMI settles fair-housing suit". *NAMI Advocate. 18,#3,23.*

Roth, J.A. and Eddy, E.M. (1967) *Rehabilitation for the Unwanted.* New York: Atherton Press.

Rubin, E.R.,and Roessler, R.T. 1983. *Foundations of the Vocational Rehabilitation Process.* (2nd Ed.). Baltimore: University Park Press.

Rushing, William A. 1971, "Individual Resources, Societal Reaction, and Hospital Commitment," America *Journal of Sociology.* 77:511-26.

Rushing, William A, and Ortega, Suzanne T. 1976. "Socioeconomic Status and Mental Disorder: New Evidence and a Sociomedical Formulation." *American Journal of Sociology.* 84:1175-1200.

Scala, M.A., and Nerney, T. N.D. "People First: The Consumers in Consumer Direction". pp. 1-6. Retrieved from "http://www.self-determination.com/publications/consumer.htm"

Schaefer, R. T. 2000 *Sociology* (7th Ed.) Boston: McGraw-Hill.

Schaefer, R.T. 2000. *Racial and Ethnic Groups* (8th Ed.). Upper Saddle River: Prentice Hall.

Scheerenberger, R.C. 1983. *A History of Mental Retardation.* Baltimore: Paul H. Brookes.

Schriner, K. 2001. "A Disability Studies Perspective on Employment Issues and Policies for Disabled People" in Albrecht, et al (Eds.). *Handbook of Disability Studies.* Thousand Oaks: Sage Publications, 642-661.

"Seattle 2000 Declaration", 2000. Retrieved from "http://www.members .home.net/directfunding/Declaration.htm" on 7-23-2001. pp. 1-8

"Section 1. Prevalence of Disabilities." Retrieved from http:// www.infouse.com/disabilitydata/chartbookprev.textgfx.html/ on 8-22-2001.

"Section 504 of the Rehabilitation Act of 1973", 1997. Pp. 1-2. Retrieved from http://www.pcc.ed/osd/504.htm on 8-13-01.

Seelman, K.D. 2001. "Science And Technology Policy: Is Disability a Missing Factor?" in Albrecht et al (Eds.). Thousand Oaks: Sage Publications, 663-692.

Seelman, K.D., 2001. "Self-Advocacy has reached the Last Frontier, p. 1 (2001) Retrieved August 1, 2001 from http://www.customcpu. com/np/alaskaapf/

"Self-Determination: Position Statement #25" 2001. pp. 1-2. The Arc. Retrieved from "http://www.thearc.org/info" on 7-26-2001.

"Self-Directed Support Corporations (Microboards)" 2001. p. 1. Retrieved from "http://www.self-determination.com/index-include.cfm?ID=67" on 8-10-2001.

"Sense of Common Identity Among People with Disabilities" 2001. pp 1-2. Retrieved from http://www.nod.org/cont/dsp_cont item_vi...Locationold+5&timeStamp. On 10/30/2001.

Shapiro, Joseph P. 1993. *No Pity: People with Disabilities Forging a New Civil Rights Movement.* New York: Times Books.

Shaw, B. (Ed.) 1994. *The Ragged Edge.* Louisville: The Advocado Press.

Simon-Rusinowitz, L. 1999. "History, Principles, and Definition of Consumer-Direction: Views from the Aging Community" Paper presented at the National Leadership Summit on Self-Determination and Consumer-Direction and Control, Oct. 21-23, 1999. Retrieved from "www://http.cdc.ouhs.edu/selfdetermination/simonrusinowitz .html." on 7-26-2001.

Smith. J.D., 2000. "Social Constructions of Mental Retardation: Impersonal Histories and the Hope for Personal Futures." In Wehmeyer, M.L. and Patton, J.R. (Eds.) M*ental Retardation in the 21ˢᵗ Century.* Austin: Pro Ed.

Sobsey, D, Lucardie, R., Mansell, S. 1995. *Violence and Disability: An Annotated Bibliography.* Baltimore: Paul H. Brookes Publishing.

"Social Security Disability Planner". 2001. Retrieved from http://www.ssa.gov/dibplan/dqualify.htm on 9-17-2001.

"State and County Psychiatric Hospitals, Inpatient Census, Beginning of 1998", 2001. Retrieved from http://www.mentalhealth.org/ databases/da...es_exe.asp?D1+AL&Type=SCPH&Myassign=list on 10-01-2001.

"Stigma Busting Network and Alerts", 2001. Retrieved from http://www.nami.org/campaign/localstigma.html on 10-1-2001.

"Stigma Watch", 2001. Retrieved from http://www.nmha.org/newsroom/stigma/index.cfm on 10-2-2001.

Stroman, Duane F. 1982. *The Awakening Minorities: The Physically Handicapped.* Lanham, Md.: University Press of America.

Stroman, Duane F. 1989 *Mental Retardation in Social Context.* Lanham, Md.: University Press of America.

"Support Broker" 2001. Pp. 1-2. Retrieved from "http://www.dds cahwnet. gov/SDPP/main/SDPilotHome.cfm" on 9-24-2001.

Swindle, R, Heller, K., and Pescosolido, B. 1997. "Responses to 'nervous breakdowns' in America over a 40-year period: mental health policy implications." Paper presented at the meeting of the American Sociological Association, Toronto: Ontario.

"Table 1. Data on Disability and Employment", 1997. Retrieved from "hhp://www.census.gov/hhes/www/disable/emperndistsi/pdr" on 9-17-2001.

"TASH", 2001 p 1. Retrieved from http://www.tash.org on 7-30-2001.

Tarrow, Sidney. 1994. *Power in Movement: Social Movements, Collective Action and Politics.* Cambridge: Cambridge University Press.

Tarrow, S. 1996. "Social Movements in Contentious Politics: A Review Article" American *Political Science Review.* 90 (4): 873-74.

"The Arc", (2001). Retrieved July 27, 2001 from http://www.thearc.org.html.

"The Criminalization of People with Mental Illness". 2001. Retrieved from http://www.nami.org/update/unitedcriminal.html on 10-1-2001.

"The *Olmstead* Decision", 1-3. 2001. Retrieved from "http://www. ncls.org.programs;health/disabil2.htm" on 11-26 2001.

The Roeher Institute, 1997, Evaluation *of the **Choices** Project in Thunder Bay Ontario: Interim and Final Reports.*

Thomas, David. 1982. *The Experience of Handicap.* New York: Methuen & Co.

Tilly, C. 1978. *From Mobilization to Revolution.* Reading, Mass.: Addison Wesley.

Townsend, John M. 1975. "Self-Concept and the Institutionalization of Mental Patients: An Overview and Critque". *Journal of Health and Social Behavior.* 17:263-71.

"Traumatic Brain Injury Model Systems" 2001. Retrieved from http://www.tbims.org/intro.html on 10-23-2001.

Trent, J.W. 1994. *Inventing the Feeble Mind.* Berkeley: Univ. of Calif. Press.

Trupin, L, Rice, D.P. and Max, W. 1995. "Who Pays for Medical Care of People with Disabilities?" *Disability Statistics Abstract.* No. 13, 1-4.

Trupin, L and Yelin, E. 1999. *The Employment Experience of Persons with Limitation in Physical Functioning: An Analysis of the 1996 California Work and Health Survey.* San Francisco: Disability Statistics Rehabilitation Research and Training Center, University of California.

Tyor, P.L. & Bell, L.V. 1984. *Caring for the Retarded in America.* Westport: Greenwood Press.

U.S. Department of Health and Human Services. 1999. *Mental Health: A Report of the Surgeon General.* Rockville. MD: U.S. Department of Health and Human Services, Substance Abuse and Mental Health Services Administration, Center for Mental Health Services. National Institutes of Health, National Institute of Mental Health.

"Voices of Positive Ability", July 23, 2001. Retrieved July 23, 2001 from http://www.wapd.org.

"Voting Laws Discriminate Against Mentally Disabled", 2001, pp 1-3. Retrieved from http://www.newswise.com/articles/2000/10/MENTAL.UAR.html on 9/25/2001.

Wagley, C. and Harris, M, 1958. *Minorities in the New World: Six Case Studies.* New York: Columbia University Press.

Ward, N., 1999. "Self Advocates Becoming Empowered: The National Self Advocacy Organization Definition of Self-Determination." pp. 1-5. Retrieved from "http://www.cdrc.ohsu.edu.selfdetermination /nward.html" on 7-26-2001.

Weiss, Gregory L. and Lonquist, Lynne E. 2000. *The* http://www.cdrc.ohsu.edu/selfdetermination/nward.html on 7-26-2001. *Sociology of Health, Healing and Illness.* (3rd Ed.) Upper Saddle River: Prentice Hall.

Weitz, Rose. 2001. *The Sociology of Health, Illness and Health Care.* (2nd Ed.). Belmont: Wadsworth/Thomson Learning.

"Welcome to the Federation of Families for Children's Mental Health", 2001. Retrieved from http://www.ffcmh.org/New%20Site/brochureTwo .htm on 10-2-01.

"Welcome to the Home and Community Based Services Resource Networks", 2001. Retrieved from "http://www.hcbs.org/" on 11-26-2001.

"Welcome to the Home of Individualized Funding Information Resources", 2001, pp 1-6. Retrieved from "http://www.members.home.net/tsalisbury" on 7-24-2001.

"Welcome to the Self-Determination Synthesis Project Homepage." 2001. Retrieved from "http://www.uncc.edu/sdsp/" on 11-15-2001.

Wenger, B.L., Kaye, H.S., LaPlante, M, 1996. "Disabilities Among Children". *Disability Statistics Abstracts.* No. 15. pp. 1-4.

Westling, D.L. 1986. *Introduction to Mental Retardation.* Englewood Cliffs, N.J.: Prentice Hall.

"What are People First Goals?" 2001 pp. 1-3. Retrieved from http://www.open.org/~people1/whatis.htm p, 3 on 8-1-2001.

"Who are People First Members? 2001, pp 1-3. Retrieved from http://www.open.org/~people1/whatis.htm on 8-01-2001.

"What is Freedom Clearing House?" 2001. Retrieved from "http://www.freedomclearinghouse.org" on 11-26-2001.

"What's New", 2001, 1-4. Retrieved from "http://www.hcbs.org/new.htm" on 12-10-2001.

Williams, P. & Shoultz, B., 1982. *We Can Speak for Ourselves.* Bloomington: Indiana University Press.

Wirth, L, 1945. "The Problem of Minority Groups," in Ralph Linton (ed.) *The Science of Man in the World Crisis.* New York: Columbia University Press. 1945. 340-356.

Wolfensberger, W. 1972. *The Principle of Normalization in Human Services.* Toronto: National Institute on Mental Retardation.

Wolfensberger, W. 1976. "The Origin and Nature of our Institutional Models" in R. Kugel and A. Shearer (Eds.). *Changing Patterns in Residential Services for the Mentally Retarded* (Rev. Ed.). Washington: President's Committee on Mental Retardation, 35-82.

Zola, Irving K. 1985. "Depictions of Disability—Metaphor, Message and Medium in the Media: A Research and Political Agenda." *Social Science and Medicine,* 22:5-17.

INDEX

Accessibility, 106-110

Activities of daily living, 6, 29, 33, 41

Activity limitations, 24, 27, 29

ADAPT (Americans Disabled for Accessible Public Transportation), 67, 105, 111, 187, 238

Adaptable design, 101

Advocacy
  definitions of , 46-47
  forms of 48-49
  for mental health, 134- 138
  for mental retardation, 160-166
  organizations, 50-64, 66-69

Agosta, J., 213

Albrecht, Gary, 18

Altman, Barbara, 24

Amalgamation, 92

American Association on Mental Retardation, 12

American Coalition of Citizens with Disabilities, 65, 74

Americans with Disabilities Act, 7, 21, 24, 75, 106, 107, 185, 188-189

Anderson, M. 44

Antisocial personality disorder, 24

Arc, The, 160

Assimilation, 92, 114

Assistive technology, 109

Bach, D., 226-227

Bank-Mikkelsen, 165

Barnartt, S., 186, 188

Barnes, C., 90, 94

Baroff, G., 156-157, 164

Basnett. I, 104, 203

Baumeister, A. 151

Beers, Clifford, 141

Berovici, S., 167

Blasiotti, E., 110.

Blatt, B., 157

Braddock, D., 152-153, 155, 168-173, 201, 203

Brain disease, 139

Boggs, E., 129

Califano, Joseph, 74-75

Cash and Counseling Program, 224

Census Bureau, 29

Census of disabled, 29

Center on Self-Determination, 236

Center for Self-Determination, 67, 234

Centers for Independent Living, 73, 101, 201-204, 212

Chamberlain, J., 137

Charlton, J., 66

Cleland, Max, 189-190

Cockerham, W., 121, 123, 127, 130

Cohen, E., 213

Conley, R., 192

Conroy, J., 230
Consortium for Citizens with
    Disabilities, 237-238
Constructionism, 9, 14
Cost shifting, 142-146, 168-
173
Consumer supports, 214
Crawford, C., 238
Crime victimization, 113
Cross-disability organization,
186
Current Population Survey,
29-30

Davis, J., 198
Dawson, S., 232, 236
Deinstitutionalization
    defined, 120-123
    of mentally ill, 123-145
    of mentally retarded, 156-
175
    of physically disabled, 190-
205
DeJong, G., 198
Demand-side model, 213
Demedicalization, 22
Developmental disabil-
    ities, 148-149
Digital divide, 110
DiNitto, D., 183
Disabled Peoples International,
68
Disabled in Action, 71, 104-
105
Disability (ies)
    causes of, 4-10
    correlates of, 34-37
    definitions of, 1-8
    demography of, 32-40
    diversity of, 1-2, 180,
    182

domains, 38-39
judicial responses to,
    173-174
legislative responses
    to, 75-80, 174-175
models of, 2, 15-16
organizations, 49-64
protests, 186-189
severity of, 5-6, 32, 34
types of, 3, 37, 180-182
Discrimination in
    employment, 97-99
    health care, 101-103
    housing, 99, 136
    transportation, 104
Doty, P., 231
Dowdall, 120, 127, 142- 143
Drake, R., 101
Dybwad, R., 46

Eaton, W., 121
Education for all Handi-
    capped Children Act
    (see IDEA)
Edwards, R., 143
Electronic communications,
    80-81
Endogamy, 86, 89
Essentialism, 14
Exclusion
    indicators of, 106-113
Expulsion, 92, 94
Extermination, 91-92

Feebleminded, 11
Federal benefit rate, 6
Federal disability legislation,
    75-80
Federation of Families for
    Children's Mental Health,
    139-140

Fiscal intermediary, 215
Fiscal management agency, 71
Fleischer, D., 15, 71, 93, 99,
    101, 104, 108, 188
Fox-Grage, W., 239
French, S., 102, 103
Functional limitation, 33
Funk, R., 70, 137
Fusion, 92, 114

Galludet University, 187
Geriatric care manager,
    221
Goffman, E., 127, 194
Goldenson, R., 191
Greider, L., 222
Gritzer, G., 184
Grob, G., 96, 120

Halpern, A., 124, 131
Halpern, J., 121
Handicaptivity, 115
Harris Poll, 98-99
Hash, M., 111
Henslin, J., 44, 46
Higgins, 18-21
IDEA(Individuals with
    Disabilities Act), 11,
    53, 70, 141
Idiots, 12-13
Identity, 88
Imbeciles, 12-13
Impairments, 25
Individual budgets, 214,
    215, 222-223
Independent funding, 214
Individualized budgets, 222
Inclusion gap, 112-113
Institutionalization
    definitions of , 121-122

Institutions for
    mentally ill, 121-124
    mentally retarded, 149-
    164
Internal advocate, 49
Instrumental activities of
    daily living, 35
International classific-
    tion of impairments,
    disabilities and health,
    24
International League of
    Societies for the Mentally
    Handicapped, 165
Integration, 164
Independent living movement,
    200-204

Kane, R., 217
Kelley, L., 94
Kemp, E., 65
Kennedy, J., 128-129, 158, 168
Kennedy, R., 158
Kent, D., 168

Lagoyda, R., 229
Lakin, K. 152
LaPlante, M., 6
Laurie, V., 200
Lerman, H., 120
Letchworth Village, 158
Linguistic minority, 88
Litvak, S., 109
Long, L., 138

Mahoney, K., 232
Major life activities, 6
Marks, D., 10, 11, 13-15
Maximalist institution,
    143
McNeil, J., 31

Mechanic, D., 130-131
Meadours, J., 237
Medicaid, 130, 142, 232, 235, 239, 241
Medical model, 14-17, 19-23
Medicare, 130, 142
Mental health care, 130-131
Mental Health Parity Act, 140
Mental Health Study Act, 128-129
Mental hospitals
  depopulation of , 121-123
  cost of, 125, 142
Mental illness
  attitudes toward, 126, 134-137
Mental retardation
  definition of, 11-12, 148-149
  extent of, 152, 155
  Stereotypes about, 149
  Models of, 149-151
Microboards, 221
Minority groups
  defined, 83-85
  types of , 84, 88
Models of disability, 4, 15-18
Monadnock Develop-Mental Services, 230
Moseley, C., 220, 230, 234
Multiple disabilities, 38-40
Myths about disabilities, 41

National Alliance for the Mentally Ill, 69, 111, 136, 139-141.
National Association of Retarded Children (see The Arc)
National Council on Independent Living, 73, 202
National Health Interview Survey, 30
National Institute of Mental Health, 126
National Mental Health Association, 139, 141-142
National Union Research, 221, 226
Nerney, T., 220, 222, 225, 234

Neumann, J, 71, 72, 74
Noble, J., 111
Normalization, 164-167

Oberschall, A., 43, 45
Olmstead decision, 233
Oregon Health Sciences University, 232

Pathology, 25, 27-28
Pelka, F., 49, 68, 72, 106, 126, 138, 158, 190, 200
People First, 47, 162-163, 237
Personal transformation movements, 44
Person-centered planning, 219, 222-223
Pharmacotherapies, 128
Physical impairments, 180-182
Pluralism, 92, 115
Pope, A., 22, 23, 182

President's Committee on
    Mental Retardation, 65
Program funding model, 217
Public residential facility,
    168

Ravaud, J., 91, 93
Reform movements, 124-132
Rehabilitation
    hospitals, 190-197
    services, 191-197
    legislation, 76-180, 183, 186
Rights of disabled, 165
Rivera, G., 158-159
Roberts, Ed, 71-73
Robert Wood Johnson
    Foundation, 229-232, 242
Roeher Institute, 238
Rolling quads, 71
Rose, D., 136
Roth, J., 192-197
Rubin, E.,183-185, 201

SABE (Self-Advocates
    Becoming
    Empowered), 232
Salisbury, M., 13, 226,
    236
Scala, M., 210
Schaefer, R., 44, 94
Scheerenberger, R., 151
Secession, 94
Seelman, K., 110, 198
Segregation, 92, 112
Self-Advocacy, 46-48, 162
Self-Determination
    defined, 208-210
    evolution of, 213-217
    groups involved in, 211-212
    models of, 213-214
    principles of, 210-211

issues in, 225-224
Shapiro, J., 71, 107, 159, 187,
    199
Sheltered workshop, 197
Shaw, B., 198
Sobsey, D., 113
Social Security Disability
    Insurance, 6
Soldier's Disability Act, 183
Stigma, 89, 135-137
Stigma Busters, 139
Stigma Watch, 141
Stroman, D., 15, 46, 84, 93,
    96, 100, 149, 165
Supply-side model, 213
Support Broker, 214, 220
Supported employment, 197
Survey of Income and
    Program Participation,
    28, 30, 33, 37
Swindle, R., 135

TASH (The Association for
    the Severely
    Handicapped), 163, 234
Tarrow, S., 46, 186
Thomas, D., 181, 198
Telecommunications and
    disabled, 109-111
Townsend, J., 121
Transbus, 105
Trent, J., 11, 13, 151, 157
Transinstutionalization, 131
Tyor, P.,151

Uditsky, 226
Universal design, 109

Vocational rehabilitation,
    183-186, 190-200

Vocational Rehabilitation
    Act of 1973, 70, 74, 185
Wagley, C., 84
Ward, N., 237
Weiss, G., 4, 15
Weitz, R., 15, 18
Westling, D., 167, 169
Wilbur, H., 11
Williams, P., 47
Willowbrook State School,
    158-159
Wirth, L., 84
Wolfensberger, W., 149-150,
    167
World Health Organi-
    zation, 8, 24
Workmens Compensation
    Laws, 183
World Institute on
    Disability, 73

Zola, I., 15, 90